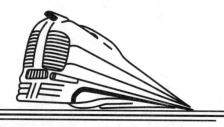

All Aboard!
The "Complete North American Train Travel Guide

Revised 2nd Edition

Jim Loomis

PRIMA PUBLISHING

Published by Prima Publishing, Roseville, California. Member of the Crown Publishing Group, a division of Random House, Inc.

Random House, Inc. New York, Toronto, London, Sydney, Auckland

PRIMA PUBLISHING and colophon are trademarks of Random House, Inc., registered with the United States Patent and Trademark Office.

Library of Congress Cataloging-in-Publication Data

Loomis, Jim.
    All aboard! : the complete North American train travel guide / Jim Loomis.
Rev., 2nd ed.
    p. cm.
    Includes index.
    ISBN 0-7615-1087-7
    1. United States—Guidebooks. 2. Canada—Guidebooks. 3. Railroad travel—United States—Guidebooks. 4. Railroad travel—Canada—Guidebooks. I. Title.
    E158.L59 1998
    917.304'929—dc21   97-37108
                                    CIP

01 02 03 04 05 HH 10 9 8 7 6 5 4
Printed in the United States of America

Second Edition

Efforts have been made to make this book complete and accurate as of the date of publication. In a time of rapid change, however, it is difficult to ensure that all information is entirely accurate, complete, or up-to-date. Although the publisher and the author cannot be liable for any inaccuracies or omissions in this book, they are always grateful for suggestions for improvement.

Visit us online at www.primapublishing.com

You get a real feeling of this country
and the people in it
when you're on a train.
HARRY TRUMAN

Contents

Acknowledgments

It's amazing how much has changed since the first edition of *All Aboard!* was published. Some trains have been cancelled, others added; some routes have been shortened, others extended; old equipment has been replaced and new equipment put into service; and we can now reserve space and order our own train tickets over the Internet.

Many, many people helped me sort all that out for this new edition, and I am most grateful to them all. In particular, thanks to Amtrak's Steven Taubenkibel, who cheerfully, efficiently, and thoroughly dealt with the multiple lists of questions I had for him.

The new chapter, which deals mostly with that incredible ride through Mexico's Copper Canyon, could never have been written without the help of Bill Braley of the *South Orient Express,* Bill Pickeral and Pat Rondelli of the *Sierra Madre Express,* Filepe Valdez from the Office of Tourism in Chihuahua City, and Oscar Ceniceros, Carlos Armenta, and Adalberto Albarran of the Ferrocarriles Nacionales de Mexico. To all of them, *muchas gracias!*

Finally, thanks to all of the onboard employees of Amtrak and VIA Rail who talked openly and enthusiastically with me about their jobs and let me watch them at their work. I continue to be impressed!

Rediscovering the Train

When I was a youngster, back in the late 1940s and early 1950s, our family would take an annual train trip from our home in Connecticut to either St. Louis or Florida, where a set of grandparents would be waiting.

Those train rides were great adventures. I remember standing on the platform of the Hartford railroad station, waiting for the train to arrive. I would crane my neck for the first glimpse, all the while being careful to keep behind the yellow warning line. According to my father, anyone standing across that line as the train rolled into the station ran the risk of being "sucked under the wheels."

The anticipation was almost unbearable. Finally, a rasping monotone would blare out over the public address system: "Your attention, please. Now arriving on Track Two. . . ."

The platform came alive with that announcement—baggage carts rattled past, last-minute passengers ran up the stairs from the waiting room, mothers anxiously corralled their kids.

The general confusion quickly subsided and then thirty or forty people were craning their necks. Still we saw nothing, just the tracks curving away beyond our line of sight. Then a black steam locomotive suddenly materialized, bearing down on us, even appearing to accelerate as it loomed larger and larger. It was always so much bigger than I had remembered. And noisier, although the locomotive's bell, clang-clanging slightly out of rhythm, was somehow clearly heard above the din as the train rumbled past.

A train ride is still a great adventure for me. I'm always anxious to board; always reluctant to get off. There is obvious irony, of course, in the fact that someone who loves rail travel has spent more than thirty years living in Hawaii, over 2,000 miles from the nearest long-distance train. Strangely, it was for this very reason that my love of train travel was revived after so many years.

Several years ago, my family was organizing a reunion in Florida around my parents' fiftieth wedding anniversary. While discussing plans to attend the event, I realized that neither my wife nor my daughter had really seen America. Both had been born and raised in the Islands and, typical of most Hawaii residents, almost everything they knew of "the mainland" was what they had seen from 30,000 feet.

Not even sure it was possible, I suggested flying straight to Florida for the reunion, then taking the train back to the west coast before flying home to Honolulu. My wife thought I was crazy, and said so. Our daughter was six at the time, and Paula had visions of trying to occupy an active youngster in cramped quarters for hours upon end. Eventually, I worked out an itinerary that included overnight stops in Williamsburg, Virginia; Washington, D.C.; Chicago; the Colorado Rockies; the Sierras in California; and, finally, San Francisco. My wife still wasn't completely convinced, but agreed to give Amtrak a try.

We had a wonderful trip. Williamsburg was charming, Washington was inspiring (and delightfully cool for June), the Rockies and the Sierras were spectacular. Just as important, our train experience was all I had hoped.

Since then, the train has become the preferred means of long-distance travel for our family. My daughter, in particular, has become a train enthusiast. A few summers ago, she and I combined two passions into a wonderful three-week excursion, logging several thousand miles on Amtrak as we followed the Boston Red Sox on one of their west coast road trips: Oakland, Seattle, Chicago, and, finally, "home" to Boston. Neither of us will ever forget it. We had a priceless opportunity for a special father-daughter time together. The scenery was magnificent, the Red Sox won six of seven games with us in the stands . . . and we did it all by train.

This book grew from those experiences. It is written for the person who is naturally inquisitive, who notices and finds delight in little things, who knows that those who hurry miss a lot. My hope is that this book will significantly add to the experience of every train ride for such a person, and I take a great deal of pleasure in that thought.

Rail Travel Information Sources

AMTRAK
Reservations, information, arrival and departure times
   From the U. S. or Canada 800-USA-RAIL
      (800-872-7245)
   Metroliner service only 800-523-8720
   Groups of 15 or more 800-872-1477
   Hearing impaired 800-523-6590
Web site http://www.amtrak.com

VIA RAIL CANADA
Reservations, information, arrival and departure times
   From the U. S. 800-561-3949
   From Canada 800-561-3952
Web site http://www.viarail.ca

MEXICO
Sierra Madre Express 800-666-0346
South Orient Express 800-659-7602

RV/RAIL TOURS
Carnival Caravans 800-556-5652
Points South, Moreno Valley, CA 909-247-1222
Tracks to Adventure, El Paso, TX 800-351-6053

American Association of Private Rail Car Owners
    202-547-5696

National Association of Railroad Passengers (NARP)
    202-408-8362
    e-mail: narp@worldweb.net

Finally, I'd like you to know about a Web site devoted to passenger train travel in the U.S. and Canada. You'll find a wide variety of rail travel information, detailed travelogues for various routes, and links to other train-related sites. I visit frequently and know you will enjoy doing so, too.

Trainweb http://www.trainweb.com

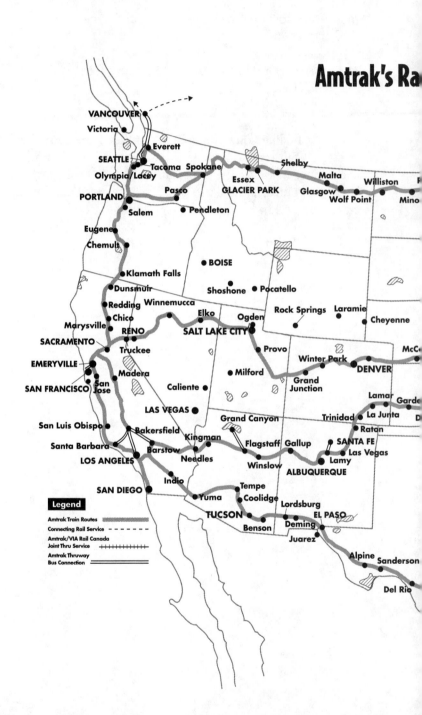

Amtrak's Ra

assenger System

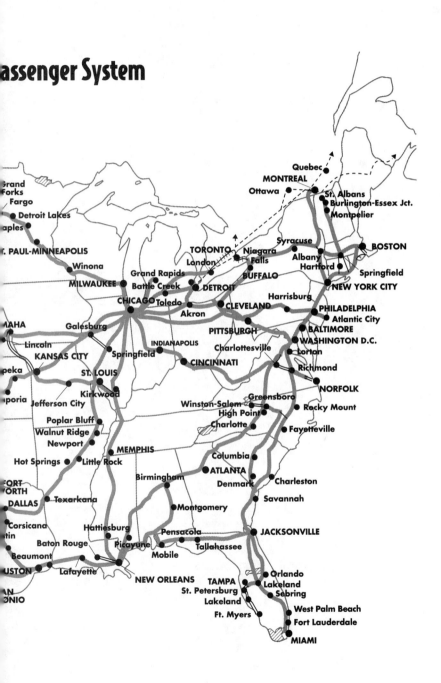

CHAPTER 1

Why Take a Train?

Sophie Tucker once said, "I've been rich and I've been poor . . . and rich is better." With apologies to the late Miss Tucker, in my many travels I've been comfortable and I've been uncomfortable . . . and comfortable is better. A lot better. In a nutshell, that's why I take the train.

There are many societal and environmental reasons for being pro-rail, which we'll talk about in another chapter, but for long-distance travel, the train is the only civilized option left for us. You think not? Consider the other choices.

See America Through a Windshield?

Forget it. Droning great distances across the country by car or—I shudder at the very thought—by bus is, for the most part, a monumental waste of time and energy. If you're the driver, it's tiring. If you're a passenger, it's boring. And either way it's confining and uncomfortable.

In his delightful book, *On the Road,* Charles Kuralt says, "Thanks to the interstate highway system, it is now possible to travel across the country coast to coast without seeing anything."

Kuralt's hyperbole can be forgiven. Unless or until you leave the interstate highways, you won't come close to much of the real America. When we build superhighways in this country, we level everything, carving a swath across the land hundreds of yards wide from horizon to horizon. When we're through, there's nothing much left to see. The only conceivable reason for traveling long distances by car is to save money, and that, I'll argue, is only possible when the cost is amortized over a number of passengers.

Flying Really Is for the Birds

Perhaps it's because of deregulation and the lack of competition that resulted. Maybe it's just the shifting economic conditions. But for the ordinary traveler, flying is no longer a pleasurable experience.

Unless you have the money, the frequent flyer mileage, or the connections to fly first class, you're forced to spend hours crammed into a narrow seat with virtually no legroom. Once, on a flight to Los Angeles, I sat next to a rather large woman. She was only moderately over-weight, but the seats were so narrow I was forced to eat my meal left-handed. Add jet lag into the mix with the cramped conditions, and a cross-country trip is exhausting. Everyone has a horror story about the routine discomforts and inconveniences of flying, yet we have come to tolerate these conditions as an acceptable trade-off for getting somewhere quickly.

Flying isn't all bad, of course. It's quite true, for instance, that occasionally—*if* you are flying during day-light hours and *if* you can arrange a window seat and *if* there is no cloud cover—you can see some pretty spectacular things from a jetliner. Once, on a flight out of Ft. Myers, Florida, I had a ringside seat for a space shuttle launch. No doubt about it, that was something to see from 20,000 feet.

But how exciting is it when the captain says, "That city off to the left of our aircraft is Wichita, Kansas"? Assuming you have a window seat on the left side, Wichita looks a lot like Topeka . . . or Boise or Duluth or Portland (Oregon or Maine, take your choice). The fact is, you don't see much of America from a plane.

Finally, the technology of modern aviation is incomprehensible to ordinary people. Instead of entering through that long, mechanized tunnel, have you ever boarded a Boeing 747 from ground level? It's unnerving. You stand on the tarmac looking up at that monstrous machine, and you know intellectually that it will not, cannot possibly, fly! Only God Himself understands how something that big actually gets off the ground. And only blind faith gets me aboard. I only know one thing for certain about a plane trip: the sooner we land, the better I like it.

A Simple Attitude Adjustment

Long-distance train travel isn't the best choice for everyone on every occasion. If you have to get somewhere fast, an airplane is admittedly the only practical answer. Also, some people simply can't gear down sufficiently to enjoy the train, whether they're in a hurry or not.

For most people, though, all it takes to enjoy a long-distance train trip is a simple attitude adjustment before starting out. Just remember that the train should be an important part of your vacation experience; the plane is nothing more than the fastest way to get there.

On the *Coast Starlight,* en route from Los Angeles to Seattle . . . (By the way, you'll notice that long-distance trains are traditionally given names as well as numbers. A nice touch, don't you think?) Anyway, on the *Coast Starlight,* you roll almost silently through the Cascade Mountains of Oregon on a single track cut through the wilderness. Heading east out of Seattle on the *Empire Builder,* you fall asleep in the Cascades and wake up the next morning in the Rockies as the train skirts Glacier National Park. The *Lake Shore Limited* takes you along the banks of Lake Erie and Lake Ontario. The *Adirondack* follows the Hudson River into New York City. If you want to gaze on some of the prettiest country anywhere, ride the *Cardinal* across West Virginia and Kentucky.

Just out of El Paso on the *Sunset Limited,* you pass a Native American boy sitting bareback on his horse, and you wonder if he is as curious about you as you are about him. From the *California Zephyr,* you see a man and a woman sitting with their arms around each other on a tractor in a field of corn that stretches to the horizon. She waves as you pass. On the *City of New Orleans,* you pass a man putting tar paper on the roof of a shack, and as he straightens and stares, you can tell that his back hurts. As you roll slowly through a South Carolina town on the *Silver Meteor,* you see an elderly woman tending a small vegetable garden in her backyard. Her tomatoes are ripe.

Twenty-four hours on a train will yield a thousand mental snapshots of America and her people . . . and the time to savor them.

More than anything, your train ride should be relaxing. That doesn't come automatically to everyone. You may have to work a bit at making that mental adjustment. Some people just can't do it. My sister once talked her husband into taking the train from Denver to Los Angeles. He enjoyed the spectacular scenery as they wound their way through the Rockies west of Denver, but somewhere in Nevada the next morning, as they were rolling along beside a highway, he suddenly sat straight up in his seat. "Good God! Those cars are moving faster than we are! They'll get to Los Angeles before we do!" Not true, of course, and he never could explain why that should matter anyway, but he was agitated and impatient for the rest of the trip.

Why travel by train? Because compared to the alternatives, it's comfortable and relaxing. Because it's civilized. And most of all, because it will broaden and elevate your appreciation and understanding of our country and its people. That's the United States of America out there, passing by right outside your living room window.

The Railroad in Everyday Language

Some are obvious, others are obscure, but many expressions we all use in our daily lives have origins that can be traced to the railroad. These are but a few.

blocked   Today it means to prevent something from moving forward, but originally the word described a train prevented from entering a stretch of track between two signals, which is called a "block."

flag someone down   This refers to the railroad practice of signaling to a train with colored flags. Radios are now used to signal the engineer to stop for passengers at remote stations, but they're still called "flag stops."

highballing down the road   Early signals were given to a moving train by hoisting colored balls onto a pole; a ball at the top of the pole meant "all clear."

something is sidetracked   This is a reference to diverting a train onto a siding until another can pass.

a full head of steam   This expression originally referred to a steam engine with maximum pressure in its boiler.

staying on track; being off the track   A railroad track is the obvious origin of these expressions.

a light at the end of the tunnel   The consensus is that this expression originated with the railroad.

derail a project or idea   A train's progress stops abruptly when this happens, too.

getting on board   There is possibly a nautical origin here, but we'll claim it anyway.

doubleheader   Originally, this term described two locomotives coupled together to pull a long, heavy train.

over the hump   When freight cars are pushed over the hump, or high point, in a rail yard, they roll easily by themselves to a siding.

hell on wheels   This expression was a reference to the gamblers and prostitutes who followed railroad crews in their own railcars (on wheels) while the transcontinental railway was being built.

CHAPTER 2

How It All Began

Railroads have been around for a long time. As far back as the sixteenth century they were used to haul coal out of mines in England and Wales. Actually, those were hardly what we would call railroads—just horses and mules pulling wagons along crude tracks—but they had the same fundamental advantage that modern railroads offer. By reducing friction, more weight could be moved with less energy. The people who ran those coal mines understood that concept in even simpler terms: the easier it was for a horse to pull one of their carts, the more coal they could put into it.

The potential of steam power had been understood for a long time, and in fact steam engines had been used for years to pump water out of those same coal mines. The big breakthrough came about 1803, when Richard Trevithick, an English mining engineer, figured out how to mount a steam engine on a movable platform. Within a few years, the very first steam locomotives were used to haul that coal from the mines to seaports, from where it was shipped all over the world. In 1825, the first rail passenger service was begun, and the news of this new means of transportation started spreading beyond England's shores. It found fertile ground in America.

It's hard to think of another new technology that had a greater impact on our country (or the modern world, for that matter) than the railroad. The railroads caused this country to *be*. It's that simple.

A Mobile Society Is Created

America's first railroad was the Baltimore & Ohio, which started service in 1830 and immediately captured the imagination of the country. That's hardly surprising. Up to that time, no human had ever traveled faster than a horse could run. Now, almost overnight, ordinary people were traveling for greater distances at higher speeds than had ever been dreamed possible. Other railroads followed on the B&O's heels.

For the average American of the early to mid-1800s, it all took some getting used to. Of necessity, families and communities had always been virtually self-sufficient. The railroads changed all of that in a matter of a few years by linking towns, then states, and finally the entire continent. Suddenly Americans had mobility; almost anyone could go almost anywhere. It's an interesting paradox that while railroads were bringing Americans together as one people, they also made it possible for the country itself to expand.

By the middle of the nineteenth century, people were heading west by the thousands, chasing after gold that had been discovered in California in 1848 or looking for some land of their own. However efficiently the railroads may have linked north, south, and east, though, they could only take people halfway into the great American West—just as far as Omaha.

The Biggest Construction Project Ever

There had been talk about extending the railroad to the West Coast for some time, but the men who proposed it were largely written off as fools. It was indeed a huge, daunting project, arguably one of the largest and most ambitious engineering projects ever attempted. Furthermore, not everyone thought California was the promised land even if the transcontinental railroad did prove feasible. Probably the best-known naysayer of the time was Daniel Webster, who described the West as a "region of savages and wild beasts, of deserts of shifting sands and whirlwinds of dust, of cactus and prairie dogs."

Nevertheless, President Abraham Lincoln decided to move ahead with the transcontinental railroad and signed the Pacific Railroad Act in 1862. Although there may have been a fair amount of foresight and vision involved, the main reason for the decision was a very real concern that California, which had become our thirty-first state in 1850, would use the Civil War as an excuse to leave the Union and become a separate nation. Then, too, with the Gold Rush in full swing, there was always the threat of attack by a foreign power, and without a transcontinental railroad the United States could never get troops or supplies to California in time to deal with the problem.

When the work finally began, it was certainly in earnest and in spite of the fact that the Civil War had begun. The Union Pacific headed west from Omaha, Nebraska, while the Central Pacific Railroad started east from Sacramento, California. The CP had problems from the outset. Most of the able-bodied men were busily mining gold, and those who were recruited proved to be largely unreliable. Finally, and as what they thought was a last resort, the railroad hired Chinese as laborers. As it turned out, they were much better workers. During the six-plus years of construction, the Central Pacific used a total of 10,000 workers, of which nine of ten were Chinese.

It was tough, dangerous work over terribly difficult terrain. In some areas, laborers were suspended from cliffs by ropes in order to hack the roadbed out of the mountainside. While digging the Summit Tunnel in the Sierras, work crews had to blast through 1,600 feet of such hard granite that in spots they were able to progress just one foot a day. A new explosive, nitroglycerin, speeded the work, but was extremely unstable in its early form—always dangerous and frequently fatal. Nevertheless, work went on from both ends, and when the crews finally met, the two holes were only a few inches off. After five years of prodigious effort, the CP crews had laid just 100 miles of track.

The Union Pacific didn't have the awful terrain to deal with and made much faster progress heading west across the Great Plains. There were still problems aplenty—finding wood from which to fashion cross ties, for instance, since there were no trees on the Nebraska prairie. To fill this obvious need, the railroad contracted with men, called tie hacks, to cut ties from trees in the western mountains, then haul the ties to meet the railroad.

The Union Pacific paid its railroad workers $1 per day, and all of them lived in railcars that followed them as track was laid. Many were immigrants of Irish and German descent, and a good many had seen service in the Civil War. As the railroad moved farther west, it entered Sioux territory. While the Sioux had ignored the occasional wagon train, they clearly considered the railroad a serious threat to their way of life. Attacks became more frequent and progress slowed as the ex-soldiers were diverted into armed units assigned to protect the remaining work crews. Through it all, fueled by relatively high wages and visions of huge profits, the work went on at a feverish pace. In fact, one Union Pacific crew laid just over ten miles of track in one day—an astonishing feat considering the backbreaking nature of the work and the lack of any kind of power equipment.

The transcontinental link finally occurred on May 10, 1869, when the two railroads met near Promontory, Utah. Sorry, but it was an ordinary iron spike, not a golden one, that was driven into the last cross tie. For that matter, the event didn't really occur at Promontory but at a site about thirty miles away. The famous photo of the event is actually of a reenactment. One other item of questionable relevance, but possible interest: America's transcontinental railroad and the Suez Canal were both completed in 1869, a coincidence that prompted Jules Verne to write *Around the World in 80 Days*.

The Stream Becomes a Flood

It's hard for us to imagine the impact on the country when the cross-country rail line was finally opened. For a quarter of a century it had taken a full six months to reach California or Oregon by wagon train from one of the several jump-off points in the Midwest, and one of every ten pioneers died during the crossing. Then, quite suddenly, a person could travel in relative safety and comfort all the way from New York City to Sacramento in a little over six and a half days. People started to do so by the thousands upon thousands.

If the western movement of people was a stream, then the mail they sent and received soon became a flood. Before the transcontinental link, mail was either carried by stagecoach or, if coast to coast, around the Horn by sailing ship—a matter of several months. Suddenly, trains had the capacity to carry large quantities of mail at low cost and at unheard of speed: coast to coast in less than a week. Mail was sorted en route in mail cars. Speed was everything. Bags of mail were thrown from trains or snatched from trackside poles as trains sped without stopping through small towns all across America. There was glamour attached to speedy mail service, and the railroads gave it top priority. Trains brought news for the masses, too— more of it and faster than ever before. Newspapers printed in major cities were delivered by train to subscribers in small-town America within hours.

America Starts Moving by Rail

By 1865, when the Civil War ended, some 30,000 miles of track crossed the country. During the next twenty-five years, steel rails spider-webbed all over America, until by 1890, well over 200,000 miles of track ran from sea to shining sea.

The federal government encouraged the spread of the railroads by giving them land, not just rights of way on which to lay their tracks but land adjacent to the tracks, too—millions of acres. The railroads sold this land at very low prices and actually gave it away in some cases. Railroads hired "colonization agents" to recruit families from the industrial East Coast. Many railroads actually operated what were called immigrant trains, which carried entire families, including personal belongings and even livestock, from the eastern United States into the newly opened areas. Thousands took advantage of this new opportunity, and as word spread across the Atlantic, European immigrants joined the flood of new settlers.

The railroads were eager, almost desperate, to encourage this resettlement, because they needed people—lots of people—wherever they laid their tracks if the railroad itself was to succeed. It worked, too, because the supplies these settlers needed to start and sustain their new lives on the American frontier were brought to them by the railroads. And, of course, as they became established farmers and ranchers, they sent their wheat and corn and cattle to eastern markets—also by rail.

In less than a quarter of a century, the railroads were prospering and so were the cities and towns they served. Chicago became a thriving center of business and trade, not coincidentally because the eleven different railroads serving that city made it the busiest railroad center in the world. New factories full of new employees sprang up to process the cattle, grain, lumber, and other raw materials being delivered to Chicago by rail from the West. And, naturally, the goods produced by these factories were then shipped by rail to consumers in every area of the country, including back to those people living in the now prosperous western towns.

It was certainly a time for people with new ideas. No doubt Richard Sears and Alvah Roebuck had a good one when they started their catalog business in 1887, but it was the railroads and their efficient handling of letters and packages that made it all possible. In fact, it's hardly a coincidence that Richard Sears, the partner who first realized the potential of the mail-order business, began his working career as a railroad agent in Minnesota. In reality, the Sears Tower that dominates the Chicago skyline today is as much a monument to the American railroad as to those two farsighted entrepreneurs.

Bigger, Better, Faster Trains

As the country grew, so did the railroads. More trains were going to more places, and they were getting there faster and more safely, too. Air brakes had been developed by George Westinghouse and were in general use on most trains by the 1880s. About that same time, a simple but significant improvement in the design of passenger cars occurred when an elastic diaphragm was added to each end of every car. These diaphragms connected when the cars were coupled together, and just like that the passageway between cars became enclosed. Until this improvement took place, the business of crossing from one lurching car to another was not for the young, the old, or the fainthearted. Once it became easy and safe for passengers to pass between moving railway cars, the modern version of the dining car suddenly became feasible.

The first regular onboard food service had begun in 1842, with credit again going to the Baltimore & Ohio. The food was prepared elsewhere, brought aboard the trains, and served cold to the passengers. Then, in 1867, George Pullman introduced a very early version of what we would come to recognize as a dining car. Actually, he called it a "hotel car," and for good reason: Since passengers didn't move back and forth between railcars, this one car contained cooking facilities, a dining area, and sleeping accommodations for as many as forty passengers.

George Pullman may have had a good idea with his hotel car, but he really hit it big when his Pullman Palace Car Company in Chicago began turning out luxury sleeping cars, which before long came to be known simply as "Pullmans." Not many people know that the railroads hauling George Pullman's sleeping cars around the country didn't actually own them. The Pullman Company retained ownership of the cars and merely leased them to the various railroads. Even the conductors and porters were Pullman employees. Pullman's "turn key operation" was several decades ahead of its time. In fact, for many years it was said that on any given night, more people were sleeping in Pullman car berths than in the beds of the largest hotel chains in the world.

George Pullman went so far as to build a small town for his workers adjacent to the Chicago plant where his railcars were built. At its peak, some 12,000 workers lived in the community created by their employer, working in his factory, living in his houses, and buying from his stores. Pullman was less a visionary than a relentless businessman, for the reality was that he made a profit on almost everything his employees bought, including the rent they paid for their homes.

Pullman's little empire began to come undone in 1893 when the country slid into a depression. As business declined and profits fell, Pullman reduced the wages he paid his employees. He did not, however, see a corresponding need to reduce the rents they paid for their housing. As the depression deepened, unrest among Pullman Company employees grew, and in 1894 they walked off their jobs in protest. Things turned ugly in short order, and in an ensuing riot, thirty-four people were killed at the Pullman plant. The U.S. Army was sent in and restored order by arresting the union leaders and tossing them in jail.

Government Regulation

For a number of years George Pullman had been regarded as an enlightened and respected businessman, but that image changed quickly after the strike. He soon found himself the object of severe criticism from many quarters. Pullman wasn't alone, either. Sharing the spotlight of harsh public opinion were a number of men who had made millions from railroads: Cornelius Vanderbilt, J. P. Morgan, James J. Hill, Jay Gould, and others.

These men were portrayed as greedy robber barons, and in truth many of them richly deserved the label. These were, after all, the days before government controls, and many railroad tycoons took full advantage of that lack of regulation through shady stock deals and shameless gouging. In many areas of the West, for instance, farmers and ranchers were at the mercy of the railroads that carried their cattle or grain to eastern markets. The railroads regularly increased their rates and were soon making huge profits while their customers continued to struggle for survival. In 1887, the federal government finally reacted, and the Interstate Commerce Commission was created by Congress to regulate the railroads, specifically to set the rates that could be charged for hauling freight.

The Unions Appear

Railroading in these early days was notoriously dangerous work. The combination of bigger, faster trains and the lack of anything approaching modern safety standards took a terrible toll. Brakemen worked on top of moving railcars in all weather. Bad track (usually laid in haste) often caused derailments. Locomotive boiler explosions were not uncommon and were always fatal to the head-end crew. It's estimated that in the thirty years leading up to World War I, railroad workers were killed on the job at the rate of some 2,500 a year, or an average of seven deaths every single day. Millions more were injured. Even everyday working conditions were often appalling. Temperatures in the locomotive cab could reach 30 degrees below zero in winter and 150 to 160 degrees in summer. Not surprisingly, these were the years when railroad unions were formed and began to gain acceptance. Gradually, the lives of railroad workers began to improve.

Storm Clouds on the Railroads' Horizon

The pendulum began swinging the other way when the country's railroads were nationalized during World War I and the government agreed to major concessions to the unions. Many of the new rules made sense at the time. For instance, an eight-hour day was established as standard for railroad employees, but at the same time, the government also agreed that a distance of 100 miles would constitute a full day's work for a train's operating crew. In those early days, that was realistic. Operating one of those early steam locomotives was exhausting work, and with stops along the route for watering and coaling, it could easily take a full eight hours to travel a hundred miles. But by the 1920s, long after the railroads had been returned to private ownership, the technology of steam locomotives had become more efficient and trains were being run at much higher speeds. The railroads were not able to change or get rid of the old union rules, so they often found themselves giving a train crew four days' pay for eight hours' work because their train had covered four hundred miles during that time.

Then trucks appeared. Actually, the value of hauling supplies by truck had become apparent in Europe during World War I, when the U.S. Army used fleets of vehicles to haul supplies and ammunition to the doughboys at the front. From that experience, it was easy to see that trucks had considerable potential for peacetime application. In 1919, a convoy of trucks set out to cross the country from Washington, D.C., to San Francisco. It took three months at an average speed of less than six miles per hour, but they did it. It was suddenly clear that the truck needed only one thing to become a new mode of transportation: a decent road. Incidentally, the young Army officer who headed up that little caravan was Dwight D. Eisenhower. During his presidency, billions of dollars were poured into the interstate highway system.

To provide jobs for the unemployed after the stock market crash of 1929, the government started building roads—the beginnings of our interstate highway system. As soon as new roads were finished, trucks began hauling freight over them. Instead of traveling city to city in a railroad boxcar, goods were traveling door to door in a truck. Then came buses—Greyhound, Trailways, and a host of small-time carriers—and the railroads started losing passenger business, too. Right behind the buses came private passenger cars. Thanks to Henry Ford and mass production, ordinary people could now pile into the family car and visit friends or relatives several hundred miles away. As if competition from trucks and buses and cars wasn't bad enough for the railroads, a few visionaries talked about airplane travel becoming feasible for large numbers of people within twenty years. To top it all off, in some parts of the country, railroads were even competing against each other for both freight and passenger business.

The Way to a Passenger's Heart

Whatever their other faults, the railroad entrepreneurs were not quitters, and they finally began to fight for their share of the passenger business. They competed by claiming faster trains, more comfortable routes, and more service amenities. But many railroads had come to realize that what passengers remembered most about their train trip was the dining experience. That's what they talked about with their friends and, as we all know, word of mouth is the most effective form of advertising. Soon, to the joy of rail passengers everywhere, competition between railroads had extended into the dining car.

During the 1930s, 1940s, and 1950s (with an interruption for World War II), it wasn't unusual to have more than a dozen entrees, including fresh fish and wild game, plus a lavish selection of desserts on a dining car menu. Many railroads became known for specific dishes served in their dining cars. Dining cars on the Great Northern, for instance, featured rainbow trout that had been caught, handed aboard the moving train, cooked, and served in the space of just a few hours.

The railroads did their best to regain passenger business after World War II by promoting rail travel to the West. They used traditional forms of advertising; in addition, many of the crack trains were given what Easterners would perceive to be Native American names: *Chief, Super Chief, Scout, Hiawatha,* and a few others.

Comes the Golden Age

Beginning around 1890 and continuing until the outbreak of World War II, Americans with the means were able to travel in real style from coast to coast and between many major cities throughout the country. It was a time that has come to be known as the *belle époque,* or the golden age, of train travel, as dozens of railroads vied for passenger business with crack trains that featured every manner of luxury and service.

The very, very rich—investment bankers, industrialists, the railroad tycoons themselves, and others of that ilk—traveled in their own private railcars, but until the railroads actually got into the business of providing it, luxury rail travel was simply not available, not even to the merely wealthy. Then, in the fall of 1911, the Santa Fe began offering once-a-week service between Chicago and Los Angeles with a train appropriately called the *de Luxe.* And indeed it was. Passengers slept in real brass beds. There were maids and a manicurist for female passengers, a barber for the men. The latest books and magazines could be found in an onboard library. Newspapers and the latest stock reports were put aboard at regular stops en route. In promoting the *de Luxe,* the railroad boasted that passengers would stay comfortable regardless of the outside temperature, thanks to a technological breakthrough the company described as an "air washing device"—a primitive form of air-conditioning.

As the years passed and passenger demand grew, the Santa Fe added more luxury trains to its popular Chicago–Los Angeles route. The *Chief* made its debut in 1926 and soon became the choice of movie stars traveling between coasts—a fact that the railroad promoted relentlessly, with publicity photos of the stars waving from the observation platform on the rear car. The lounge car featured a barber, a hairdresser, a manicurist, and a hostess. In the *Chief*'s dining car, the menu offered a dizzying variety, expertly prepared and served with a flourish. There was even a private dining room where Hollywood moguls could dine and make their blockbuster deals in private.

The *Chief* proved very popular. To meet the additional demand and broaden its passenger base, the Santa Fe added other new trains to the route. The *Scout* wasn't as fancy as the *Chief,* but it catered to middle-income families traveling on a budget and helped bring long-distance train travel to a whole new market. The *El Capitan* was an all-coach train, and the *California Limited* served only first-class passengers. Finally, in 1936, Santa Fe introduced the *Super Chief,* which soon became a standard in its own right. Gradually the traditional Pullman cars gave way to gleaming stainless-steel consists (any combination of locomotives and cars making up the entire train), with the now-classic bullet-shaped observation/lounge car bringing up the rear. Even after auto and air travel forced rail passenger service into serious decline, the Santa Fe steadfastly maintained its standards of quality and service to the very last.

Competition for passengers among railroads was probably fiercest on the routes between Chicago and New York City. A number of railroads served those cities, but most of the competition was between the Pennsylvania Railroad's *Broadway Limited* and the pride of the New York Central System, the famous *20th Century Limited.* Both trains ran at high speeds, both offered fine dining and many service amenities, and, for a time anyway, both left Chicago heading east at about the same time. Old-time Chicago train watchers tell of waiting at any one of several vantage points in the suburbs to see which train would be leading as they came thundering past, still running on parallel tracks at that point.

Other railroads were also contributing to the lore and legacy of the American luxury long-distance train. The Baltimore & Ohio operated a number of excellent trains but probably considered the *Capitol Limited,* running between Washington, D.C., and Chicago, to be its flag-ship. One of the Great Northern's best was the *Oriental Limited,* so named by the railroad's founder, James J. Hill, because he thought that his northern route from Chicago to Puget Sound would open the way for a vast amount of trade between the United States and Asian markets.

The Wabash Railroad's *Cannon Ball* began providing daylight service between St. Louis and Detroit in 1946.

Curiously, even though the famous song had been around for decades, there is no record of any train with that name before the Wabash got around to using it.

During this so-called *belle époque,* dozens of railroads operated literally hundreds of trains. Many developed their own identity and reputation: for speed, service, color scheme, a special dish in the dining car, or just its own peculiar *élan.* And, of course, in that wonderful railroad tradition, they were all given names. Some were clearly regional (*Connecticut Yankee, Southern Belle*), while others touted destinations (*Dixie Express, Orange Blossom Special, Texas Eagle*). Some trains were named for people, both real and fictional (*Commodore Vanderbilt, Pocahontas, Rip Van Winkle*). Some names were highly evocative (*Black Diamond, Flying Cloud, North Wind*), and at the other end of the spectrum, some tried to be clever (*Silent Knight*) or cute (*Seven O'Klocker*).

Many of us actually remember riding some of those trains, and they certainly were wonderful, maybe even as luxurious as we remember them. Still, the fact is that during all those so-called glory years of rail travel, most Americans rode on trains that were quite ordinary—slow and probably neither very clean nor very comfortable. Then as now, luxury was for the fortunate few.

First It Rained, Then It Poured

When trouble came for the passenger trains, it came from many directions at once, and it wasn't pretty. Trucks by the hundreds of thousands began hauling commodities of all kinds over a new system of interstate highways. Mom and Dad and their 2.5 kids traveled wherever they wanted to, coast to coast over that same highway system in a family car that ran on gasoline costing twenty-five cents a gallon. Airplanes became larger and faster, which meant they carried more people farther, faster, and cheaper than ever.

With all those fast, new jets flying everywhere, the U.S. Post Office decreed that all first-class mail would henceforth travel by air. (Remember? We used to pay one rate for letters sent by surface and a higher rate for airmail.) Revenue from first-class mail carried on fast passenger trains had been an important source of income for the railroads. Any one of those factors would have hurt; all together they were fatal.

Some railroads had seen it coming and tried to fight back, but one after another they all came to realize that it was a losing battle. At that point, the problem became how to get out of the passenger business. It wasn't easy in those days before deregulation. The same Interstate Commerce Commission that had been created in the late 1800s was now a way of bureaucratic life for the railroads. The Commission approved requests for routes and reviewed and approved the fares the railroads charged. Unfortunately, from the railroads' perspective, the Commission also had to approve whenever a railroad wanted to cut out passenger service. Usually, approval would only be given if the railroad could demonstrate that there was little if any demand for the service.

And so the game began. Railroads allowed both their equipment and their service to deteriorate in the hope that train travel would become such an unpleasant experience that passengers would turn elsewhere for their transportation. Certainly a lot did, but for many unlucky souls, the train was the only way to get where they had to go. (By the way, that's still the case today in many rural communities, where an Amtrak train is literally the only way in or out of town.)

Gradually, the situation settled into a standoff between the federal government and the railroads. The government refused to let the railroads stop providing passenger service; the railroads refused to provide more than the most basic service. The traditional dining car soon gave way to dirty lounge cars where vending machines dispensed stale packaged food. Sleeping cars on overnight trains were replaced with coaches, forcing passengers to sit up all night—even those willing and able to pay for first-class accommodations. It was a frustrating, maddening situation that went on for years. And everyone knew that sooner or later it could end only one way.

CHAPTER 3

Amtrak to the Rescue

The great trains are gone. Of course it's a pity, but with the advantage of 20/20 hindsight, most people agree it probably wasn't realistic to think that a nationwide system of privately operated passenger trains could have survived. It certainly hasn't worked out that way anywhere else in the world.

Anyway, after a decade or more of struggle, by 1970 it had become clear that the private railroads were simply not going to provide the country with anything even remotely resembling a nationwide rail passenger system. Even government oversight and regulation of the railroad industry wasn't going to save the passenger train. The railroads' claim that their financial health would be threatened if they were forced to continue providing passenger service was quite true in most cases. In fact, the Interstate Commerce Commission had all but officially acknowledged the plight of the railroads during the 1960s by granting various railroads permission to eliminate what amounted to almost 60 percent of the nation's passenger trains. Even that relief wasn't enough help for some, however, and private railroads continued to go broke at an alarming rate.

Time for Some Hard Decisions

Politicians had been watching these convulsions in the railroad industry with consternation. It had become clear to most members of Congress that sooner or later they would have to confront a very fundamental question: Did America really need some kind of rail passenger system? There were loud and vocal arguments on both sides, but the answer finally came up "yes," helped along at least in part by the fact that there was already a mandate to that effect on the books (the High Speed Ground Transportation Act, passed by Congress in 1965). The Act had created and funded a federal office to look into the feasibility of, among other ideas, high-speed rail. Some of the funds had gone into the study of far-out futuristic schemes, but a lot was put to practical use—helping the Penn Central begin high-speed Metroliner service between Washington, D.C., and New York, for example.

Things came to a head during the summer of 1969. After a great deal of argument and discussion, several different members in both the House and the Senate introduced a variety of bills. There was the usual dithering as the several versions slowly began working their way through the legislative process. Then, in June of 1970, the Penn Central collapsed into bankruptcy, and the resulting shock waves galvanized Congress into action. What emerged was something called the Rail Passenger Service Act, which finally allowed the private railroads to give up their passenger service. It also created a half-private, half-public company to take over the job of providing the country with a nationwide rail system. Although a bit short on specifics, the bill was nevertheless a commitment of support for passenger trains by the federal government. It was also pretty much a bipartisan effort. (Cynics have noted—in fact, they continue to note—that support of rail passenger service has less to do with political philosophy than with whether or not there are trains serving the district of any given member of Congress.)

The method of funding devised to launch this company was pretty complicated. Essentially, it allowed private railroads to make a cash payment to the new entity in exchange for permission to get out of the passenger business. On a case-by-case basis, railroads could also elect to make payment in the form of passenger equipment or operating crews. By the time it all shook out, twenty railroads had given nearly 1,200 pieces of equipment and a total of just over $197 million in cash. Congress added to the pot with $40 million in cash and another $100 million in loan guarantees, giving the company some $340 million to begin operations.

The final hurdle was a presidential signature. Richard Nixon had been keeping a low profile on the subject, but in retrospect that part of the process was probably never really in doubt. Nixon was already looking ahead to his reelection campaign in 1972 and worrying about how the unpopular war in Vietnam would affect his chances. Politically, he couldn't afford having the death of the passenger train laid at his doorstep, too. He signed the bill on October 30, 1970.

Any sighs of relief from pro-rail people were premature, however. Many who were there at the time now believe that the intent of the Nixon administration, if not actually the president himself, was to give lip-service support to the creation of the new rail system and then quietly kill it behind the scenes. These suspicions were subsequently borne out by a succession of power plays and roadblocks aimed at undermining the new company. They were usually orchestrated by Nixon aide John Erlichman (later of Watergate fame).

A Shortage of Know-How

The formal name for this new public/private corporation was the National Railroad Passenger Corporation and, as a matter of fact, that's still its name. Given the American propensity for nicknames, it's not surprising that the company almost immediately became known simply as Railpax, "pax" being common shorthand in the travel industry for "passengers." Within months, supposedly because a few critics of rail travel had begun referring to the new company as Railpox, the name was changed to Amtrak, an acronym for AMerican TRavel by trAcK. A new logo was also adopted—the same arrow-shaped mark still in use. It was almost instantly dubbed "the pointless arrow" (proving, I suppose, that someone will always find something to pick on).

As President Nixon named directors to the board of the brand-new company, not one railroad person was among them. Then, continuing this puzzling precedent, the board's choice for Amtrak's first president was Roger Lewis, who was available for the job by virtue of having been recently fired from his position as head of General Dynamics. Lewis assumed his new job just one week before Amtrak's scheduled start date. Don Phillips, a Washington-based journalist whose credentials include stints as a transportation writer at UPI and the *Washington Post,* came to like the man personally but publicly speculated on Lewis's real assignment: "I am persuaded that [Lewis] took the job with orders from the White House—direct or indirect—to oversee an orderly shutdown [of Amtrak]."

Some were startled by Lewis's priorities as he undertook what was undeniably a daunting job. One early Amtrak employee, Kevin McKinney, recalled in a *Trains* magazine story that the first memo Lewis distributed to his staff complained about the appearance of the reception area outside Amtrak's executive offices. The memo further directed that thereafter the number of magazines permitted on the coffee table would be limited to no more than four.

In putting together his team, Lewis surrounded himself with other executives equally unfamiliar with the business of railroading. Graham Claytor, himself a future Amtrak president and head of Southern Railway at the time, grumbled that "Amtrak doesn't have a railroader above the level of trainmaster" and dourly predicted that the new Amtrak brain trust, people Claytor considered near-hopeless amateurs, would "screw it up beyond . . . redemption."

Organizing a coast-to-coast system of passenger trains would be a monumental task under even the best of circumstances. It took a while, but the first train to operate under the Amtrak banner rolled out of Washington, D.C.'s Union Station headed for New York City on May 1, 1971.

A Rocky Start

An old Madison Avenue axiom says, "Nothing can kill a business faster than great advertising." Translation: If you create demand for a product or service, it had darn well better meet customer expectations; if it doesn't, the negative word of mouth can destroy you. Amtrak stumbled into that trap in its early days with a catchy advertising slogan: "We're making the trains worth traveling again." Unfortunately, they weren't.

From day one, Amtrak people found themselves with a maintenance and operations nightmare on their hands. Being saddled with a variety of equipment collected from more than a dozen railroads caused some nasty surprises. Amtrak soon discovered, for example, that the electrical systems in one or two passenger cars of a train's consist were incompatible with the rest of the train. Rolling stock, most of which had been old to begin with, was deteriorating rapidly, and little money was available for repairs, let alone any kind of orderly maintenance program. Worst of all, in Amtrak's first few years, locomotive failures occurred at the rate of ten per day. *Per day!* There was no money for new ones, of course, so Amtrak had to scrape together whatever cash it could and go back on the used locomotive market, buying poor equipment to replace terrible equipment.

In many areas of the country, Amtrak had to haul all that run-down equipment over poor track, adding to the woes of beleaguered passengers. Railroads were in poor financial shape after the disastrous 1960s, and rather than spend money to maintain their track, most simply let it deteriorate, reducing the speed of their freight trains accordingly. Amtrak passenger trains running over that same track had two options: run at the highest safe speed possible and cause discomfort to their passengers from the bouncing and swaying, or reduce speeds and frustrate their passengers with slow trains and late arrivals. Some choice!

Finally, many of the onboard crews, which Amtrak had inherited from private railroads along with all that run-down equipment, brought with them casual if not downright unpleasant attitudes. After all, they had probably been working for a railroad that had been actively trying to discourage passenger business for years.

For the record, a few railroads continued to guard their reputation for quality and service. One was the Santa Fe, which had begun operating the deservedly famous *Super Chief* between Chicago and Los Angeles in 1948. Amtrak had taken over the route, but Santa Fe's chairman, John Reed, was so distressed at the level of service being provided on the train that he indignantly withdrew permission for Amtrak to use the *Super Chief* name. That decision was never reversed, and today, although it has become one of the company's better trains, it is still called the *Southwest Chief.*

Too Many Trains, Not Enough Dollars

Despite these very serious concerns, Amtrak's biggest problem was financial. Within months, the company's deficit had begun to mount alarmingly. For one thing, start-up costs had been huge. For another, Amtrak's route system was highly political from the get-go, with influential pro-rail members of Congress demanding trains into their districts whether or not there was any serious demand for the service. As an example, early in its existence, Amtrak began service between Washington, D.C., and Parkersburg, West Virginia, at the behest of Harley O. Staggers, the powerful and influential congressman from guess which state? In its first several years of operation, and despite increasing deficits, the Amtrak system had actually increased from some 23,000 miles to more than 27,000 miles.

About the only thing holding steady during Amtrak's turbulent early years was the public's support for rail. That support was reflected in the opinion polls, which, as we all know, are avidly read by the politicians. So, while Congress remained committed to the passenger train, it nevertheless recognized that too much was being demanded of the company and that a cutback in service would be necessary. After months of hand-wringing— no one in Congress wanted *his* train eliminated—the Amtrak system was reduced by about 14 percent, which ironically left the company just about the size it was on its very first day.

After several years of operations to provide some kind of track record, Congress at last began to evaluate Amtrak in a more realistic light. Clearly, the notion that Amtrak could operate at a profit had not been realistic— not as long as every other manner of public transportation, from airplanes to sidewalks, was being subsidized by government at one or more levels. In 1978, Congress formally acknowledged Amtrak's need for government support by ordering the company to generate enough revenue on its own to cover at least half of its operating costs. Then, a few years later, Congress finally dealt with the problem created by its own members. Specific monetary guidelines were set up for judging every train in Amtrak's system. Trains that fell below certain minimums for ridership and revenue would face elimination, even over the inevitable objections of individual members of Congress.

No Friend in Reagan

Somehow Amtrak managed to muddle through the 1970s, meeting and at least trying to deal with one obstacle after another. Another obstacle would come along in 1981, when Ronald Reagan took office as the country's fortieth president. Reagan was opposed to any subsidy for Amtrak, and with Budget Director David Stockman at the point, the first of many attempts to reduce or eliminate the flow of federal dollars to Amtrak was not long in coming. Instead of proposing plans for the future, Amtrak found itself having to justify its very existence with an administration that was almost blindly anti-rail. (Ironically, for many years Ronald Reagan had appeared in advertising campaigns extolling the virtues of the Union Pacific's passenger service.)

Another Change at the Top

It had taken almost four years, but influential pro-rail members of Congress had finally gotten the idea that Roger Lewis was not the right man to run Amtrak. One clue came when in spite of all Amtrak's problems Lewis would not support a request to Congress for additional funding. Responding to congressional pressure, the Amtrak board replaced Lewis with Paul Reistrup. Reistrup was a railroader, all right, but he proved artless when it came to dealing with the politicians. After a three-and-a-half-year hitch, he was replaced by Alan Boyd. Once again Amtrak found itself with a nonrailroad man as its president, but Boyd had been the country's very first Secretary of Transportation and was a consummate Washington insider. During his four-year tenure, and despite Reagan's policy of benign neglect toward Amtrak, Boyd managed to bring about some kind of political stability among the various players.

During most of Amtrak's first dozen years, however, the timing for its top leadership somehow seemed to be wrong. When circumstances cried out for someone with operational know-how, they got a politician; when they needed someone who could talk turkey with the power brokers on Capitol Hill, they got a railroader. Fortunately for Amtrak, Graham Claytor became the company's fourth president in the summer of 1982.

The Cavalry Arrives Just in Time

W. Graham Claytor, Jr. was a railroad man first and foremost. He was known to "walk the train" on every Amtrak trip he took, relentlessly looking for the smallest out-of-place detail. But Claytor also proved to be a skilled politician. Already greatly respected by his peers, he was soon viewed in the same way by members of Congress as well, many of whom felt a good deal more comfortable about continuing federal support for Amtrak with the no-nonsense former president of Southern Railway in charge. Unlike most of his predecessors, Claytor was able to speak from experience and with authority. Happily, under Claytor's leadership, Amtrak began to deliver.

Claytor began a shape-up program at Amtrak that would continue through the 1980s. Training improved for employees, and gradually (due to elaborate procedures required by union contracts) those with unsatisfactory performance records were weeded out. As did the railroad barons of a century before, Claytor knew that what passengers most remember is having a meal in the dining car. Little by little—when you're habitually underfunded, there's no other way—plastic was replaced by china and stainless-steel utensils in Amtrak diners, and airline-type food gave way to meals prepared on board. Claytor was a hands-on leader who took a personal interest in every aspect of the Amtrak operation. Many an Amtrak passenger who had written a letter of complaint about some lapse in service was surprised to receive a personal letter from

Claytor himself in response, including an assurance that the matter would be addressed.

One day at a time, Amtrak began working through many of its problems. Engineers and conductors, who had continued to be employees of the freight railroads, became Amtrak employees. New contracts with labor unions resulted in more productivity from onboard crews. In addition to support for operating expenses, Congress provided funds for new equipment: bi-level Superliners to replace traditional railcars on Amtrak's western runs were ordered in 1975, followed by an order for new locomotives in 1976. In the late 1980s, Amtrak placed an order for a new generation of passenger car, dubbed the Viewliner, which would enable the company to start getting rid of the old single-level coaches and sleepers still operating on eastern routes. In 1993, a new locomotive appeared, the first one in several decades specifically designed for passenger train service, and a new order for updated Superliners was placed.

The End of an Era

In December of 1993, Graham Claytor retired; in May of 1994, less than six months later, he died at the age of eighty-two. It is universally agreed that Amtrak would probably never have survived without him.

A New Hand on the Throttle

In succeeding Graham Claytor, Thomas M. Downs became Amtrak's fifth president. Downs had his hands full from the start. Minimal funding during the eight-year Reagan administration had continued under George Bush and was beginning to take its toll. Replacement and maintenance for locomotives and cars were being deferred because of a lack of funding; and equipment failures, the same problem that had plagued Amtrak in its start-up years, was happening all over again. President Bill Clinton was vocally pro-rail, but his budget requests for Amtrak, generous compared to those of Reagan and Bush, were drastically reduced by a suddenly conservative Congress.

During his first year at Amtrak's helm, Downs moved quickly to streamline the company's operations, transferring both responsibility and authority further down toward frontline employees. As a direct result, and with reduced costs clearly part of the picture, some 600 middle-management people were laid off. In December of 1994, Downs had the dubious distinction of announcing the most drastic reduction in service in Amtrak history—more than 20 percent.

Since then, there have been even more cutbacks as Amtrak, under constant attack by a Republican Congress, has struggled to achieve breakeven. Additional trains have been eliminated, some routes have been shortened, and schedules of one or two popular long-distance trains have been reduced from daily to just three or four days a week. In some cases it has helped, but some of the cutbacks (the schedule reductions, for example) have had an opposite effect and in one or two instances were rescinded.

All this is not to say, however, that there aren't some very positive signs. In some cases, state governments have stepped in and provided funds to make sure their citizens continue to have rail service. California helps fund the *San Joaquins* and the *Capitols;* Vermont helps underwrite the cost of operating what was called the *Montrealer* but has since been appropriately renamed the *Vermonter;* and Illinois has stepped in to ensure continuation of rail service between Chicago and several cities downstate as well as St. Louis.

As noted earlier, Amtrak has made a real effort to move both responsibility and authority further down the chain of command. For example, a product line manager is now responsible for each of Amtrak's long-distance trains—that means the train's profitability in addition to the train's operation. The result has been better service, special menus with tasty regional dishes served in dining cars, and happier passengers. In fact, Amtrak recently received national recognition for "most improved customer service" from Knowledge Exchange, a publishing firm specializing in financial analysis.

To generate additional revenue, Amtrak began carrying freight in 1997 and several high-speed boxcars may now be seen at the end of many passenger trains. There may well be a downside, however. Although Amtrak's freight business is a tiny drop in the bucket by comparison, it nevertheless means that they're now in competition with the freight railroads over whose tracks Amtrak trains must travel. The concern, of course, is that these other railroads will now be even less inclined to worry about Amtrak's on-time performance.

As 1997 was ending, Congress finally passed legislation that would provide the railroad with funding that would ensure continued operations for at least several more years. And, in a move that surprised many, Tom Downs resigned as Amtrak president and chief executive officer, triggering a search for a successor.

It has been a rocky road and there are still real concerns for the future of passenger rail service in the U.S., but the fact is every day Amtrak trains continue to carry Americans to and from thousands of cities and towns from one end of the country to the other. In terms of cost to the taxpayer, it's all being done at bargain prices. In its first years of operation, Amtrak depended on the federal government for almost 60 percent of its operating costs. Today, revenues from the sale of rail tickets and other sources (carrying the mail for the U.S. Postal Service, for example) cover some 80 percent of the company's operating cost, making Amtrak the most cost-effective public rail transportation system in the world.

Considering the obstacles that have been overcome and notwithstanding the difficulties lying ahead, that's quite a record.

CHAPTER 4

Planning Your Own Train Trip

I f you want to fly between two large U.S. cities, there will
probably be several airlines from which to choose. But if
it's a long-distance train ride you're after, then Amtrak is
your only option. The Amtrak system covers most of the
continental United States, which means you can reach or
get close to most major cities by train. (See the Amtrak
System Map on pages xvi–xvii.) Before you begin to work
out the details of any rail trip, however, you should know
a few things about present-day train travel and you ought
to consider a few others.

Beware of Great Expectations

To avoid disappointment, it's important to have a clear
understanding of what you can reasonably expect from
your train trip—and, probably more important, what you
shouldn't expect. One Amtrak car attendant I spoke to is
still astonished about the couple on a cross-country honey-
moon train trip who had somehow gotten the idea that
there would be a fireplace in their compartment. Many of
these misunderstandings, at least according to the onboard
crews, are caused by advertising that gives people the idea

A Superliner coach. Most passengers ride on the upper level of these cars. (Photo courtesy of Amtrak)

that a train is like a cruise ship. There are indeed similarities, but the two experiences are opposite in the most fundamental way: Cruise ships focus on a wide variety of on-board activities, because most of the time there's nothing to see but ocean beyond the railing. Trains, on the other hand, offer constantly changing scenery outside the window and for the most part leave passengers to create their own activities and diversions.

Things You Should Know Before You Start

First, and probably most important, do your planning as far in advance as possible. Your first priority should be deciding on specific dates for your train travel. Most long-distance trains, especially the sleeping-car accommodations, sell out very quickly. That's particularly true during the busy summer months, but no matter when you travel, it's a very

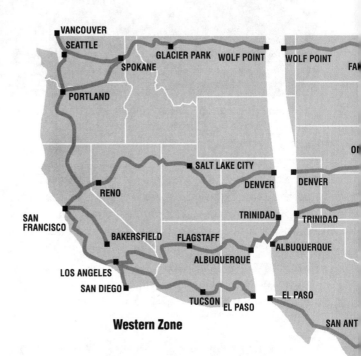

Amtra

Western Zone

are Zones

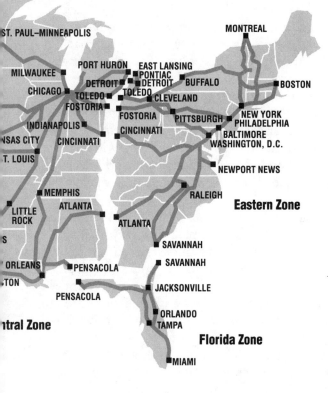

ST. PAUL–MINNEAPOLIS

MILWAUKEE
PORT HURON   EAST LANSING
PONTIAC
CHICAGO   DETROIT   DETROIT   BUFFALO   BOSTON
TOLEDO   TOLEDO   CLEVELAND
FOSTORIA
FOSTORIA   PITTSBURGH   NEW YORK
INDIANAPOLIS   PHILADELPHIA
CINCINNATI
NSAS CITY   CINCINNATI   BALTIMORE
T. LOUIS   WASHINGTON, D.C.

NEWPORT NEWS

MEMPHIS   RALEIGH
ATLANTA   **Eastern Zone**
LITTLE
ROCK
ATLANTA
S
SAVANNAH
ORLEANS   SAVANNAH
TON   PENSACOLA
JACKSONVILLE
PENSACOLA
ORLANDO
ntral Zone   TAMPA
Florida Zone
MIAMI

MONTREAL

good idea to make your train reservations at least ninety days in advance—sooner if you can.

For years, trains operating east of the Mississippi River were comprised of the traditional single-level railcars, while long-distance trains running west of the Mississippi were equipped with Amtrak's two-level Superliner cars. However, new equipment has been steadily replacing the old cars. Today, Superliners are being used on a number of eastern trains: the *Capitol Limited,* the *Cardinal,* the *City of New Orleans,* and *Auto Train,* for example. New Viewliner sleepers are now in use on the trains running between New York and Florida and on the *Crescent* and *Twilight Shoreliner* (which up until fairly recently was called the *Night Owl*).

On all long-distance trains, Amtrak offers its passengers a choice between two distinct types of service: coach or first class. On those trains, the term "first class" always refers to the sleeping cars (also called "sleepers"). In fact, the two terms are interchangeable. Some all-coach trains also have two levels of coach class, referred to as "coach" and "club coach" (also called "parlor car," usually by the old-timers). With club coach, you will get wider, more comfortable seats and complimentary food and beverages served at your seat. There is, of course, a surcharge for these extras.

The information and suggestions in the following pages are intended to help you plan a rail trip that's best suited to your individual preferences and budget. While most of the examples refer to longer and more detailed itineraries, shorter rail trips deserve no less attention. Whether you're considering a four-day excursion through New England to admire the fall colors or a four-week rail tour of the West, the planning process should be the same—as thorough and as unhurried as possible. After all, any vacation, whether short or long, requires an investment of your leisure time and your money, neither of which should be wasted.

Consider a Package Tour

This chapter is about planning your own train trip because it's fun to do and you can design it exactly the way you want. You should be aware, however, that Amtrak has packaged a wide variety of rail tours of varying lengths, which include train fare, hotels, and some sightseeing. These trips can usually be scheduled at your convenience, and the cost will probably be somewhat lower than if you book the identical itinerary yourself. You are limited to the preplanned itineraries, however. For information and a detailed brochure, call Amtrak's Great American Vacations at 800-321-8684.

A Word About Rail Fares

When traveling by train, all passengers pay a basic rail fare that covers the cost of a seat in coach class. That fare will vary, depending on how far you're traveling. If you opt to travel in first class—meaning in one of the several different sleeping car accommodations—you'll be upgrading your ticket by, in effect, paying a first-class surcharge. The cost of the upgrade will vary, depending upon the type of accommodations you select and how far you're traveling. Both the basic rail fare and the first-class surcharge will fluctuate, depending on the time of year you travel—you'll pay more during the busy summer months and less at other times.

Special Fares

With Amtrak's special Explore America fares, you can add a surprising amount of traveling to a simple itinerary without increasing the cost of your basic rail ticket. And, unlike most airline fares, these are easy to understand.

Amtrak has divided the country into three zones: **East** (basically, from the Atlantic seaboard inland as far as Detroit and Atlanta), **West** (from Denver to the Pacific Coast), and **Central** (everything in between). There is also a kind of subzone that includes all of Florida and as far north as Savannah, Georgia. How much you'll pay on an Explore America fare depends on whether you travel through one, two, or three zones.

You can use an Explore America fare as long as you aren't traveling for more than forty-five days and don't stop off in more than three places. Stick to those guidelines, and there will be no increase in your basic rail fare no matter how many miles you travel, including round-trip itineraries. Just remember that this is the basic rail fare for which you get a coach seat. If you want to travel in a sleeping car, you'll pay the first-class surcharge on top of this special fare.

Look for Other Discounts

Your age (at either end of the spectrum) can also save you money. Children under two years of age travel free. Those between ages two and fifteen pay half fare when accompanied by an adult. Seniors aged sixty-two and over get a 15 percent discount on their rail fare when traveling Monday through Thursday. For a $20 annual fee, full-time students can obtain a Student Advantage card, which also yields a 15 percent discount. (Call 800-333-2920 to order this card.) Are you a member of AAA? That's worth a 10 percent discount. There is also a 15 percent discount for passengers with disabilities (some form of documentation will be required). Be advised, however, that none of these special discounts apply to sleeping-car accommodations, and there may be other restrictions. For instance, the senior discount doesn't apply on *Auto Train* or for Metroliner service between Washington, D.C., and New York on weekdays. As noted already, fares vary according to the season, so once you have tentative dates, check with Amtrak to see when those changes in price occur. It may be that you can save some money just by changing the dates of your trip by a week or so.

The North American Rail Pass

As this edition was being sent off to the printer, Amtrak and VIA Rail in Canada were introducing the North American Rail Pass. Modeled after the very popular Eurail Pass, it offers unlimited travel for thirty days on both the Amtrak and the VIA systems. These passes may be purchased through travel agencies or directly from Amtrak or VIA Rail. Again, I would recommend using a knowledgeable travel agent because prices will vary according to the time of year and there are a number of restrictions. For example, the pass will not be valid on *Auto Train,* on Metroliners, or on Canadian trains not operated by VIA. Another important note: It will be valid for coach travel only; if traveling first class, you'll still have to pay the usual supplemental charge for sleeping-car and club coach accommodations.

Who Should Plan Your Trip?

There's no reason at all why you can't do all the preliminary planning yourself. For me, that's part of the fun. Besides, the more personal thought you put into your trip, the more successful and rewarding the whole experience is likely to be. Get as far into the details as you want, even selecting the specific trains you want to take. Once you think you're ready to make reservations, though, you should probably turn matters over to a knowledgeable travel agent. Usually, no additional cost is involved, since the agent is paid a commission by Amtrak (as well as by airlines, rental car companies, cruise ships, hotels, and others) for handling the details and your ticketing. I suggest letting the travel agent double-check what you've done and take care of the reservations and the ticketing. A good one will know a few tricks of the trade, which could mean you'll pay a lower fare.

How to Find a Knowledgeable Travel Agent

Ah, therein lies the rub! Notice I've used the word "knowledgeable" as opposed to "experienced." The unfortunate fact is, most travel agents—even those who have been in the business for a long time—don't necessarily know much about train travel. I tell you that from bitter experience. It's easy to have the train trip you've always dreamed about turned into a nightmare by the wrong travel agent. Never fear. I have a few suggestions to help you find the right one.

First, here's a simple one-question quiz to find out if your local travel agent knows very much about booking rail travel: Simply ask him or her if any of the Amtrak sleeping cars have windows for passengers sleeping in upper berths. If you get a lot of hemming and hawing, be careful! (The correct answer: Yes, but only in the new Viewliners.)

Every year, Amtrak presents Golden Spike Awards to a very small percentage of travel agents across the United States and Canada. To be recognized with one of these awards, a travel agent must have written a lot of Amtrak tickets. Chances are good that most of them will be able to handle even a complicated rail itinerary. (A list of Golden Spike travel agencies, along with a few travel agents who actually specialize in booking rail travel, is included in Appendix D.)

You might also stop by a local newsstand and look for one of the popular magazines directed at the serious railfans, such as *RailNews, Railfan & Railroad,* and *Trains.* Any travel agent advertising in one of those publications had better know his or her stuff!

Going to Do It Yourself? Start with a Timetable

To get started, just take things in a logical order, starting with the two most important decisions: How long will you be gone, and where do you want to go? Everything else is simply a matter of filling in details, and that's when you'll need an Amtrak timetable. You can usually get one free by calling Amtrak's nationwide toll-free number: 800-USA-RAIL (872-7245). They'll mail one to you, although it may take several weeks to arrive. If you don't want to wait, contact the closest Amtrak office or try your travel agent, who may have a few. Just be sure to ask for the National Timetable (sometimes referred to as the System Timetable), which includes schedules for all Amtrak trains from coast to coast. There is also a Northeast Timetable, which provides a detailed schedule of trains running between New York and Boston. You may want to ask for both. Or just get on the Internet, call up Amtrak's web page at *http://www. amtrak.com,* and go to the schedules. The current timetable for every train in the Amtrak system is right there for you. For that matter, you can also order printed copies of the timetables from the web page.

Learn How to Read the Timetable

Amtrak has done a good job with its timetables. The format is simple and well presented, making the tables easy to read. The timetables contain much more than just train schedules. Depending on your specific itinerary, much of the information may be of little or no concern, but some could be very important.

Below each schedule, for instance, is a paragraph describing the different services available on that particular train. That's where you can find out if your train has a dining car serving full meals or only a lounge car serving snacks. Most of Amtrak's long-distance trains run daily, but others

California Zephyr

Chicago...Denver...
Salt Lake City...Reno...
Oakland (San Francisco)

5			◄ Train Number ►		6
Daily			◄ Days of Operation ►		**Daily**
Read Down	Mile	▼		Symbol ▲	Read Up
3 05P	0	Dp	Chicago, IL-Union Sta. (CT)	⚐ ♿ Ar	4 20P
3 41P	28		Naperville, IL	♿	2 59P
4 51P	104		Princeton, IL	● ♿	1 47P
5 50P	162		Galesburg, IL-S. Seminary St.	♿	12 55P
6 38P	205		Burlington, IA	● ♿	12 04P
7 13P	233		Mt. Pleasant, IA	⚐ ♿	11 30A
7 59P	280		Ottumwa, IA	⚐ ♿	10 44A
9 17P	360	▼	Osceola, IA (Des Moines)	● ♿	9 23A
9 52P	393		Creston, IA	● ♿	8 47A
🚌 Amtrak Thruway Bus Connection-Kansas City, MO/Omaha, NE-Schedule Below					
12 06A	501	Ar	Omaha, NE	⚐ ♿ Dp	6 57A
12 31A		Dp		Ar	6 32A
1 35A	555	Ar	Lincoln, NE	⚐ ♿ Dp	5 07A
1 45A		Dp		Ar	5 01A
3 22A	652		Hastings, NE (Grand Island)	⚐ ♿	3 28A
4 10A	706		Holdredge, NE	● ♿	2 38A
5 20A	784	▼	McCook, NE (CT)	● ♿	1 30A
6 42A	960		Fort Morgan, CO (MT)	● ♿	10 05P
8 39A	1037	Ar	Denver, CO	⚐ ♿ Dp	8 47P
9 35A		Dp	(Colorado Springs 🚌)	Ar	8 02P
11 30A	1100		Fraser-Winter Park, CO	● ♿	5 17P
12 00N	1113		Granby, CO (Rocky Mtn. Nat'l Park)	● ♿ 4 52P	
3 15P	1222		Glenwood Springs, CO (Aspen)	⚐ ♿	1 42P
5 25P	1311		Grand Junction, CO	⚐ ♿	11 57A
7 19P	1390		Green River, UT	● ♿	9 13A
8 37P	1488	▼	Helper, UT (Price)	● ♿	8 10A
10 42P	1564		Provo, UT	● ♿	6 05A
12 13A	1608	Ar	Salt Lake City, UT	⚐ ♿ Dp	5 15A
1 05A		Dp	(MT)	Ar	4 50A
4 18A	1871	▼	Elko, NV (PT)	● ♿	10 58P
6 25A	2009		Winnemucca, NV	● ♿	8 53P
9 40A	2180	Ar	Sparks, NV	● ♿ Dp	6 20P
9 55A		Dp		Ar	6 05P
10 06A	2184		Reno, NV	⚐ ♿	5 45P
10 59A	2218		Truckee, CA	● ♿	4 48P
1 07P	2284		Colfax, CA	● ♿	2 37P
2 13P	2319		Roseville, CA	● ♿	1 47P
3 05P	2337		Sacramento, CA	⚐ ♿	1 20P
3 25P	2350		Davis, CA	⚐ ♿	12 43P
3 49P	2377		Suisun-Fairfield, CA	● ♿	12 15P
4 11P	2393		Martinez, CA (San Joaquin Trains)	⚐ ♿	11 53A
4 40P	2413	▼	Richmond, CA-BART Sta.	♿	11 21A
4 55P	2420		Emeryville, CA	⚐ ♿	11 10A
5 40P	2425	Ar	Oakland, CA-Jack London Sq. (PT)	⚐ ♿ Dp	10 40A

Connecting Services

🚌 Amtrak Thruway Bus Connection—Emeryville, CA 36/San Francisco, CA						
5 10P	0	Dp	Emeryville, CA (PT)	⚐	Ar	10 45A
			San Francisco, CA 🚌			
5 40P	9	Ar	-Ferry Building	⚐	Dp	10 25A
5 55P	10	Ar	-Fishermans Wharf, Pier 39	● 26	Dp	9 55A
6 10P	11	Ar	-S.F. Shopping Cntr., 835 Market		Dp	9 40A

This is a recent timetable for the *California Zephyr*. Read down for Train 5's schedule (Chicago to Oakland) and up for Train 6 (Oakland to Chicago). The Symbol column indicates if there is checked baggage service and/or if the platform is handicapped accessible at that particular station. The black dot means that tickets are not sold at that station but may be purchased when you board the train.

don't—the *Cardinal* or the *Sunset Limited,* for example. When you select a specific train for your itinerary, it's important to know if it runs every day or just three days a week. The timetable will give you that and other information.

Some cities not served by Amtrak may be reached by buses scheduled to connect with the trains. That information is also in the timetable, along with the locations of all Amtrak stations and whether or not you can check baggage there.

One more thing about timetables in general: Remember that minor changes in train schedules occur frequently. A train that is listed in the current schedule to depart at 10:00 A.M. today could leave thirty or forty minutes earlier three months in the future when you're planning to travel. So once you've worked out your itinerary and are ready to book your reservation, be sure to confirm all departure and arrival times for your specific dates, either by calling Amtrak directly or through your travel agent. Then check again a few days before you leave.

Study the sample Amtrak timetable for a few minutes, and you'll discover that there is order and logic to the format. The schedule for the westbound *California Zephyr,* Train 5, runs top to bottom in the left-hand column, while the schedule for the eastbound *Zephyr,* Train 6, is listed bottom to top in the right-hand column. (Please note that this is just an example of a typical timetable's format. The *Zephyr*'s current schedule will no doubt have a number of changes.)

Deciding on Your Destinations

Study the map of Amtrak's coast-to-coast system (pages xvi–xvii) and settle on a primary destination. Then, assuming you have the time, consider adding two more stopovers. Using those special Explore America fares, you can do that with very little increase in your basic rail fare . . . and there will be *no* increase if you stay within the same number of zones.

For instance, suppose you live in Washington, D.C., and want to spend some time with your favorite Aunt Mabel in Atlanta. Of course, the obvious thing to do is hop Train 19, the *Crescent,* to Atlanta, spend a few days with your aunt, then return home on the same train. But by taking advantage of the Explore America fare, look at the nifty vacation you can arrange for yourself:

- Washington, D.C., to Atlanta to visit Aunt Mabel
- Atlanta to New Orleans for some jazz and Creole cooking
- New Orleans to Chicago to see the Washington Redskins play the Chicago Bears
- Chicago back home to Washington, D.C.

At the time I put together this hypothetical example, Amtrak's regular round-trip coach fare between Washington, D.C., and Atlanta was $170.50. By switching to the Explore America fare, even after adding New Orleans and Chicago to the itinerary, the cost of the rail fare only increased to $218—less than $48. If you want to go first class, you'll pay extra for each additional night spent in sleeping-car accommodations. Sure, it'll cost more, but the upgrade is certainly worth considering. You'll save the cost of a hotel room for each night on the train, and your meals in the dining car will be free!

One of the main reasons for taking the train is to see the country, so bear that in mind when working out the details of your rail itineraries. These special fares can help you do that.

The Plane/Train Option

There's still another possibility to consider: Amtrak has arranged special joint fares with United Airlines that permit you to fly one way and take the train the other way. For instance, you could take the train from Los Angeles to Seattle to Chicago, then fly back to L.A. from Chicago. By the way,

I've talked to a good number of people who have tried this train/plane option, and all agree that they enjoyed the experience more when they took the train to their vacation destination and flew home. A knowledgeable travel agent can plan an air/rail trip for you, or to make your own arrangements, call this special toll-free number: 800-440-8202.

A Little Research Will Pay Off

After you make a list of places you want to visit, find out something about those areas *before* deciding how long you'll stop there. Any good bookstore will have travel guides for most major cities and for every region of the country. Public libraries are also excellent sources for free information, as are the tourism promotion offices in each of the various states.

For example, if you want to visit historical sites associated with the opening up of the American West, you'll probably head for Nebraska and Wyoming. Both state governments fund offices whose function is to get promotional literature into the hands of people exactly like you. Call them! Information operators in Lincoln and Cheyenne, the two states' capitals, will almost certainly be able to find the right phone numbers for you. If not, take an easy shortcut: Ask for the number of the governor's office and call there. The staff there will know exactly whom you should contact for your information and will be delighted to tell you.

You'll find that the research you do will pay big dividends in the form of a better trip. There's a wealth of information out there, and most of it is free.

Bus Connections

Almost every Amtrak train passes near but not through one or more large towns or cities. In many of those cases, Amtrak provides connecting bus service. For instance, say you're traveling from Los Angeles to Phoenix on the *Sunset*

Limited; Tucson, 120 miles southeast of Phoenix, is the closest station stop. No problem. Amtrak has a bus that will take you there, and it will be waiting at the station when the *Sunset* pulls into Tucson. Book the bus when you make your train reservations, so your ticket to Phoenix will be right there in your Amtrak ticket booklet when you board the bus.

Starting Your Itinerary

Okay, so you know how long you can be gone and where you want to go. Now you're ready to begin developing a detailed itinerary. Some travelers refuse to prepare itineraries in the mistaken belief that they will somehow become locked into a rigid schedule from which they can't deviate. What nonsense! A carefully prepared itinerary is nothing more than relevant information compiled in an orderly fashion. Not having one with you as you travel is foolish; not leaving one behind with friends or family in case of emergency is irresponsible.

Begin with a rough worksheet listing the days you'll be gone. At this stage, don't worry about specific dates. Remember that trip to New Orleans and Chicago via Aunt Mabel's? Here's how it would look on a worksheet, planned to fit neatly into a two-week vacation:

Day 1	Dep. Washington, D.C.
Day 2	Arr. Atlanta
Day 2–5	Aunt Mabel's
Day 6	Atlanta to New Orleans
Day 7, 8	New Orleans
Day 9	Dep. New Orleans
Day 10	Arr. Chicago
Day 11, 12	Chicago
Day 13	Dep. Chicago
Day 14	Arr. Washington, D.C.

Next, plug in real dates for your trip, beginning with those you can't change. In this example, you'll have to start with Day 12, when our hypothetical Redskins-Bears football game will be played. That's your one firm date, around which the rest of your itinerary must revolve. Once that's done, use your timetable and add specific trains to the rough itinerary.

Oct. 15	Dep. Washington, D.C., Train 19, *Crescent,* 6:50 P.M.
Oct. 16	Arr. Atlanta, 9:05 A.M.
Oct. 16–18	At Aunt Mabel's
Oct. 19	Dep. Atlanta, Train 19, *Crescent,* 9:25 A.M. Arr. New Orleans, 8:00 P.M.
Oct. 20, 21	Tour New Orleans
Oct. 22	Dep. New Orleans, Train 58, *City of New Orleans,* 2:10 P.M.
Oct. 23	Arr. Chicago 9:10 A.M.
Oct. 24, 25	Tour Chicago
Oct. 26	**Bears vs. Redskins**
Oct. 27	Dep. Chicago, Train 30, *Capitol Limited,* 7:45 P.M.
Oct. 28	Arr. Washington, D.C., 1:47 P.M.

Your itinerary may go through many additions and changes before you actually leave, so keep things simple until seats are booked and hotel rooms are reserved. (See the example of a finished itinerary at the end of this chapter.)

A Word of Warning About Connections

If you're flying, a missed connection seldom turns out to be a big deal. Chances are there will be another plane from either the same or a different airline before long. It's different with Amtrak. There are no other passenger railroads, and most of Amtrak's long-distance trains run only once a day. In fact, some, like the *Cardinal* or the *Sunset Limited,* operate just three days a week.

When you're traveling by train, a missed connection can be a real disaster, perhaps even a vacation buster. So as you prepare your rail itinerary, be careful of any close connections. If there's a later train that would allow more time to make the connection, choose that one, even if it means spending a few extra hours somewhere. Or consider stopping at that point, spending the night, and continuing your journey the next day. (Note: If you're traveling on an Explore America fare, you're permitted a total of three stopovers once your trip begins. If that extra night's stay counts as a stopover and puts you over the limit, it will affect the price of your ticket. Check that detail with Amtrak or your travel agent.)

How Safe Is a "Guaranteed Connection"?

If a connection can't be avoided, be sure to find out if it's a "guaranteed connection." If it is, Amtrak will do everything within reason to make sure you and other passengers affected make your connections. Usually that means holding the second train until yours arrives. As a practical matter, however, they can't delay the departure of a train for very long since it will undoubtedly be connecting with another train somewhere else.

If you do miss a guaranteed connection with a train that runs once a day, any of several things could occur. As a first choice, Amtrak will pay for your overnight stay in a hotel and put you on the same train the next day—assuming there's space, of course. Unfortunately, if you're traveling in a sleeper during one of the frequent busy periods, available space is not likely. In that case, even though you're holding a first-class ticket with a guaranteed connection, you could end up riding overnight in a coach seat. The eventual refund of your sleeping-car accommodation cost will be small consolation. If the entire train is sold out the next day, you could be sent on your way by plane or, depending on your destination, by bus, which is hardly the way you would expect your carefully planned train trip to end up.

Many factors could affect how your missed-connection problem is solved, but keep in mind that the final decision is up to Amtrak. (For more on this subject, see Chapter 8, "When Things Go Wrong.")

Should You Ride in Coach or in First Class?

You'll have to choose whether to go coach or first class before you book your train reservations. There are a number of factors to consider.

With a coach ticket, you'll ride in one of fifty or sixty seats in a standard passenger railcar and seventy or more in a Superliner coach. A first-class ticket puts you in small but private accommodations that include a bed to sleep in at night. In the next few pages I'll discuss other differences, but that's it in a nutshell.

For short trips, even if it's an all-day ride, the choice is easy—coach is the way to go. For overnight journeys, the coach versus first class decision becomes much more difficult, although the differences are easily defined: It boils down to cost and comfort.

Save Big Bucks in Coach

The biggest difference between coach and first class is cost. Coach is cheaper. In fact, it's a lot cheaper. Depending on the time of year, it's possible to travel from coast to coast and back again for less than $250, as long as you ride in coach class. That same trip in a sleeping car could cost $1,200 or more, depending on the type of accommodations you choose.

Here's an example: Let's assume you're traveling around the middle of September between Los Angeles and

Chicago on Train 4, the *Southwest Chief*. Here's how the cost of riding in a first-class economy bedroom compares with that same trip on the same train in coach. Remember, this is a two-night trip each way.

Los Angeles–Chicago, One Way

Class of Service	Coach	Sleeper
Basic Rail Fare	$235	$235
First Class Surcharge		$281
Total Cost	$235	$516

The cost differential between coach and first class really widens if you're traveling round-trip. There's only a slight increase in the coach fare, but now you're paying for a total of four nights in the sleeper.

Los Angeles–Chicago, Round-Trip

Class of Service	Coach	Sleeper
Basic Rail Fare	$242	$242
First Class Surcharge		$562
Total Cost	$242	$804

If two people are sharing the economy bedroom, remember that the first class surcharge is per room, not per person, so the second person will pay only the basic rail fare.

These costs will fluctuate depending on the time of year. The basic rail fare I quote here assumes you're using Amtrak's Explore America fare, which does have a few restrictions. The bottom line: Coach travel wins hands down if cost is your most important consideration. There are other considerations, however, and I'll get into those just a bit further on.

One Other Coach Option

On several of its short-haul routes, Amtrak offers some-thing called "Club Coach" service. Basically, it's a higher class of service provided in an all-coach train, and natu-rally it comes at a higher fare. Club coach passengers traveling along the Northeast Corridor are located in a special section of a coach that includes a snack bar. The surroundings are somewhat more plush, and a free tray meal is served to you in your seat. Go for it if you have the money and are into traveling first class. On other routes, principally the Los Angeles to San Diego trip, the club coach surcharge is minimal, but so is the difference in service.

The Unreserved "Reserved" Seat

You already know that securing a coach seat on any of Amtrak's long-distance trains requires a reservation. You also need to know that your reservation does not mean you have a specific seat assignment; it means simply that there will be one empty coach seat for you somewhere on that train. This is a small but important detail—especially if several people are traveling as a group. See Chapter 5, "Packing and Last-Minute Details," for suggestions on what you can do ahead of time and during the boarding process to get a good seat and to help make sure that your family will be seated together.

Can You Sleep Sitting Up?

The seats in coach class are wide and comfortable, and there is ample legroom even when they're fully reclined. Many seats are equipped with special extenders for your feet and legs so you can really stretch out. All things considered, your coach seat on the train will be compara-ble to a first-class seat on an airplane but with much more legroom. Make no mistake, however: It may be comfortable and roomy, but it's still a chair and you'll still have to sleep in it! If experience tells you that sleep just won't come under those conditions, consider opting for a sleeping car.

Are You a People Person?

Is privacy a big consideration for you? Coach seats are comfortable, and the car itself is spacious; but if the car is full, you'll be in fairly close proximity to fifty or sixty other people. If you're traveling alone, you could be lucky and end up with an empty seat beside you, but you could also be sitting next to a stranger or find a young mother with a couple of restless toddlers directly behind you. Some people see this as a great way to meet people and make new friends; others soon find themselves longing for the chance to be alone. Before letting cost alone dictate your decision, think about how much value you put on your privacy.

Comfort and Privacy in First Class

Life in the sleeping cars is undeniably luxurious compared to coach class. While none of the first-class accommodations can be described as spacious, they are private and, come nighttime, you've got your own room and a real bed to sleep in. Most but not all first-class accommodations are equipped with their own toilets. Sheets, blankets, pillows, and towels are all provided. For some travelers, the privacy and comfort found in the sleeping cars is an essential luxury for which they're happy to pay.

Free Meals: A First-Class Bonus

While all passengers are welcomed in the diner, the cost of dining car meals is included in the price of your first-class ticket. Coach passengers pay the regular menu prices for their meals. Since the prices in Amtrak dining cars are quite reasonable and you can always bring food aboard or purchase sandwiches and snacks in the lounge car, this may not be a major issue for you.

Other First-Class Extras

Amtrak serves up additional extras for sleeping-car passengers that add to the pleasure of the trip. On most trains, you'll receive a complimentary copy of a morning newspaper. The attendant in each sleeping car will provide a number of other services either automatically or on request. Some of these include wake-up calls, free juice and coffee each morning, making up your berth each evening, and serving food or beverages in your room.

Which First-Class Accommodation Should You Choose?

Coach seats are all pretty much alike, but when it comes to sleeping-car accommodations, there will be several choices, depending upon the specific train you've chosen. Eastern trains with Viewliners offer a choice between standard and deluxe bedrooms. Both types of rooms have an upper and lower berth, and both have toilet facilities in the room. Doors between adjoining bedrooms can be opened to provide four-bed compartments for families. Superliners operating west of the Mississippi River and on a number of eastern trains offer economy bedrooms for one or two people, deluxe bedrooms for two and possibly a small child, and family bedrooms that sleep two adults and two young children. Special rooms designed for passengers with disabilities are also available in both Viewliner and Superliner sleepers. Note that the cost of first-class accommodations is based on the room, not on the number of people occupying it. That means the first-class surcharge for an economy bedroom on a Superliner, which has two berths, is the same whether it's occupied by one or two people.

**Insider Tip: How to Cut the
Total Cost of a First-Class Ticket**

Suppose you're traveling overnight between Tampa and Baltimore. Train 90, the northbound *Silver Palm,* leaves Tampa just before midnight and arrives in Baltimore at 7:43 the next evening. Book a standard bedroom between

Tampa and Charleston, South Carolina, where the train arrives at about 9:00 A.M., and a coach seat the rest of the way. You'll have a comfortable bed to sleep in during the night and a coach seat for the daylight portion of the trip. The savings? Over $100.

Finding and Booking the Right Hotel

Unless you have several Aunt Mabels scattered around the country, one or more nights in a hotel could well be part of your train trip. For some people, a hotel is just a place to sleep, and almost any one will do. Others want their hotel to be another interesting and enjoyable part of the experience. In other words, where you stay during your stopovers is also a matter of your own personal taste and budget.

You can always turn the matter over to a travel agent. Just give your agent some idea of the type of hotel you want and a price range, and he or she will suggest a place to stay and take care of the booking.

If you want to make the arrangements yourself, the easiest approach is to call the central reservations number for one of the national hotel chains. They'll probably have a hotel where you want to go, and at least you'll know your room will meet the minimum standards of that particular chain. If, however, you prefer smaller hotels that may offer more in the way of taste and charm, your best bet is to browse in the travel section of your local bookstore. They'll have any number of guidebooks to help you make your choice, be it deluxe accommodations or a listing of quaint bed-and-breakfast spots. Once you find a hotel that seems to meet your requirements, call or write for rates and a brochure.

If all seems to your liking, go ahead and book your room. Do it by phone if you wish, but be sure to have the hotel send you a written confirmation. At the very least, ask for and make note of a confirmation number. It's standard practice for the hotel to ask you to guarantee your reservation with a credit card. If you would prefer not to, make sure the hotel will still honor your reservation. And be aware that without the credit card to guarantee it, your reservation will cancel automatically, probably at 6:00 P.M. on the day you're supposed to arrive.

What Is All This Going to Cost?

After you've done it a few times, you'll be able to estimate the cost of your train tickets fairly accurately. But why guess at it? Once you've decided when and where you're going, just call Amtrak (800-USA-RAIL) for a fare quote.

Now start on estimates for the other costs connected with your trip. Do not try to anticipate every individual expense. Instead, think in terms of daily averages, either per person or for the whole party, whichever is appropriate. The following guidelines are the ones I use, and they should provide you with a rough starting point. Adjust your own guidelines according to personal tastes and preferences.

Using your rough itinerary, figure out how many nights you'll be in hotels. For big-city hotels, allow no less than $100 to $120 per night; for hotels in smaller cities and rural areas, figure room rates at half to two-thirds of those amounts.

For food costs, figure $35 per day per person for adults and kids over twelve years of age. That's $7 for breakfast, $10 for lunch, and $18 for dinner. Yes, it could be less, and obviously it might well run much more, depending on where and what you eat. For younger children, reduce your estimate appropriately. (Remember that a first-class rail ticket includes the price of your dining car meals. If you're riding in a sleeper, figure out how many meals you'll be having on board the train and don't budget for those.)

Will you be renting a car somewhere along the way? Allow $40 per day. (Remember that there will likely be a "drop charge" or you'll be paying a higher daily rate if you return the car to a different location. Check that out ahead of time.)

How much sightseeing will you be doing? Better figure at least $10 to $20 per person per day. Don't count the days you'll be on the train. All of that sightseeing is free!

Going to be shopping and buying souvenirs? Don't guess at an average daily amount. Instead, decide what you can afford, and budget that lump sum for the entire trip. If you're traveling with children, I'd suggest deciding on an appropriate shopping allowance for each of them, then giving each child the money up front—and when it's gone, it's gone.

You'll also have small but frequent miscellaneous expenses, such as tips, snacks, fees for checked baggage, and film. Allow a total of $15 to $20 per day for such costs.

Be realistic, work with daily averages, and you'll be amazed at how accurate your estimate will be. A good estimate of your travel expenses done now is an important reality check that your trip will be affordable. It will also be a valuable guide to keep you on budget during your vacation.

Book Your Space Early!

Make your rail reservations as soon as your dates of departure and return are definite, when you've decided on your destination and other stopovers, and when you know whether you want coach or first-class seats. The other details—hotel rooms, rental cars, sightseeing tours, and the rest—can be filled in later. Early booking is especially important if you want sleeping car accommodations. They're very popular and fill up rapidly, particularly in the summer months. One important note: Amtrak now requires that you purchase your tickets within seven days after making a reservation, and sooner than that if you're booking for travel less than a month away.

Booking Through a Travel Agent

When it comes to making the actual reservation and getting your tickets, you can either work through a travel agent or handle it yourself directly with Amtrak. Personally, I prefer working through a knowledgeable travel agent. It won't cost you any more, and it's always a good idea to have a pro double-check your work. On one of my recent trips, for example, the travel agent I used knew that a lower fare was about to go into effect. He saved me almost $50 just by waiting a few days before writing my tickets.

Booking Direct with Amtrak

If you do elect to call Amtrak for reservations (800-USA-RAIL), you'll find the reservation agents very capable and usually extremely helpful. Do not call Amtrak direct if you're still uncertain about significant details of your itinerary. The agents are usually very busy and will not be able to give you the help you might need to make up your mind. They may try, but that's when some small but important detail is sure to fall through the cracks. Besides, filling in those details is how a travel agent earns his or her commission.

Whether you use a travel agent or call Amtrak direct, be sure to cover these important items with them before you hang up:

- Ask if they're sure you've been quoted the lowest possible fare.
- Ask if there are any changes you could make in your itinerary that might further reduce the cost.
- Ask if there are any connections in the itinerary that could be a problem.
- To avoid some of the less desirable accommodations, be sure to request specific room numbers if you're booking sleeping-car accommodations (see Chapter 9, "Passenger Train Equipment").

- Be sure to ask for the cancellation date for your reservation. You must purchase your tickets by a specific date once you've booked the space. If you don't pay for your tickets by that date, your reservation will cancel automatically, and your seats will go back into inventory for sale to someone else.
- Get a reservation number when you book. *This is important!* If you need to make any changes in your itinerary or if a problem should occur during your trip, that number will help Amtrak locate your complete record quickly.
- Be sure to look at your tickets carefully when they arrive and check each date and train number against your itinerary.

Booking via the Internet

You can also handle everything from start to finish online. Both Amtrak and VIA Rail in Canada offer interactive web sites that will permit you to review the timetables, select the trains you want, choose your sleeping car accommodations, make a reservation, and pay for the tickets. Both programs indicate that they will automatically select the lowest available fare for you. Frankly, these programs are still relatively new, and I'd still limit your online activity to checking schedules and preparing your itinerary. Then have a savvy travel agent double-check your work, make the reservations, and do the actual ticketing.

You can reach Amtrak's web page at *http://www.amtrak.com* and VIA Rail at *http://www.viarail.ca*. Incidentally, you'll also find lots of other information at both of those sites, including current news releases, system maps, descriptions, and photos of accommodations.

Do You Need Special Services?

If you or someone traveling with you should require any kind of special assistance or service—a wheelchair or a special diet, for instance—call Amtrak (800-USA-RAIL) at least seventy-two hours before you leave. It would also be a good idea to call the Amtrak representative at the station ahead of time. And then plan to arrive at the station early.

Insider Tip: How to Get Last-Minute Sleeping-Car Space

If you have to make a train trip on short notice, you may find that no sleeping-car space is available. Don't despair. It might not be a convenient hour for you, but at about 5:00 A.M. eastern time, call the Amtrak reservation number (800-USA-RAIL). Every morning around 4:00 A.M., the Amtrak computer is purged of passengers who have canceled space and at that hour you'll probably be first in line if a vacancy has occurred for the train you want. If worse comes to worst, board the train with your coach ticket and ask the conductor right away if there's a vacancy in one of the sleepers. There are no-shows more often than most of us would imagine.

Paying for Your Tickets

If you book with Amtrak direct, you can pay for your tickets by phone with a major credit card, and they will be mailed to you. If you live near an Amtrak station or office, you can pick up and pay for your tickets there. If you wish, you can pay for tickets through a travel agency, whether it handled the details or not. All the agent will need is your reservation number. By the way, it's a good idea to pay for your tickets with a credit card. It automatically provides you with a record of the purchase and a measure of protection should there be any solvency problems with the travel agency.

Make Copies of Your Tickets

Before you leave on your trip, make two photocopies of your tickets. Give one copy to a friend or relative, and take the other set with you. Just be sure to keep that second copy in a different place than your original tickets. This is a basic precaution that should be taken routinely by all travelers. As a matter of fact, you should photocopy all important travel documents, especially passports and plane or train tickets.

If You Need a Refund

Should your plans change or circumstances force you to cancel your trip, there's a right way to go about getting a refund. Go back to the travel agency if that's how you bought the tickets, or contact Amtrak if you booked direct. Either way, you will need the original tickets for a prompt refund. There are some restrictions and you will probably be charged a service fee, but generally speaking, Amtrak has a fairly liberal refund policy, even handling many refunds by mail.

What About Travel Insurance?

Travel agents sell this insurance. The policy will compensate you if you have to cancel your trip, either before you start out or while you're traveling. Almost any reason will constitute a valid claim. Think carefully before buying, because it's a better deal for some people than it is for others. Realistically, what are the chances that you'll have to cancel your trip at the last minute or interrupt it in progress? How old are you? How's your health? Are there other family or business circumstances that could cause you to abort your plans? There are several kinds of travel insurance, so talk it over with a travel agent. Before you decide, however, remember that he or she receives as much as a 30 percent commission for each sale. The bottom line is that it's a crapshoot and only you can make the call.

Putting Your Itinerary into Final Form

The last step in the planning process is to produce a final version of your itinerary. Remember that an itinerary is much more than just a day-by-day schedule; it should be your one written source of information, including everything you need to know about your trip: train arrival and departure times, addresses and phone numbers of all hotels, confirmation numbers for all reservations (train, hotel, and rental car), and other pertinent information and relevant notes.

The format may vary, but every itinerary should record information in appropriate chronological order. As an example, here's a section from one of my itineraries as it existed about a month before departure. I note relevant details, such as reservation and confirmation numbers, in the third column.

Monday, April 28

10:30 A.M.	Dep. White River Junction, Amtrak Train 55, *Vermonter*	Res. #882563 Custom class
7:35 P.M.	Arr. Washington, D.C.	
	Phoenix Park Hotel 520 N. Capitol Street, NW 202-638-6900	Conf. #C35D113 AAA rate

Wednesday, April 30

7:15 P.M.	Dep. Washington, Amtrak Train 19, *Crescent*	Car 1910, bedrm. 10

Thursday, May 1

8:57 A.M.	Arr. Atlanta	
	Ritz Carlton Buckhead Hotel 3434 Peachtree Street 404-892-6000	Conf. #226799 Early check-in OK'd

Sunday, May 4

9:12 A.M.   Dep. Atlanta,   Coach seating
                 Amtrak Train 19,   (check cost of
                 Crescent   upgrade)

7:50 P.M   Arr. New Orleans

                 Maison DuPuy   Conf.
                 1001 Rue Toulouse   #106216
                 504-586-8000;   Late check-in
                 800-535-9177   OK'd
                                                        Room
                                                        guaranteed

Monday, May 5

3:15 P.M.   Dep. New Orleans,   Car 130,
                 Amtrak Train 1,   bedrm. 5
                 Sunset Limited

Wednesday, May 7

6:05 A.M.   Arr. Los Angeles
                 Taxi to LAX

12:15 P.M.   Dep. Los Angeles,   Check-in
                 Hawaiian Airlines,   required
                 Flight 3   Seat 15B

2:45 P.M.   Arr. Honolulu

When finishing up your itinerary, avoid unnecessary verbiage but include everything you will need to know once you've left home. While you're away, this will be your bible, and you'll refer to it many times each day. *Make three copies of your itinerary:* one for your shoulder bag, one for your suitcase (in case the shoulder bag is lost or stolen), and one to leave at home with a neighbor or relative.

That's it. You're just about ready to leave.

CHAPTER 5

Packing and Last-Minute Details

$\int$ omeone who no doubt learned the hard way once said, "There are only two kinds of travelers—those who are traveling light and those who wish they were." Certainly, when you travel by train, you're permitted to bring more baggage than the airlines allow. But why would you want to?

When in Doubt, Leave It Out!

If you pack intelligently, you can be away from home almost indefinitely and get along very well with only one medium-sized suitcase. All you need is the resolve to do it.

Before you start packing, go over your itinerary. What's the longest stretch you'll be without access to a washing machine? Four days? Okay, then give yourself a margin for error and pack in fives.

- For a man, that means five shirts, five changes of underwear, five pairs of socks, and so on. Pack two pairs of pants, making sure they'll both work with all of the shirts.

- For a woman, take two or three slacks and skirts, plus five tops that will go with all of them.
- For men and women, take two pairs of shoes—one casual and one a little dressy (both comfortable). Wear one pair and pack the other.

When it comes to toiletries, don't bring large sizes of anything with you, be it toothpaste, mouthwash, Kleenex, or whatever. Instead, buy the smallest available tubes or packages, then replace them along the way if necessary. Some items you use every day at home can be left out altogether to save space and lighten your load—that big bottle of aftershave, for instance. Ladies should be sure to bring an adequate supply of sanitary supplies; they are not sold aboard the train.

A Catchall Carry-on Bag

In addition to your one suitcase, take a nice, roomy shoulder bag. There will be exceptions, but it's best to assume that while you're on the train, getting to your suitcase won't always be convenient. The shoulder bag, on the other hand, will stay with you in your room or at your seat. Knowing that, pack each bag accordingly, with your short list of essentials in the shoulder bag and everything else in the suitcase. You'll quickly develop your own list of shoulder-bag items. To get you started, here's mine:

- Toothbrush
- Toothpaste (small tube)
- Razor (an electric razor is much easier while you're on board)
- Shave cream (small tube)
- Clean shirt
- Clean underwear and socks
- T-shirt (to sleep in)

- A plastic zip-lock bag (for wet facecloths, and so on)
- Reading material
- Spare glasses
- Two pens and a notebook
- Postage stamps
- Small calculator (I'll explain this later in Chapter 6)

The bottom line when it comes to packing: less is better. As travel writer Rick Steves notes, how many people do you know who brag that they take a little more baggage with them on each trip? You get the idea—the lighter and smarter you travel, the happier you will be every step of the way.

What About Electric Appliances?

If you can't do without your electric hair dryer or razor, you won't have to. Standard AC outlets of 120 volts are provided in all first-class rooms and in all lavatories, both coach and first class. But before you stick either of those items into your bag, stop for a reality check: Do you want to deal with the bulk and the weight?

Packing for Kids

In addition to the usual items your kids will need during the time you'll be away, be sure to pack an assortment of books and games to occupy them while they're on the train. Adults may be able to enjoy the passing scenery for hours at a time, but not youngsters, who need plenty of distractions. In particular, be sure to bring each child's favorite thing. When he or she gets tired or bored or cranky or sick, that one item—blanket, teddy bear, doll, pacifier, whatever—will help make things all right.

Riding Coach? Bring a Blanket!

Amtrak coaches are air-conditioned, and sometimes the system is hard to regulate. Even during the summer it can get quite chilly at night in those large cars. Amtrak does not provide complimentary blankets for coach passengers, so if you're riding coach, bring your own blanket. There ought to be a limited supply of small, lightweight blankets for sale in the lounge car, but often none are available, and they don't help much anyway. Heed this advice, and you will thank me for it. I know, I know—a minute ago I told you to pack light, and now I am advising you to bring a blanket. It doesn't have to be a big one. A small thermal blanket or one for a twin-size bed that can be folded in half for extra warmth will be fine. Don't pack it; roll it up and tie it to your carry-on bag.

And Perhaps a Pillow

Amtrak does provide all coach passengers with a pillow, and while it's considerably larger than the puny ones handed out by the airlines, it's still less than what you're probably used to. I found a small down-filled travel pillow in a mail-order catalog some years ago and bring it along on every trip. During the days, I compress it into a tight roll that fits neatly in my suitcase. Come nighttime, I'm thankful for it whenever I find a hard foam-rubber pillow waiting for me on a train or in a hotel room. The contoured inflatable kind are okay, too.

Coping with Baggage

All Amtrak coaches, whether on short- or long-distance runs, have overhead racks running the length of the car to accommodate luggage. While the rules are not strictly followed, each passenger is allowed two pieces of baggage of "reasonable" size and weight. Additional items are no problem as long as common sense is applied.

If your baggage includes larger suitcases or boxes, they can sometimes be stacked at the end of the car or, in the case of the Superliners, in baggage racks on the lower level. My first recommendation is that each person travel with just one medium suitcase and a shoulder bag to avoid this very problem. However, if you must have large, heavy baggage, I really recommend using Amtrak's Checked Baggage Service. Be at the station at least thirty minutes prior to departure to arrange that. Each extra piece of baggage will be tagged and placed in the baggage car. If the total weight of your baggage is more than 150 pounds, expect a small additional charge. Just remember that these pieces will be unavailable to you during your trip.

Be advised, however, that it's not always possible to check baggage. Either the station where you board or at your destination may not offer the service, or your train may not include a baggage car in the consist. This information is included in the Amtrak timetable or you can always call Amtrak at 800-USA-RAIL to make sure.

If you have an unusual amount of baggage or if you are not able to handle it yourself for any reason, call Amtrak's 800 number at least seventy-two hours before your departure.

Will the Train Be on Time?

If you're boarding at the train's point of origin, it will almost certainly leave on time. There could be a delay in departure if your train is held for passengers making connections from an incoming train, but under no circumstances will your train depart ahead of schedule from any station—ever!

If you're boarding somewhere along its route, there is a real possibility that the train will be late. That means you should find out exactly when it will arrive before you leave for the station. After all, if the station is a ninety-minute drive from your home and the train is due at 5:45 in the morning, you would probably like to know if it's going to be two hours late on that particular day! Here's what to do:

First, try calling the Amtrak office at the station where you'll be boarding. If no one is there (you may need to leave home before Amtrak personnel arrive at the station), call Amtrak's toll-free number, 800-USA-RAIL. If they say the train is running on time, head for the station as originally planned. However, if they say the train is significantly late, beware! Their information could be old, and since Amtrak pads its schedules, your train could have made up a lot of that lost time since they got that information. The fail-safe method is to call the Amtrak station one or two stops up the line from your departure point a few minutes before the train is due there. By then, they'll know exactly when the train will arrive, and the timetable will tell you the running time from there to your station.

Whatever You Do, Don't Miss Your Train!

Someone once said that the only way to be sure of catching a train is to miss the one before it. Maybe that was true in the good old days, but miss one of Amtrak's long-distance trains, and you've got a real problem. Most operate just once a day, so at best you'll have to wait twenty-four hours for the next train. During peak travel times, however, you may find the train sold out for the next day . . . and the next, and the next. That's especially likely if you're riding on a first-class ticket.

For heaven's sake, allow plenty of time for the drive to the station. Any number of things could delay you, so allow for the unexpected. You may end up sitting in the station for a while, but at least you'll be waiting calmly. Don't begin your train trip with anxiety and stress.

It is commonly assumed that times listed on railroad schedules are arrival times. Not so. When only one time is listed for a specific station stop, that indicates when the train departs. If the train is running on time, it will actually arrive several minutes before that time, so plan accordingly. In most stations, the train won't be there very long—sometimes just sixty seconds or so.

The point is, don't be casual about the business of getting to the station and boarding your train. It's easy to miss a train, and when you do, getting things straightened out is at best a minor inconvenience. At worst, it can be a nightmare.

Things to Know About Boarding

Some Amtrak trains do not offer reserved seating, which means that your seat is not guaranteed. Usually, however, that system is used on short-haul trains that run fairly frequently and are not often sold out.

In coach class, that "reserved seat" status guarantees you a seat on the train, but usually no specific seat has your name on it. This is particularly important to remember if you are traveling with one or more friends or as a family, because you will undoubtedly want to sit together. While there are no guarantees, you can do a few things to make sure you board quickly and, hopefully, end up in the seat or seats you want.

If you're boarding the train at its point of origin, you should have no problem. Just make sure you all get to the station early and check in right away with the Amtrak official at the gate. He or she will know how full the train is. Even if it's sold out, the gate official can arrange for your family to board first, if not ahead of the other passengers.

If you're boarding the train en route, however, the train could be nearly full by the time it gets to your station. Here's what to do:

- Call Amtrak at 800-USA-RAIL several days before departure and ask them to inform the onboard chief of your needs.
- When you arrive at the station, ask an Amtrak employee where to stand on the platform so you won't find yourself several hundred feet from the coaches when the train comes to a stop. The object is to be among the first to board.
- Better yet, designate someone in your party, unencumbered with kids or baggage, to hop aboard and look for seats as soon as the train stops.
- Once on board, if you cannot find enough seats together, ask the car attendant for help. If he or she is unable to help, ask the conductor who takes your tickets or the chief of onboard services. One of them should be able to accommodate your family.

One of the perks of riding first class is that specific accommodations have been reserved for you. All you need to do is find the right car and the attendant will direct you right to your room.

Finally, this may seem obvious but make sure to board your train at the station stop showing on your ticket. A friend of mine once held tickets for sleeping-car accommodations between Miami and Washington on the *Silver Star.* At the last minute, he had to change his plans, and he boarded his train in Orlando instead, some 250 miles north of Miami. However, thinking that his bedroom would be waiting for him no matter where he boarded that train, he did not change his tickets or bother to notify Amtrak. Wrong! He was considered a no-show in Miami, and the conductor had sold his bedroom to a coach passenger who had asked for an upgrade.

Metropolitan Lounges

If you're boarding your train in Washington, D.C., New York, Chicago, or Portland, Oregon, be sure to take advantage of the comfortable accommodations Amtrak has for sleeping-car passengers in those stations. These waiting rooms, called Metropolitan Lounges, are nicely furnished with easy chairs, current magazines and newspapers, and complimentary coffee, juice, soft drinks, and snacks. Telephone and fax facilities are also available. The lounge in Chicago actually has a working fireplace.

An attendant will ask to see your ticket when you enter, and you will be welcomed into the lounge only if you have just arrived or are about to depart on a first-class ticket. Amtrak sticks to this rule quite strictly. I was once refused entry to the Metropolitan Lounge in Chicago because the first three-hour leg of my trip (Chicago to Galesburg) was in coach class, notwithstanding the fact that I was traveling first class from there to Oakland.

Welcome Aboard!

Okay, you've planned your trip, packed carefully (and light), arrived at the station early, boarded without a problem, and have just settled into your seat. The train starts rolling before you realize it, and you're on your way. Now you're ready to experience everything that is relaxing and fun about a rail journey.

Life on Board

Today's long-distance trains provide passengers with most of the comforts of home. Despite all the improvements and refinements, however, don't expect things to be perfect. A train is not a cruise ship on wheels. With several hundred people living together in close quarters for as long as three days, there are bound to be inconveniences. Bear that in mind, and before making an issue out of something, ask yourself if you're being unreasonable under the circumstances. I once listened to a woman in an adjoining room berate the car attendant unmercifully because he had been unable to silence a minor rattle somewhere in her room. The poor man had tried several times to find it without success, and clearly it was time she thanked him for his effort and made the best of it. So, before boarding, resolve to lighten up. There's too much to enjoy on the train to let minor issues spoil your trip.

Where to Stow Your Baggage

If you're traveling on one of Amtrak's coaches, whether an older type or a newer bi-level car, you'll find room for one or two medium-sized suitcases in the rack above your seat.

There will be plenty of space for a small carry-on bag in the same rack or on the floor under your feet. Superliner coaches also have a large storage rack for luggage on the lower level just as you enter near the middle of the car.

In the new Viewliner sleeping cars, which operate on many of Amtrak's long-distance eastern routes, you'll find room for a couple of small to medium-sized suitcases in the standard bedroom and a bit more in the deluxe bedroom. The sleeping-car accommodations in Superliners really have no place to store baggage conveniently. Like the coaches, however, each sleeper has a large, easily accessible luggage rack on the lower level. In my experience, the best method is to stow most of your baggage there, taking only a small carry-on or shoulder bag to your room.

Your Onboard Crew

You'll come in contact with a number of crew members during your trip, including your car attendant, the conductor, possibly a chief of onboard services, dining-car staff, and a lounge-car attendant. (For a complete explanation of the duties and responsibilities of each crew member, including the engineer and the assistant in the locomotive, see Chapter 7, "Who's in Charge Here?")

Traveling in Coach

As a coach passenger, you have not been preassigned a specific seat. That means you should just climb aboard and sit where you want. On short-haul trains, you'll be pretty much on your own. The only members of the train crew you'll encounter are the conductor or the conductor's assistant. On overnight trains, you'll probably be directed to a specific car, but usually you can choose any seat you wish in that car. Sometimes, to help keep track of where people are getting off, coach passengers on overnight trains will be assigned to specific seats by car attendants. Most are quite reasonable about shifting people around, so if you have a problem with your seat assignment, ask if you can be reassigned.

Where to Sit

For a smoother, quieter ride, try to locate a seat near the middle of the car and, if riding a Superliner, on the upper level. Some Superliner coaches do have a few lower-level seats, but these are usually reserved for disabled or elderly passengers. Unless you require such accommodations, avoid these seats when you board. You get a better view from the upper level.

Be Careful About Changing Seats

After you board, the conductor will take your ticket and slip a cardboard seat check into a slot in the baggage rack over your head. That tells the conductor and the car attendant where you will be getting off. Don't change seats without notifying either the conductor or the car attendant or without taking the seat check with you. This is especially important if you're on an overnight trip and have to leave the train in the wee hours. Many a passenger has changed seats during the night and slept through his stop because the car attendant couldn't locate him. When that happens, the car attendants invariably get the blame—which explains why they may be uptight if you change seats without telling them.

Traveling First Class

"First class" on Amtrak means private accommodations in a sleeping car. It also means that the cost of your meals in the dining car is included in the first-class surcharge you paid when you bought your ticket. (Actually, most Amtrak crews don't commonly use the term "first class." Instead, they say that you are "in the sleepers.")

As a sleeping-car passenger, you have been assigned a specific room in a specific car. The room and car numbers will appear on your ticket. Each car's number will be visible from the platform, usually near the door where you enter. In any event, the first member of the train crew you see on the platform will be able to direct you to your car.

Your car attendant will be at the car entrance. He or she will have a list of all passengers assigned to that car and will be expecting you. The car attendant should offer to carry your bags from the platform into your room if you need help doing so.

Once you're shown to your room, take your time and settle in. The car attendant will offer to show you where everything is and how it all works. You'll find everything very compact. In fact, first-time riders are sometimes startled at how small the accommodations appear. However, the rooms are well designed, very efficient, and generally quite adequate.

What to Wear

In another day and time, people dressed up to travel. Cramped spaces on planes changed all that, and today casual dress is acceptable, if not always appropriate. Anyway, feel free to dress comfortably for your train trip. That's especially good advice if you're traveling in coach, where you'll be sleeping in your clothes. Jeans or slacks and a sport shirt are fine for men; a skirt or slacks and a blouse are equally appropriate for women. You will see shorts, tank tops, T-shirts emblazoned with messages of questionable taste, and the like, but for the most part, passengers comply reasonably well with today's minimum standards. One more thing: Ladies, forget the high heels. They are definitely not the thing to be wearing in a moving train.

Washroom Facilities

Superliners, both coaches and sleepers, have four lavatories located on the lower level of each car. All include washbasins with hot and cold water and a toilet. Some include changing tables for infants, and one lavatory is usually over-sized. (Find and make note of that one early in your trip.) Superliner sleepers have a shower on the lower level and an additional lavatory on the upper level. All six deluxe bedrooms have toilets and showers in the room.

Viewliner sleepers have toilet facilities in all bedrooms, and both the deluxe bedrooms and the special bedroom also have shower facilities. There's also a shower at one end of the car for passengers occupying the standard compartments.

Short-haul coaches and coaches used on eastern long-distance trains have lavatory facilities at the end of the car, including a washbasin and a toilet. There are no shower facilities.

Ever since railroads began carrying passengers, waste water from washbasins and toilets was dumped directly onto the tracks below. That is no longer the practice, at least as far as Amtrak is concerned. As the result of a federal mandate, Amtrak has systematically converted all toilet facilities to the self-contained type found on airplanes. The cost has been horrendous, and while obvious aesthetics were involved, the fact is that there was never any evidence of valid health concerns caused by the old practice.

Smoking

Amtrak's policy on smoking has changed often over the years, and every time I ask someone at Amtrak for an update it seems as though there has been another one. And no wonder. No matter what the policy is, someone is always going to be unhappy. With that in mind, here's the smoking policy as this edition went to press: No smoking on all short- and medium-distance trains. On all overnight trains, smoking is not permitted in the coaches, sleepers, or dining car. On most overnight trains, smoking (cigarettes only, by the way) will be allowed in one designated area of the train, for example, in the lower level of the Superliner lounge car. On the *Sunset Limited,* the lower level of one coach has been converted into a smoking lounge.

Whatever the current policy, the chief of onboard services on all overnight trains should make regular announcements over the public address system. And, of course, the car attendant will be able to tell you. One other option for you smokers: Take a look at the train's time-table. You'll see several stops along the way that are scheduled to take ten to twenty minutes, usually to unload trash, rewater the cars, and refuel the locomotives. It's also your chance to hop off and have a cigarette on the platform.

Pets

Pets are a no-no. Not at your seat, either in or out of a container, and not even in the baggage car. At first I thought this policy was too severe, but after hearing a number of horror stories from crew members about pets running loose on trains, I've come to agree that it's the only approach. An exception is made is for certified guide and service animals, for which documentation is required.

Things That Go Bump in the Night

Many a passenger has bedded down for the night in a cozy sleeping-car room, only to become aware of a persistent rattle or squeak coming from somewhere inside the compartment. It's not unusual, and it may happen to you.

If you're bothered by such things, just get up and track it down. Most of the time, it's something easily located—a coat hanger swinging with the motion of the train against the sides of the skinny little closet or a ladder not stowed quite right in the upper berth. It's amazing how effectively a washcloth wedged into a crack can silence a rattle. If you can't locate that elusive noise, call the car attendant. He or she has found and fixed many a rattle and will probably have better luck.

Security for Your Belongings

It is an absolute fact that incidents of thievery are rare aboard Amtrak trains, but that doesn't mean you can ignore everyday common sense. The best rule is to leave real valuables at home. If you must bring them aboard, take them with you whenever you leave your seat. That's true for sleeping-car passengers, too, by the way. You can lock the door to your private room once you're inside, but the doors don't lock from the outside. My advice to both coach and sleeper passengers is to always carry your identification, your money, your credit cards, and your tickets with you. Always! Sleeping-car passengers can feel comfortable about leaving other items—cameras, tote bags, even handbags—in their rooms, but put them someplace out of sight and close the drapes and door to your room securely when you leave. If the car attendant is around, tell him or her that you're going to be out of your room for a while. Notify the attendant if someone opens the door to your room, apparently by mistake. (Don't be overly concerned, however. It's almost always a case of right room, wrong car.)

Personal Food and Drink

Passengers are permitted to bring food and drink aboard the train. My advice, however, is to eat in the dining car or get snacks from the lounge car. The food is quite good and is moderately priced, and it gives you an opportunity to get up, move around, and meet some of your fellow passengers. Besides, how would you like it if someone next to you started eating a can of sardines?

If you're riding in coach, don't bring any alcoholic beverages aboard, because you are not permitted to consume them in your seat. Beer, wine, and a variety of mixed drinks are available in the lounge car and must be consumed there. If you're in a sleeping car, you may bring your own alcohol aboard, but it must be consumed in your room. Amtrak train crews generally have a low tolerance for passengers who overindulge and cause problems. Conductors can and do put offenders off the train . . . literally a sobering experience, I'm sure.

Dining on Board

Part of the enjoyment of train travel is the unique experience of eating in a rolling restaurant, and a pretty good one, too. Amtrak is into food service, big time. The system-wide total is impressive: Best estimates are that an average of more than 10,000 meals are served every day year-round, and that will increase to as many as 14,000 meals a day in peak season. There has been steady improvement since the early 1980s, when budget problems brought the Amtrak dining experience to its lowest ebb. Today, considering the long hours and the busy, crowded conditions under which they work, Amtrak's food service crews do an incredible job. As an example, the dining-car crew on the *Silver Meteor* will serve as many as 450 meals on a busy day. On a western train like the *Sunset Limited,* which has a larger diner with a bigger crew to serve more passengers, as many as 600 meals a day will be prepared.

There are fewer choices on the menu than you would find in a restaurant, because storage space in a dining-car kitchen is quite limited. Nevertheless, the portions are generous, the food is good and reasonably priced, and the service is usually cheerful and efficient. Happily, despite the added costs, Amtrak has pretty much phased out the Styrofoam plates and plastic utensils that became necessary during the budget-slashing years. On long-distance routes, plastic has been replaced with real china and stainless-steel tableware on linen tablecloths. Hooray!

In a full-service dining car, the kitchen crew consists of a chef and at least one food specialist. In the Superliner kitchens, there are always two and sometimes three food specialists to assist the chef, depending on the passenger load. In fact, as real china replaced the disposable plates, an additional worker has been added to help with the dishwashing. In the dining area itself, there will be either a steward or what Amtrak calls a lead service attendant, plus as many as four service attendants, again depending on the type of equipment and the number of passengers on board for that trip.

The dining car is usually located near the middle of the train so no one has to walk the length of the train to reach it. When you enter the diner, wait for the dining car steward or the attendant in charge to seat you. Meals are family-style in Amtrak dining cars, meaning that you'll be seated with one or more fellow passengers. In my experience, it's best to take the initiative and break the ice immediately. Introduce yourself and get the conversation started: "Where are you from? How far are you traveling? Are you enjoying your trip?" I've met some very interesting people in Amtrak dining cars. Besides, the alternative is to sit in uncomfortable silence for the better part of an hour.

Kids are welcomed in the dining car. Booster seats are not always available, although they are supposed to be. In the Superliner dining cars, the top portion of the seat lifts off and can be used for youngsters to sit on. For whatever reason, most dining car crews either don't know about this feature or don't volunteer it, so you'll have to ask.

Menus will vary from train to train. Long-distance trains feature dishes that are appropriate for the part of the country through which you're traveling. Furthermore, individual chefs are given a fair amount of latitude in what they serve and how it's prepared, so it's hard to generalize about dining-car food. Nevertheless, here's an idea of what you can expect in terms of selection and cost when you enter an Amtrak dining car. Remember, coach passengers pay for their meals while sleeping-car passengers pay out-of-pocket only for soft drinks, beer, or wine.

Breakfast The dining car is usually open for breakfast from 6:30 A.M. (double-check the exact time with your car attendant) until about 9:30 A.M. You'll hear announcements over the train public address (P.A.) system when the diner opens. The busiest hours are usually between 7:00 and 8:30 A.M. Since you are seated on a first-come, first-served basis, to avoid a wait, try to get to the diner just as it opens or wait until 9:00 A.M. Usual breakfast fare is served: fruit juice, cereal, eggs (fried or scrambled), pancakes, French toast (a tradition of train travel), bacon or sausage, toast, and tea or coffee. Grits are served on most trains traveling to or through the South. Cost: $4–$5.

Lunch Dining-car service begins around 11:30 A.M. and continues until everyone is served, closing usually about 1:30 P.M. As with breakfast, there are no reservations. The lunch menu will probably include soup, a choice of a hamburger or cheeseburger, chicken sandwich, individual pizza, or a salad plate. For dessert, there's pie, cake, or ice cream. Drinks include coffee, tea, milk, soft drinks, beer, and wine. Cost: $5–$8.

Dinner On long-distance trains, dinner in the dining car will be by reservation. Normal procedure is for the dining-car steward to move through the train assigning passengers to the various seatings, starting at 5:00 or 5:30 P.M. Usually, he or she will be able to seat you when you would prefer to eat, especially if you're in first class.

Again, P.A. announcements through the train will tell you when to head for the diner. The evening menu is quite a bit more extensive than lunch. There will be several entrees, probably a choice from among a chicken, fish, or pasta dish, a steak or perhaps roast beef, and a chef's special, which will very likely be a regional dish. Dessert includes pie, cake, or ice cream. Coffee, tea, milk, soft drinks, beer, and wine are the beverages. Cost: $8–$15.

You can pay for your meals in the dining car with cash, personal check, or credit card. As already noted, when you travel first class on Amtrak, all your meals are included at no additional charge. If you're traveling first class, either the chief of onboard services or your car attendant will provide you with a meal voucher shortly after you board. Just present it each time you have a meal in the dining car. You have a full choice of the menu and will not be charged except for beverages other than coffee, tea, milk, or juice.

Coach passengers are also welcome in the dining car, of course, and can choose from the same menu as folks from the sleeping cars. The only difference is that meals are not included in the cost of the coach ticket.

Amtrak has some interesting ideas under consideration to improve the food service on board its trains. One is to serve only the appetizer and main course in the dining car, having passengers move into the adjacent lounge car for dessert and coffee. This system would permit the dining car to serve more people in a shorter period of time and eliminate the problem of requiring some passengers to choose between very early or very late seatings.

As noted elsewhere, your car attendant will bring meals from the dining car to sleeping-car accommodations if you request it. But unless you're unable to move throughout the train without difficulty, why do that? Part of the train experience is going to the dining car and meeting fellow passengers over a meal. If you do elect to eat in your room, be advised that it could take a while to arrive and will probably not be piping hot.

The Lounge Car

The other dining option available to all passengers is the lounge car, where a variety of hot and cold sandwiches, snacks, and drinks are almost always available. The attendant does stop serving several times a day for meals and an occasional break, but generally the lounge car will be open from 6:00 A.M. until midnight. On shorter runs, the lounge car will remain open for the entire trip. Sleeping car passengers do have to pay for their purchases in the lounge car, by the way.

Beware the "Denver Cocktail"

If you're on one of the western trains and would like a mixed drink or two in the lounge car or perhaps wine or beer with your meal in the diner, don't forget that altitude increases the effect of alcohol on the human body. For example, the *California Zephyr* climbs to more than 9,200 feet as it crosses the Continental Divide west of Denver. At that altitude, one glass of wine will have the effect of two. This physiological phenomenon is usually the reason that otherwise sedate passengers are occasionally seen tottering back to their seats from the dining car as the eastbound *Zephyr* begins its descent into the Denver area.

What About Bathing?

Taking a bath in the literal sense can't be done. However, you can manage to approximate one with a little effort and some ingenuity. As with almost everything else, a lot depends on what kind of accommodations you have.

Superliner sleeping cars have a shower on the lower level. It's a bit cramped (especially if you're tall) and a little tricky, but it works. The prescribed method is navy-style: water on, get wet, water off...soap up...water on, rinse off, water off.

There is a shower in each deluxe bedroom in the Superliners. Actually, it's a compartment the size of a phone booth that contains both a toilet and a shower. The shower works like the one on the lower level, except that you have even less room to maneuver because of the toilet. Be careful not to press the shower button when you mean to flush the toilet. You'll need a good sense of humor if you do.

If you're much over six feet tall, showering on the train can be an awkward task. Even when riding in a sleeper, I usually opt for an all-over sponge bath instead. It's just easier and faster. Towels and washcloths are supplied in the sleeping cars, but if this is your choice, ask the car attendant for an extra towel to stand on.

Superliner coaches don't have showers. There are simply too many passengers to convert a much-needed washroom into a shower. When traveling overnight in coach, whatever the equipment, the only solution is the sponge bath.

Viewliner sleeping cars, in service on Florida trains and other eastern routes, have a toilet and washbasin in each bedroom. There are also showers in the deluxe bedrooms and an additional shower at the end of the car for passengers in the standard bedrooms.

Sleeping in Coach

Any way you cut it, you'll still be sleeping in a chair. That's not nearly as bad as it sounds, though, because Amtrak's coach seats are large and comfortable, they recline, and most have leg rests. In fact, they're pretty much like that nice recliner in your living room, the one you fall asleep in while watching Jay Leno. The major difference is the noise and motion of the train and the other people around you. Some passengers don't manage this part of the train experience very well, but some tips can make it easier:

- Bring a blanket and your own pillow (as mentioned earlier, one of those small, down-filled kind you can roll up and pack in your suitcase).
- Don't eat a huge dinner, and skip the caffeinated beverages.
- Change into loose clothing—an extra-large sweatshirt and sweatpants are ideal.
- Stay up as late as you can, reading or chatting quietly with your seatmate; don't even try to sleep until you're really ready for it.
- Earplugs and a sleep mask will help.

Sleeping in First Class

Most people (and I'm one of them) don't truly appreciate their sleeping car accommodations until bedtime. Once I'm under those clean sheets and into a good book, glancing up occasionally as we pass through a town, I have a feeling of contentment that makes that extra fare worth every dime. I get the same feeling all over again when I wake up the next morning after spending a restful night in reasonable comfort.

Remember that the car attendant has a lot of beds to prepare—as many as forty-four if you are traveling in a Superliner and the car is full. Try to give him or her as much advance notice as possible when you're ready for bed. Ideally, get one of the later seatings in the diner and let the attendant know when you're heading off to dinner. Your bed will be made up when you return.

Here are a few suggestions to help ensure a good night's rest in your first-class bedroom:

- You won't need to bring a blanket, but you might want to bring a pillow (again, one of those small, down-filled kind you can roll up and pack in your suitcase).
- Don't overdo it at dinner, even though your meals are free, and avoid the caffeine.
- Stay up as late as you can reading; turn out the light only when you're really sleepy.
- You can easily darken your room, so a sleep mask won't be necessary. Consider using earplugs.

Incidentally, the car attendant would rather you didn't try to prepare the bed yourself. Also, don't try to close it up in the morning, especially if you're going to be occupying the room for another night. There's a right way to do it, and the attendants would rather you left that job to them.

Tipping

For some reason, the issue of whether to tip members of the train's onboard crew confuses many travelers. Fear not, here are the ground rules:

- Do *not* tip the conductor, the chief of onboard services, or the dining car steward.
- *Do* tip the car attendant. In the sleepers, a good rule of thumb is $5 per night per passenger. Increase that appropriately if you ask to have meals brought to your room. I suggest at least an additional $2 per person per meal. In coach class, assuming you've been helped with baggage and have received cheerful and friendly attention, my suggestion is $1 or $2 for a one-night trip; $3 or $4 for two nights. Most passengers tip the car attendant as they leave the train at their final destination, although others prefer tipping after each

special service is provided. (By the way, I've inter- viewed numerous car attendants during my many travels on Amtrak, and although it's deplorable, all agree that female car attendants tend to receive lower tips than their male counterparts. Please be sensitive to that inequity.)

- *Do* tip the lounge-car attendant. Extra change left behind on the counter after each purchase is appropriate.
- *Do* tip the service people in the dining car. Follow the same rules you would in any other restaurant: Start with the standard 15 percent, moving up for really good ser- vice and down for casual or unfriendly service.

Some first-class passengers have the misconception that they're under no obligation to tip dining-car staff be- cause their meals are complimentary. Not so! If you have the means to ride first class, you can afford to tip gener- ously where warranted. Please do so. The IRS assumes you will be tipping these people, by the way, and requires them to pay income tax on an amount equal to 8 percent of each meal check they serve.

If done right, no jobs on a long-distance train are easy. Car attendants routinely put in eighteen- to twenty-hour days; the dining car staff often prepares or serves 500 to 600 meals a day; the lounge-car attendant is on duty al- most nonstop for eighteen hours, sometimes, I'm sorry to say, in a smoke-filled environment. Crews working the cross-country trains are on duty for forty-five or fifty hours straight, spend one night in a hotel, then work the same train back home. I would encourage you to recog- nize and reward people who perform efficiently and cheerfully under those conditions.

Finally, you should be aware that official Amtrak policy says no employee shall solicit tips. I have never once run into it, but should it happen to you, especially if it's flagrant, I would encourage you to report the individual to the onboard chief. It's not that the sin is so great; it's just a pretty good indication of a bad employee.

Taking Pictures

If you enjoy taking photographs on your vacation trips, traveling across the country by train will provide you with a limitless number of photo opportunities, both inside and outside of the train. I carry two cameras when I travel—a good-quality "idiot-proof" camera with a built-in flash for interior and nighttime shots and a more sophisticated model that allows me to set the shutter speed and to focus manually. Between them, I'm able to cover almost any photo opportunity.

Taking interior shots on a train is no more difficult than taking photos in your own home. For shots of a party in the lounge car or of that nice couple from England you met over dinner, the little automatic camera is perfect.

Unfortunately, it's not as easy to get really first-rate shots of the scenery passing by outside. Shooting through the tinted train windows is the biggest obstacle to really good pictures. Unlike European railroads, the windows in American coaches and sleeping cars cannot be opened (although they can be pushed out in an emergency). Final results may not be perfect, but there are things you can do to improve the quality of those important souvenir photos.

Photos taken through tinted windows tend to come out looking a little "flat." To compensate a bit, use a color print film. If you prefer to shoot slides, as I do, use Kodachrome, which provides more contrast than Ectachrome. Other manufacturers have equivalent film types, which your dealer can help you select. If you have a more sophisticated camera, a compensating filter will probably help. Which filter you need will depend on your choice of film. Again, consult someone knowledgeable where you buy your film.

A film speed of 100 or 200 is appropriate. Anything less will require faster shutter speeds; anything more will yield grainy results.

Get the camera's lens as close to the window as you can *without touching it.* A lens pressed against the window or a camera body braced against any other part of the train can transmit the train's vibration to the camera. Result: blurry photos.

If you can control the adjustment, switch your camera from automatic to selective focus. Some cameras with the automatic focus feature will focus on the transparent window pane instead of that gorgeous passing scene outside. Controlling the focus yourself will avoid that problem. Usually you won't have time for much adjustment, so often the best advice is to set your focus on infinity and forget about it.

Again, if your camera is so equipped, switch from automatic to selective shutter speed, then set the shutter speed to 250 or 500. Because the train is moving, slower shutter speeds can result in blurry photographs.

If you take the ultrasimple approach and use one of the so-called "idiot-proof" cameras exclusively, you probably won't be able to make most of those adjustments. My advice? Don't worry about it! Your photos won't be up to *National Geographic* standards, but they'll still make dandy souvenirs.

If you have time, check for any reflections in the window and block them with your body before shooting. Don't use the automatic flash for photos taken through the train window. It will probably cause a photo-wrecking reflection, and besides, it's of no use for objects more than fifteen or twenty feet away. Do use the flash for interior shots, even during daytime hours.

Please don't try for clearer photos by opening the windows in the train's exit doors, either in the vestibules or on the lower level of the Superliners. You run the risk of injury from flying debris kicked up by the train, from passing trains, or from stationary objects at trackside.

One more thing: Don't be too disappointed when you get home and find that quite a few of your photos have been ruined by what I call the "green blur"—bushes or trees that suddenly zoom in front of the camera just as you press the shutter. I'm an expert on the green blur and have hundreds of shots to prove it.

Onboard Activities

Most of the organized activities occur in the Superliner lounge cars, simply because they are so much bigger than their single-level counterparts. You'll hear about them over the train's public address system. Movies are shown and, toward sundown, there's usually a happy hour. Depending on how "with it" the onboard chief is, games involving the entire train are often played, with prizes offered for answering trivia questions or for producing the greatest number of objects in a scavenger hunt.

Finding something to do on the train is more of a problem for some passengers than for others. Many people (I'm one) can just gear down and dreamily let the hours roll by along with the miles. Others need to change their activities rather frequently. Having something available to do is important, especially at night or when there is nothing much passing by outside to hold your attention.

Enjoy the Scenery

The view, of course, is the main reason for traveling by train, so take full advantage of it. On most long-distance trains, Amtrak provides passengers with printed route guides identifying the major points of interest along the way. These include a written description and a schematic map that tells you on which side of the train each feature will appear and about when to start looking for it.

Superliner lounge cars provide panoramic views of the passing scenery. (Photo by the author)

Frequently, a member of the crew—usually one of the conductors, since they know the route best—will provide commentary about the passing scenery over the P.A. system. Unfortunately, there really isn't any standard when it comes to this kind of live narrative. Some passengers enjoy it; others would prefer not to have to listen to it. Some conductors have a real feel for this kind of thing and do a wonderful job; others don't or won't do it at all.

Several of Amtrak's trains feature special lecturers who offer commentary over the P.A. system about the country-side through which the train is passing. For instance, during much of the year a Native American volunteer boards the eastbound *Southwest Chief* in Gallup, New Mexico, and provides a fascinating narrative about the area and the people who have lived there for thousands of years. He or she leaves the train three hours later in Albuquerque and, later the same day, catches the westbound *Chief* back to Gallup, once again lecturing all the way. A few other trains—the *California Zephyr* and the *Cardinal,* for example—often have volunteers from local historical societies who come aboard to perform similar services. Without exception, I've found these people interesting, articulate, and well informed. All deserve thanks and appreciation for their dedication and effort. Please make it a point to acknowledge them should you be on one of those trains.

Compute the Train's Speed

The train's speed varies greatly, depending upon track conditions, grade, the amount of rail traffic, weather, and other factors. The maximum speed allowed for Amtrak trains is 125 miles per hour along the northeast corridor from Washington, D.C., to Boston, and 79 miles per hour almost everywhere else in the country. "How fast are we going?" is almost certainly the question asked most often. There is an easy way to figure it out, quickly and accurately. You'll need a sweep second hand on your watch and a calculator, unless you don't mind working out the math yourself. You'll also need to be able to see the mileposts passing by outside your train. (Information about mileposts can be found in Chapter 10, "How It All Works.")

The formula is simple: Divide 3,600 (the number of seconds in an hour) by the number of seconds it takes you to travel one mile (the distance between two mileposts). For example, if it takes the train 53 seconds to travel one mile, it is going 67.92 mph. The engineer in the locomotive cab carries a stopwatch for the same purpose, by the way. He's required to operate right at the speed limit and regularly checks the accuracy of the speedometer in the cab using this same method.

If you'd rather not bother with the math, here's a chart that will shortcut the process for you:

Time Between Mileposts	Speed (mph)
2:00.0	30
1:43.0	35
1:30.0	40
1:20.0	45
1:12.0	50
1:05.5	55
1:00.0	60
:55.4	65
:51.4	70
:48.0	75
:45.0	80
:42.4	85
:40.0	90
:37.9	95
:36.0	100
:34.3	105
:32.7	110
:31.3	115
:30.0	120
:28.8	125

There is another, much less accurate way to compute the train's speed. Count the number of "telephone" poles passing by in a fifteen-second period, and multiply that number by six. Most of the time, that will give you a rough idea of the speed. (Incidentally, those are not really telephone poles. They were originally installed by the railroad to bring electricity to its signals and switches.)

Track the Train's Progress

Bring along a soft-cover road atlas of the United States, and as you travel from town to town, mark the train's progress on the maps with a colored highlighter pen. If you don't want to bring the entire atlas, just photocopy the appropriate pages before you leave home. Personally, I'd bring the whole atlas, because it does provide a nice record of your train trip—even more so if you're a frequent train traveler.

Estimate Your Arrival Time

I enjoy figuring out whether we're gaining or losing time along our route. It's quite easy, because departure times for each station stop are listed in the Amtrak timetable. You can probably get one from the car attendant or conductor, and you may find one at your seat or in your room when you board, but I always bring one with me. Just for fun, I use this to log our progress and to predict the exact time we'll arrive at our final destination.

Because there is plenty of time, and as the mood strikes me, I sometimes keep a running account of how we're doing in some detail. For example, here's a portion of the log I once kept aboard Train 97, the *Silver Meteor,* between Jacksonville and Orlando. One little thing you discover through this exercise is where the schedule has been padded. Note that the timetable shows twenty-five minutes between DeLand and Sanford; in actuality, at least on this particular day, it only took eighteen minutes.

Station Stop	Schld Dprt	Schld #Min	Actl Dprt	Actl #Min	No. Miles	Avg Speed	Time Gnd/(Lst)	Total Time Gnd/(Lst)	Est Arvl Orlando
Jcksnvle	12:37	—	12:37	—	—	—	—	—	3:54
Palatka	1:43	:66	1:48	:71	59	49.9	(:05)	(:05)	3:59
DeLand	2:31	:48	2:39	:51	52	61.2	(:03)	(:08)	4:02
Sanford	2:56	:25	2:57	:18	16	53.3	:07	(:01)	3:55

By the way, to compute the train's average speed over longer distances, use the following formula:

$60 \times$ no. of miles $\div$ no. of minutes = mph

As an example, in the log shown above, it took Train 97 a total of 51 minutes to travel the 52 miles between Palatka and DeLand, Florida. Here's the math to figure out the train's average speed over that leg:

a. $60 \times 52 = 3,120$
b. $3,120 \div 51 = 61.2$ mph

Many people won't want to bother with these kinds of calculations, but others enjoy keeping tabs on how their train is doing.

Listen In on Train Talk

It's done with a device called a scanner, a radio receiver about the size of a cellular phone that picks up conversations between members of the operating crew—usually the engineer and the conductor. These little devices rapidly scan across radio frequencies used by police, fire departments, civil defense, railroads, taxi companies, and others, and automatically stop whenever they come across a channel in use. For years, I thought only the real hard-core train nuts carried one of these little electronic toys, but I must confess that I bought one a couple of years ago and have enjoyed using it when I travel by train. You can pick up not only conversations between members of your train crew but also those from yard workers, passing trains, and the recorded voices of the hot box detectors you pass. (There will be a number of other references to a "hot box" in later chapters; see an explanation of the term in "Railroad Terms and Slang.") Scanners provide a fascinating look at railroad operations and are perfectly legal, but there are a couple of things to remember:

- Use the earphones that come with the scanner, so the periodic squawking won't disturb other passengers.
- Some high-end scanners also include the ability to transmit, permitting two-way conversations. You certainly don't need that feature, but in any event the inflexible, carved-in-stone rule is listen but do not talk! People who do talk have no sense and if discovered are likely to find themselves standing on a platform watching their train disappear in the distance without them.

You can buy a serviceable scanner in most electronics stores for around $150. They're powered by a rechargeable battery, which typically will operate the scanner for five or six hours. If you're traveling in a sleeping car, you can save your battery and operate the device by plugging the adapter into the electric receptacle in your room. The battery can be recharged in the same manner. Just be sure the model you buy will pick up the frequencies commonly used by the railroads (160.215 to 161.565 megahertz). There's also a nifty little publication called *Trak Tables,* which lists Amtrak frequencies by train numbers. To order a copy, contact Three Rivers Press, Box 70285, Bellevue, Washington 98007.

Take a Walk

Once or twice between each meal and usually after each stop, the conductor "walks the train," literally passing through from one end to the other. The conductor does this to collect tickets from passengers who have just boarded or just to make sure that there are no problems. You should do it to get the juices going a bit and just for the exercise. After all, before you know it, you'll be back in the dining car for another meal! You'll find it's more exercise than you might think, since you are working more than normal to keep your balance in the moving train.

Read a Book or a Newspaper

Most of us have any number of books we haven't been able to get to because of our busy daily schedules. Here's the perfect opportunity to start on that tome you've been holding on to. I try to save most of my reading for the evening, when there's little or nothing to see outside.

Sleeping-car passengers usually get a morning paper delivered to their room by the car attendant, and sometimes there will be other copies in the lounge car for coach passengers. These newspapers are put aboard the train at major stops early every morning. For example, Train 48, the westbound *Lake Shore Limited,* stops in Cleveland, Ohio, a bit after 6:00 A.M., so first-class passengers will usually find the Cleveland newspaper under their door upon waking. I enjoy looking through these unfamiliar newspapers, since I'll probably pass through some of the towns and cities they're writing about. Sometimes, instead of the local paper, *USA Today* will be put aboard, but either way you'll feel in touch with what's going on in the world.

Listen to Audiotapes

A number of mail-order catalogs feature audiotapes, and most good bookstores stock a large selection, too—everything from children's stories to classic literature to old radio shows from the 1940s and 1950s. (Take it from me: These are a *must* if you're traveling with kids!) I once sat gazing out the window of Train 7, the *Empire Builder,* as it rolled through the farm country of Minnesota while listening to an audiotape of Garrison Keillor spinning some of his wonderful yarns. It was rather a strange feeling. I fully expected to see a passing sign proclaim our impending arrival at Lake Wobegon.

Do Puzzles and Games

Bring along a book of crossword puzzles. Most also include other games: anacrostics, cryptograms, and other word games. Bring a deck of cards (or buy a souvenir deck in the lounge car) for solitaire or other card games with your traveling companion or new friends in the lounge car. If you're traveling with children, by all means pick up a book of games for kids in your hometown bookstore before you leave. Several are available, and each can give you lots of new ideas for games and other diversions you'll all enjoy.

Write Letters

Finally you have the time to write to friends and family—and something to tell them about, too. You can buy Amtrak postcards in the Superliner lounge car, but bring some along or buy a few in the station before you leave just in case. Be sure to bring your own postage stamps, or better yet put stamps on them before you leave home.

Otherwise, you're likely to carry those cards and letters with you the entire way.

Watch a Movie

There are TV monitors in Superliner lounge cars, usually one at each end of the upper level and another downstairs. Recent feature films are shown in the evening, usually twice, and often video entertainment geared toward youngsters is presented in the afternoons. In any case, as on the airlines, all movies shown will have been sanitized for family viewing. The new Viewliners have video monitors in all of the sleeping compartments, and as new equipment is added and older cars refurbished on the eastern trains, video monitors will appear in those coaches with headsets available for rental.

There's Romance on the Rails—Literally

Some passengers take the idea of a romantic train trip quite literally. For them, an overnight train trip seems to have a direct affect on the libido. Train crews grin and shake their heads when asked about some of the more inventive means passengers have taken to have sex on board a long-distance train. Amorous couples have been discovered in the baggage car, in vestibules, in the lounge car, in the washrooms (quite a trick, given their size), and wherever else opportunity, desire, and, I suspect, a sense of mischief or daring collide.

Because of the lack of privacy at their assigned seats, coach passengers are most often the ones who seek somewhat more secluded locations for these activities. But not always. Sleeping-car passengers are occasionally discovered having sex in parts of the train other than their rooms. And it's not unknown for couples safely ensconced in private accommodations to deliberately leave their window shades up during their lovemaking as the train flashes—sorry, no pun intended—through small towns.

For the most part, Amtrak crews try to look the other way when encountering these situations. The unofficial commonsense response seems to have a lot to do with whether or not other passengers are being disturbed or offended.

By the way, those who successfully engage in these amorous onboard activities are said to have joined the Eighty-Mile-an-Hour Club, the rail equivalent to the Mile-High Club of the airline industry.

A Few Do's and Don'ts

Most of these suggestions probably apply more to coach passengers because of the communal seating arrangement. But whether you're sitting in coach or a sleeper, you're still living with a lot of other people in fairly confined circumstances. Being a good neighbor is really just a matter of common sense and basic courtesy.

- Use earphones with radios, tape and CD players, and scanners. (Amtrak will enforce this.)
- Loud conversations, even in private sleeping-car accommodations, can be very disturbing to people located nearby, many of whom will be relaxing, reading, or dozing.
- Tidy up after yourself in the washroom. One car attendant cannot possibly keep all of them clean all of the time.
- Let your car attendant know right away if you find something wrong—a malfunctioning toilet, for example. Early attention to these problems will minimize inconvenience to fellow passengers and can frequently prevent things from getting worse.
- Don't hog a seat in the lounge car if other passengers are obviously waiting for their turn.
- As pleasant as it may be, don't linger in conversation for more than a few minutes over coffee in the dining car.

There's either another seating scheduled or the dining-car crew is ready for a well-earned break.

- Unless it's truly important, don't bother a member of the crew who's on a meal break in the dining car. It's a tough job, and they deserve that short time to themselves.

- If you're traveling with children, don't let them run around the train without supervision. It's dangerous, especially in the vestibules between the cars, and it can be very annoying to other passengers.

One last word on the subject of behavior: Some passengers are under the impression that there are no laws on board a train and actually think they can indulge in drugs, liquor to excess, and any number of other illegal activities with impunity. Wrong! Wherever the train happens to be, the laws of that particular state apply to everyone on board. Passengers can be removed from the train and arrested in exactly the same way they can be kicked out of a hotel or a restaurant and into the waiting arms of the law. It can and does happen.

Train travel is meant to be an enjoyable experience. Agitation and impatience are simply incompatible with a leisurely cross-country train ride, so once on board and settled into your surroundings, relax. Gear down. Start noticing the new and the different in the passing scenery. Meet some of your fellow passengers. In fact, try to adopt the philosophy of an English gentlemen I met over lunch in the *Empire Builder*'s diner a few years back. The conductor had stopped by our table to inform us that we would be at least two hours late into Seattle because of work being done on the tracks. My English friend fairly beamed at the news. "Jolly good!" he exclaimed. "We're getting our money's worth and then some, aren't we!"

CHAPTER 7

Who's in Charge Here?

The success of any company, whether a manufacturing firm or a railroad, depends on its employees and, ultimately, how well they perform their jobs. When it came into existence in 1971, Amtrak inherited thousands of employees from private railroads. Along with all those new people came a kind of compendium of pecking orders, systems, and procedures that somehow had to be forged into one way of doing things. In many respects, the resulting operation didn't work out well; in some instances, change for the better has taken years.

When Thomas M. Downs took over as Amtrak's president in 1994, more than two decades after the company was created, he was startled to discover that he was the first supervisor that both a conductor and a chief of onboard services had in common. Largely due to Downs' urging, Amtrak reorganized its systems and introduced newer and better management techniques. Happily, that included the granting of more authority to front-line employees, and today, at least in theory, key members of the onboard crew can take action on the spot to rectify most problems.

A Word About Race and Gender

Although there are still some inequities in a number of areas, Amtrak has consistently demonstrated a progressive approach to the problem of discrimination by race or gender. The most obvious example is the position of car attendant. In the days of the Pullman porter, these jobs were limited to African American males. Today, however, it's not unusual for passengers to find that their car attendant is, for example, a white female.

This enlightened attitude also extends to giving women an opportunity to work in other railroad jobs that were traditionally the exclusive province of men. Women are now serving in every capacity on both freight and passenger trains, including the head end. For traditionalists, not to mention sexists, that will take some getting used to. My brother Pete was on a short-haul trip in the Midwest recently when a railfan, seated across the aisle from him, turned on his scanner to listen in on chatter among the crew. The man suddenly sat bolt upright in his seat and exclaimed to everyone within a twenty-foot radius, "Holy ——! The engineer's a girl!"

Who Does What and Why

First, you should know that a distinction is made between the operating crew (the engineers and the conductors) and the service crew (everyone else working on board). As the terms imply, the operating crew is responsible for actually running the train, while the service crew looks after the needs of passengers. There is another significant difference: The service crew usually stays with the train for the entire trip, while the engineers and conductors are restricted by federal law to working no more than twelve hours in a row. They join and leave the train at designated stops along the route.

Most Amtrak crew members tend to become quite close and treat each other like family. For instance, car attendants will switch off during the night, with one person covering two cars through a couple of stops so the other one can get a bit more sleep. If one of the dining-car crew becomes ill, it's not unusual for the chief of onboard services to pitch in and help out. Often one train crew will help out another. Once, while I was traveling eastbound on the *Southwest Chief,* our train slowed to a stop when we met our westbound counterpart so that several cases of soft drinks and a bag of ice could be handed from our lounge car to theirs.

The ability to get along with people is certainly a pre-requisite for anyone considering a job with Amtrak. By the time someone becomes a veteran employee, he or she has seen it all and can deal with most of it pretty darn well.

There are, of course, many other key jobs in the opera-tional structure of a railroad, but this section focuses on those employees who are directly responsible for getting you to your destination safely and for looking after your needs along the way.

Engineer

This is the job many of us wanted when we were kids and if you've ever been one of the privileged few to ride in the cab of a locomotive, you'll know why. It's a thrill to sit up there with all that horsepower, grandly acknowl-edging the waves from kids of all ages as you thunder past. But make no mistake—it's a tough job, and while it's generally agreed that being a freight engineer is more demanding, the men and women who haul Amtrak trains around the country are acutely aware that they're respon-sible for the lives of as many as 500 passengers.

Becoming a locomotive engineer isn't easy. It's particu-larly difficult if your goal is the head end of a passenger train and not quite so hard if you're after a job as a freight engineer. Basically, it boils down to supply and demand.

Most engineers, or at least the older, married ones, seem to prefer working for Amtrak because of convenience. An Amtrak engineer works a set schedule and thus has the luxury of knowing in advance when he or she will be at home or away. A freight engineer, however, is usually on call and goes off to work when needed.

Then there's the matter of training. Before someone can even be considered for an engineer's job, he or she has to spend six weeks in a classroom. One section covers instruction in the mechanical aspects of the equipment, another deals exclusively with air brakes (reflecting the obvious importance of knowing the hows and whys of stopping a train weighing many thousands of tons), and the third is a detailed review of the operational rules of railroading. From the classroom, an engineer trainee moves into the cab of a locomotive as an assistant to the engineer for a minimum of 480 hours of on-the-job training. Even after the classroom and on-the-job experience, there's still no guarantee that the trainee will be selected. Some would-bes are rejected because, according to one veteran engineer, they "just don't seem to have a feel for it." No matter how long they've been on the job, all engineers go through refresher training periodically and must take regular exams to qualify and requalify for the specific territory they work.

Of course the engineer is the person who controls the locomotive that pulls the train, alternately operating the throttle to start the train in motion and keep it moving and the brakes to slow or stop the train. The engineer also controls the whistle and constantly uses the radio to communicate with the conductor and the dispatcher.

To start the train, the engineer opens the throttle, which causes the diesel motors to run faster, generating more electricity and increasing the flow of power to the traction motors on each of the locomotive's axles. At the same time, the engineer often leans out the window and looks straight down at the ground. In that way, he or she can tell the instant the train starts to move and can adjust the throttle accordingly to keep the wheels from slipping. A slipping wheel is a real no-no, because it can cause a jerk that can be felt throughout the train. Passenger train engineers pride themselves on their smooth starts, so starting with even a small jerk is embarrassing.

Because freight trains are longer than passenger trains, there is a lot more slack, or "play," built into the coupling mechanism hooking each car together. As a freight starts moving, the slack is taken up in one car after another down the length of the train. Brakemen in the cabooses would hear the jolt coming toward them and hang on. As the slack is taken up in car after car, it builds in intensity. By the time it gets to the last car of a long train, it can literally knock you off your feet.

As strange as it may seem, freight engineers must handle their trains very gently. Taking up slack abruptly while a freight train is rolling can actually snap a coupling and break the train in two. In fact, to prevent massive derailments, the knuckle in the coupling device is deliberately designed as the weakest link in the chain so it will break under severe stress. How many times an engineer breaks a train is one way of measuring his or her performance and abilities. Sometimes it happens because the engineer caused it, but other times a knuckle gives way from metal fatigue or because it's old and rusted. When that happens, the engineer will replace the defective knuckle (spares are carried in freight locomotive cabs) and keep it to show as proof that the break was not his or her fault.

Once under way, the engineer's attention is almost always directed toward the track ahead, looking out for obstructions and also watching for signals, speed-limit signs, whistle posts (to blow the whistle for an approaching grade crossing), and other trackside markings. The locomotive cab is equipped with two large side mirrors, which the engineer uses to inspect the rest of the train as it rounds a curve for problems such as smoke from an overheated bearing or shifting loads in the case of freights. The assistant engineer does the same on the other side of the cab. Traditionally, the engineer sits on the right side of the locomotive cab, because in the days of steam locomotives, that was the side of the tracks where all the signs and signals were placed.

The visual inspection was also an important function performed by railroad personnel riding in cabooses at the end of freight trains, but both the cabooses and the people who rode them have been replaced by an electronic device mounted at the end of the rear car. Called FRED by railroad people (an acronym for Flashing Rear End Device), it picks up reports from the automatic detectors alongside the track and relays them by radio to the engineer in the head end.

Unlike the smooth ride passengers are treated to, it's pretty bouncy in the cab of a locomotive, and the rough ride can affect the accuracy of the speedometer. Because trains must run at or close to the prescribed speed for any given stretch of track, most engineers carry a stopwatch, which they use regularly to determine precisely how fast the train is moving. This is done by recording the exact time it takes the train to pass between two mileposts, then computing the speed from that. (See the table on page 97.)

Most Amtrak engineers came to the job with freight experience, and most agree that being a freight engineer is the more difficult of the two jobs. Because freight trains are so long—a 150-car train can be over a mile and a half from end to end—the engineer of a freight train often finds one part of the train coming up a hill and the other part heading down the other side at the same time. Just to complicate matters, the number of cars on either side is constantly changing as the train passes over the crest of the hill. That's very tricky, because the engineer must make sure to be pulling all the cars all the time. Now suppose there's a curve in that stretch of track. That means the engineer also has to think about centrifugal force affecting the part of the train that's going around the curve.

Veteran engineers will tell you that in many ways their job is tougher and more demanding than that of an airline pilot. The cockpit of a modern jet certainly looks complicated, but as one engineer friend of mine says, "Those are all fancy gizmos to help the pilot do his job. We don't have any of that stuff to help us." And he's quite right. In that sense, there is indeed a greater burden placed on a locomotive crew. If the train is running in fog or snow, there is no radar to help the head-end crew. The engineer must be so familiar with the route that he or she can "see" the track ahead in the mind's eye.

Another apt comparison between the locomotive engineer and an airline pilot is that both are expected to operate their machines in a manner that will minimize the use of fuel. The pilot does it by adjusting the attitude of the aircraft in flight so it passes through the air with the least possible resistance. The locomotive engineer conserves fuel in much the same way the driver of a car does—with a delicate touch, both on the throttle and the brakes.

Federal law permits an engineer to be on duty for no more than twelve hours. For that reason, one pair of engineers does not stay with a long-distance train for the entire route. For instance, along the westbound route of the *California Zephyr,* operating crews change in Galesburg, Illinois; in Lincoln, Nebraska; in Denver and again in Grand Junction, Colorado; in Salt Lake City, Utah; and so on all the way to Oakland, California. Usually, a crew coming off duty will sleep overnight at one of those points, then the next day take the eastbound train back to where they started. Under no circumstances is an engineer permitted to continue operating a train after reaching the twelve-hour limit. If a train has been delayed because of weather or track conditions and it appears that the operating crew will "go dead" before reaching its scheduled crew-change stop, Amtrak must anticipate the problem and arrange for a fresh crew to meet the train somewhere along the route before that happens.

Engineers are intimately familiar with the track in their territories, that is, with the stretch of track over which they operate their trains. They know that track the same way a commuter knows the roads between home and work. They have to—and must take regular tests to prove it. In many cases, probably most, they also get to know some of the people who live along their regular routes. These folks sit in their windows or step out into their backyards to wave as the trains go by. The crews get to know their "regulars" and wave back when they appear, usually with a friendly toot from the whistle, too.

One more tidbit I found interesting: Unlike the airlines, where meals are provided for the cockpit crews, head-end crews on Amtrak trains bring their own food in lunch pails. The only thing they're permitted to get from the dining car is coffee. On occasion, a chef will bend the rules and send up food that would otherwise spoil and be thrown out, but the steak or half chicken that can be used another day stays in the diner's freezer.

As with almost any job, there is a downside to being a railroad engineer. The first thing a visitor to the head end discovers is that it's noisy up there. That shouldn't be surprising, since the engineer is sitting just a few feet in front of as many as 4,000 horses. All that power makes quite a racket, and it's magnified several times whenever the train enters a tunnel. The real culprit, however, is the whistle, which is blown constantly. Earplugs are provided, but they aren't practical because a lot of necessary conversation is going on. Amtrak's newer locomotives are air-conditioned, permitting the crew to keep the windows closed. That has been a big help in alleviating the whistle noise problem.

There is only one real negative to the engineer's job, but it's a big one. Many engineers, whether freight or passenger, have struck and killed someone while at the controls of their locomotives. Perhaps the person thought he or she had plenty of time to drive across the tracks before the train reached the crossing. Maybe a teenager was playing chicken with the train on a dare. Maybe some poor soul has decided it would be a quick way to end it all. Whatever the circumstances, they're all equally tough on the person who happens to be the engineer that day. Spend a few hours riding in the head end and you somehow sense a touch of uneasiness as every grade crossing is approached. Most engineers manage to keep it in perspective. One told me, "As long as I've done everything possible—if I wasn't speeding, used the whistle, and applied the brakes—I can't take it personally." There is, of course, no way in the world to stop in time, although they always try.

Amtrak engineers are assigned to specific runs, which range from ninety minutes to ten hours in length. They are paid for no less than eight hours for every day they work, so it's Amtrak's responsibility to schedule their hours efficiently.

Assistant Engineer

Once upon a time, even after steam locomotives had been taken out of service, these people were called firemen. Today, the assistant engineer provides a second set of eyes and ears in the locomotive cab, calling out the signals as they're passed, noting any change in the speed limit, sending and receiving messages on the radio, and generally assisting with the many details, which allows the engineer to focus on the primary task of driving the train. Assistant engineers are fully qualified to operate the locomotive and regularly do so, spelling the engineer along the route. As a rule, the only difference between the two is years of experience. Assistant engineers are used on all long-distance trains, but on short-distance runs (between New York and Washington, for example), only one engineer is in the cab.

Conductor

There is a conductor on every train—passenger or freight, long or short, and whether it travels 1,000 miles or 1,000 feet. This is the person who is actually in charge of the train, roughly equivalent to the captain of a ship at sea. That means the conductor has to be thoroughly familiar with both railroad operations and the train itself.

Anyone who is an Amtrak conductor has worked his or her way up the ladder and knows a lot about railroad operations. Every new conductor goes through an initial training program of 244 hours, which includes train operations, emergency procedures, passenger relations, and all procedures necessary for handling tickets. There are periodic refresher courses after that.

As do engineers, each conductor works a specific territory, usually a section of the route just a few hundred miles long, and knows it intimately—every switch and every crossover. Conductors are required to take an annual test on the operating rules, which is based on the specific territory they work. If a conductor changes residence, a new test must be taken and passed before he or she can begin working a new territory. By the way, it takes a grade of 85 percent or better to pass those tests. Conductors are also required to pass a physical exam every two years.

The conductor is in regular contact with the engineer by radio throughout the trip and, in this manner, stays up to date on the train's progress, track conditions, other rail traffic, and any number of other details. If there's some kind of mechanical problem with the locomotive, the conductor (in consultation with the engineer) decides when or if the train can continue on its way. While the train is en route, it's the conductor who must deal with all the little idiosyncrasies that are found in every car: a bedroom door that comes off its track, a circuit breaker that trips for no obvious reason, and who knows what else?

The conductor also has the authority to deal with any other problem if it involves the safety or well-being of the passengers. If a passenger becomes ill, the conductor can arrange for an ambulance to meet the train at an upcoming stop. If a passenger becomes disorderly, the conductor has the authority to stop the train and put the person off.

Being so thoroughly familiar with the train's route, the conductor is usually the one to make periodic announcements over the public address system about points of interest along the way. It's also the conductor's responsibility to inform passengers of the reasons for any delays that may occur. (Some conductors don't do this, however, which is a real sore point with many frequent passengers. In my opinion, there is simply no excuse for not informing passengers about delays that are longer than a few minutes.)

There is also paperwork to do. The conductor officially notes all arrival and departure times (which is confirmed with the engineer by radio). Should the train be late, the conductor is responsible for filling out a Delay Report, which includes both the length of the delay and the reason it occurred.

Finally, the most obvious duty: the responsibility of collecting tickets and supervising the loading and unloading of passengers and baggage. Even when nothing apparent is going on, most conductors "walk the train" once or twice every hour just to keep an eye on things.

Assistant Conductor

Originally, this person was called a trainman, flagman, or brakeman. Today, the assistant conductor has the same duties and responsibilities as the conductor but in a subordinate role. One vestige of the old job remains, however, since the assistant conductor is often assigned to look after the rear portion of the train.

Coming back to the issue of gender once again, if the assistant conductor happens to be female, many passengers assume that she has little or no responsibility other than taking tickets. Not so. She takes the same tests, meets the same requirements, and must have the same knowledge of railroad operations. Usually the only real difference between the conductor and assistant conductor position is their length of service.

Chief of Onboard Services

The chief of onboard services is immediately responsible for the quality of service on your train. Earlier in the company's history, quality control for onboard service was the responsibility of train inspectors, who would board unannounced to conduct random inspections. This changed in the mid-1980s, when chiefs were put aboard all long-distance trains. By the time the 1990s came around and cost-cutting was clearly a factor, the chiefs were eliminated on some trains. It's easy to justify having an onboard supervisor for trains such as the *California Zephyr* or the *Silver Meteor,* which have service crews of more than twenty people. Having an extra person on a train where the entire service crew is just five or six people makes much less sense.

Whether you're riding in coach or first class, you should be able to spot the chief within the first thirty minutes of your trip. He or she sports a navy blue blazer with gray slacks or skirt and is quite clearly someone in authority. While the conductor is primarily concerned with the operation of the train, the chief of onboard services is responsible for just about everything else that goes on inside the train. He or she double-checks all supplies, greets passengers, distributes meal vouchers to first-class passengers, makes regular public address announcements, and keeps tabs on every aspect of service during the trip. On long-distance trains, it's usually the chief who organizes activities in the lounge car or offers prizes for trivia contests or scavenger hunts conducted over the P.A. system.

About the only way to become a chief is to work one's way up through the ranks. And a good thing, too, because the chief must be prepared to pinch-hit for another crew member in the event of illness, accident, or, as sometimes happens, if a regular crew member is a no-show.

After the car attendant, the chief is your best recourse for any problem you might encounter. In fact, a good chief will anticipate and deal with problems before they occur—like finding a more appropriate seat for the mother with two youngsters who was seated right behind a retired couple, or taking a teenager aside and quietly asking that he change that T-shirt with the obscenity on it. A chief's constant focus should be the safety and comfort of the passengers and on keeping the rest of the crew on its toes. When you get a good chief, you know it right away. Unfortunately, Amtrak still has a few "invisible chiefs" who are seldom seen or heard throughout the trip.

Dining-Car Steward

There are fewer and fewer stewards these days, and personally I think that's a pity. Being greeted by a polished maitre d' as you enter the dining car certainly adds to the overall experience. In most cases now, that function is performed by the lead service attendant (LSA), who also waits on tables.

The steward is responsible for the quality of the service in the dining car. He or she seats people, distributes the meal checks on which the order is noted, records the complimentary meals of sleeping-car passengers, and collects payment from the coach passengers. The steward is also responsible for all cash collected in the dining car. Over the duration of a two-day trip, that can amount to many thousands of dollars. The accounts had better balance at the end of the trip, too, because any difference must be made up from the steward's personal funds.

Theoretically, the LSA has the same responsibilities as the steward. Because the LSA must also work tables, however, there just isn't as much time to spend on the niceties of dining. Lacking a steward, the emphasis is necessarily on getting people seated and served in a reasonable amount of time.

Whether a steward or an LSA, this person is responsible for making sure everyone gets fed—whatever that entails. If a power failure knocks out all the ovens in the diner's kitchen, for example, the steward will dash to a telephone at the next stop and arrange for hot meals to be delivered to the train at a station up ahead. (I've often tried to imagine the scene in a KFC restaurant when the phone rings and an Amtrak steward wants 250 chicken dinners delivered to the local station when the train pulls in ninety minutes later.)

Service Attendants

This is Amtrak's gender-neutral term for waiter or waitress. Call it what you will, on a long-distance train, it's a tough job. Each day, they start serving breakfast in the dining car as early as 6:30 in the morning, and the final seating for dinner often lasts until 9:00 P.M. In between, the service attendants may have served as many as 700 meals. It's quite true that the chef and the assistants in the kitchen had to prepare all those meals, but the service people had the added responsibility of maintaining a cheerful disposition throughout that sixteen-hour day. It's especially grueling on one of the western trains, which take two nights to reach the West Coast. After a scheduled fifty-hour trip from Chicago to Oakland, crews working the *California Zephyr* spend one night in a hotel, then depart the next morning for the trip back home—two more tough sixteen-hour days. A compensating factor, usually the most important one for Amtrak crews, is that they get six or seven days off before the next trip.

In addition to waiting on tables, each member of the service crew has other specific duties: setting the tables, filling the salt shakers, sorting and stocking the packaged condiments, and performing a host of other tasks—pretty much the same things you would do to prepare for a dinner party in your home.

In Amtrak's early days, most crew members were veterans of the railroad, many being third or even fourth generation. Some of these folks remain, but through normal attrition and as more women have been hired, their numbers have diminished.

Chef

Once you enter the kitchen in an Amtrak dining car, you're on the chef's turf, and a good chef keeps a sharp eye on everything that happens within his or her domain. The chef boards the diner several hours before the train departs to make sure the kitchen has been left in proper order by the previous crew. Occasionally things are not shipshape. In such cases, a long trip begins by cleaning up after someone else.

Amtrak's computer determines in advance the amount of food and supplies that should be put aboard the diner before each trip. The first order of business for the chef is to check supplies against that list to be sure that everything the computer ordered has arrived. That's important, because every steak and piece of chicken must be accounted for at the end of the trip, and anything missing must be paid for out of the chef's own pocket. Some food is prepared or cooked ahead of time. Bacon, for example, is precooked, then heated prior to serving.

Amtrak chefs are permitted a fair amount of latitude within the framework of the current menu. The chicken dish can take many savory forms depending on how the chef chooses to prepare it, for example, and the "chef's special" offers another outlet for culinary creativity. Although there isn't a lot of variety on the menu due to limited storage space, many chefs bring their own personal collection of spices on board to give several items on the bill of fare an additional bit of individuality.

A few years ago, in a determined effort to improve the quality of onboard meals, Amtrak began sending its chefs to "Chefs College," otherwise known as the Culinary Institute of America in Hyde Park, New York. Everyone agrees it worked, and in a domino effect, morale among the entire dining-car crew has gone up, too. It's pretty simple: Better food means happier passengers, who leave more generous tips.

Once under way, and as mealtime approaches, activity in the diner's kitchen increases to a pace that's somehow frenzied and orderly at the same time. The chef is still clearly the one in charge and handles most of the actual cooking. Orders come in, are filled, and sent out (or up via dumbwaiter, in the case of Superliners) with amazing dispatch. They'd better be! On some of the more popular trains, as many as 250 meals have to be prepared and served over a four-hour period. A Superliner dining car can seat seventy-two passengers at a time, and even under optimum conditions that translates into four one-hour seatings. Meals have to be prepared and served efficiently, or the dinner hour will stretch into bedtime—annoying to passengers, exhausting for the dining-car crew.

One veteran Amtrak supervisor who worked his way up through the ranks says that a chef has the toughest job on a passenger train.

Food Specialist

Food specialists are the people who work in the kitchen under the supervision of the chef. Responsibilities are divided, but include the same tasks we all perform at home in our own kitchens, from putting the groceries away to cleaning up the pots and pans after the last meal is served. The days are long and the work is hard. As with many other onboard employees, what makes it all worthwhile is good pay for the hours worked and lots of time off for leisure or, in many cases, another job for additional income. Newly hired food specialists go through an initial training program of 105 hours, and they must take a number of trips and perform satisfactorily under the watchful and usually very critical eye of a veteran chef.

Car Attendant

These are the folks who look after the comfort of passengers on all of Amtrak's long-distance trains. There are no car attendants on short-haul trains or on trains that may cover a lot of distance but don't operate overnight.

Note that the correct term is car attendant and not porter. It's not a major issue with most, but in the minds of some, porter is a term that carries a reminder of another time. Its origins date back to the days when virtually all sleeping cars were manufactured, owned, and operated by the Pullman Company. Only African American males were hired to staff those cars. The jobs were highly prized, especially during the Great Depression, and those who got them took justifiable pride in the quality of their work. Not surprisingly, however, a good deal of latent racism came with the territory. It became the unfortunate custom for many passengers to call every porter "George," after the company's founder, George M. Pullman. Hearing that every day from passengers who neither knew nor cared what their given names were was certainly a humiliating and dehumanizing experience for many Pullman porters and, it seems to me, accounts at least in part for the passing of the term. Incidentally, that bit of history is one reason Amtrak has made a point of providing all employees with name badges.

New hires go through a minimum training program of 105 hours. There are periodic refresher programs, and as with all new hires in any of the onboard jobs, car attendants have to take a number of "student trips" and perform up to standards before they are made permanent employees.

I had always assumed that brand-new attendants would start out working in coaches and gradually work their way up to sleeping cars, but that's not necessarily true. Amtrak people bid for their assignments, and whether or not they get their request is determined partly by seniority and partly by how popular the particular trip is. Whether or not an attendant works in coaches or sleepers seems pretty much a matter of choice; in fact, many attendants prefer the coaches. Sleeping-car attendants make more money because of tips, but even under normal circumstances they work harder and their passengers can be much more demanding.

Amtrak assigns one car attendant to every sleeping car, whether it's one of the new single-level Viewliners or a bi-level Superliner. Not so with coaches. You'll find one car attendant for every three coaches on eastern trains, while one attendant looks after two coaches out west in the larger Superliners. (By the way, in Amtrak slang these folks are known as "tacos," an acronym for Train Attendant, COach.)

Whether working in coach or sleeper, many of the attendant's duties are the same: boarding passengers, helping to stow their baggage, maintaining a seating chart, keeping the car orderly and the bathrooms clean, making sure each passenger gets off at the right stop, and generally doing whatever is necessary to make sure the trip goes pleasantly for everyone. Coach attendants distribute pillows throughout the car and retrieve them after each passenger leaves the train.

Sleeping-car attendants have fewer people to look after but much more to do. I once had a wonderful conversation with a long-time car attendant who provided the best description of the job I've ever heard. "This here sleeper," he said, "is just like a small hotel . . . and I'm the only employee!" That about sums it up, too. The attendant is doorman, receptionist, bellhop, maid, room-service waiter, and concierge all rolled into one. Spend forty-eight hours watching a good one in action and you'll have a real appreciation of what a demanding job it is.

A sleeping-car attendant reports for duty about three hours prior to the train's departure, making sure every room is in order and has towels, facecloths, soap, a route map and timetable, and anything else that's supposed to be there. The attendant cleans mirrors, removes any dirty linen, stocks and cleans the rest rooms, and looks for anything that may not be in working order. (If a toilet doesn't function properly, now is the time to find out and get it fixed!) He also checks to be sure all the beds have already been made up. Most of the time they have, but not always. In those cases, he'll have to do it himself.

Even if everything is in order, there's a great deal of bed-making in the life of a car attendant. When a passenger is ready to retire for the evening, the berth has to be lowered into position and arranged for sleeping; on two-night trips, it must be made up again the next morning. Often there is as much as a 50 percent turnover of passengers on a forty-eight-hour trip, meaning half of the bedrooms could be occupied by different individuals on successive nights. The first passenger may ride overnight from Chicago to Denver, with the second traveler boarding in Salt Lake City for the trip from there to Oakland. The attendant must pull off the old sheets and remake the bed before the new arrival boards, ready for a good night's sleep.

There's even more bed-making to do on turnaround trips. The *California Zephyr*, for instance, originates in Chicago and is turned around in Oakland. The car attendant makes up the berths twice on the westbound trip, remakes them with clean linen in Oakland during the layover, then twice again on the return trip to Chicago. A Superliner sleeper can carry a total of forty-four passengers, which translates to more than 200 bed-makings over one round-trip.

You'll first meet your attendant on the platform, where she will check your name off against her passenger manifest and direct you to your room. Once the train is underway, she should also take the time to make sure you understand where everything is in your room and how it all works.

Some sleeping-car passengers enjoy the idea of room service and ask the attendant for beverages or meals served in their rooms. Strange as it may seem (since the dining-car experience is one of the unique things about train travel), it's not unusual for a sleeping-car passenger to have all meals brought to the room for the entire trip. Of course, that's the norm for passengers with disabilities and anyone having difficulty moving about the train.

The sleeping-car attendant will also give you a wake-up call if you would like one or if you're going to be leaving the train at an early morning station stop. The attendant will offer to bring juice or hot coffee to your room at whatever time you might wish in the morning. Also, the same attendant will usually slide a morning paper, put aboard at a major city the train passed through in the wee hours, under the bedroom door. In theory, attendants are still supposed to shine passengers' shoes during the night, but in actual practice it doesn't happen. The shoe shine is one of the last vestiges of the days of the Pullman porter and is highly symbolic for many Amtrak car attendants. There is almost universal agreement that it's no longer appropriate for them to perform that service.

The car attendant is the person you should first contact with any problem or need. Whatever it may be, you can be sure that the attendant has heard it before and will take it in stride. (I always make it a point to ask the attendant in my car to tell me about some of the unusual experiences he or she has had. They all have dozens of stories, some so bizarre they couldn't possibly be invented.) Coach attendants usually occupy one of the rear seats in their car. Sleeping-car attendants are usually assigned one of the rooms in the car. Some will make a point of telling you which room they're in, should you need something during the night. If your attendant doesn't volunteer that information, ask. But, please, be considerate. Don't roust the poor soul in the middle of the night for a trivial request. By the same token, don't hesitate to call if you have a legitimate need—illness, for example.

Car attendants work a base of 180 hours a month. It figures out to just over 40 hours per week, but that's deceiving. The typical workday for a car attendant is 16–18 hours long. It would be worse than that, except they help each other out—one attendant will handle the boarding of passengers for several cars in the middle of the night so a colleague can get a bit more sleep. The upside is the time off. Every attendant I've talked to lists this as a major benefit to the job. Although it varies according to the schedule of the employee, car attendants average four days off for every three they work.

Lounge-Car Attendant

The specifics of this job vary somewhat according to the kind of equipment involved. On eastern trains, especially the short-haul trains without a dining car, it's a particularly busy job. The attendant operates behind a counter in a galley located in the middle of the lounge car and provides hot and cold sandwiches and a variety of beverages for passengers. On western trains, the attendant is located in a similar facility on the lower level of the Superliner lounge car.

The lounge-car attendant's schedule is a killer: On the long-distance trains, he or she will be up at 5:00 A.M., making coffee and preparing the little galley to open at 6:00. The attendant takes three forty-five-minute meal breaks during the day and finally closes down around midnight. For most of that eighteen-hour day, the lounge-car attendant is on his or her feet, serving a constant stream of passengers—heating packaged meals in the galley's microwave oven, serving potato chips and other snacks, pouring cold drinks, selling decks of cards or souvenir blankets, and making change—all the while maintaining a cheerful disposition.

(As an interim measure in its smoking policy, Amtrak did away with smoking anywhere on the train but in the lounge car. Most passengers applauded, but it made life miserable for the lounge-car attendants, who found themselves working that grueling schedule in a constant haze of tobacco smoke. When new policies eliminated smoking entirely from some trains, no one was happier than the lounge-car attendant.)

Product Line Manager

As part of the decentralizing of authority, Amtrak has placed specific individuals in charge of each long-distance train and made those people responsible for virtually every aspect of that train's operation. Each product line manager (isn't that an awful title?) can now make many decisions affecting the train which in former times could only have been made by someone (or more likely, a group of someones) at Amtrak's corporate offices in Washington, D.C.

For instance, Brian Rosenwald, product line manager for the *Coast Starlight,* has added a parlor car. Now, as the train rolls through California's famous wine country, sleeping-car passengers are invited to the parlor car to enjoy an afternoon snack and sample wines produced in some of the very vineyards passing by outside the window. Needless to say, the parlor car has proven to be a very popular addition to what was already Amtrak's most popular train. The point is, whether adding a parlor car to the train's consist, overhauling the dining car menu, or deciding to eliminate smoking on board, the product line manager now has the latitude to initiate a wide variety of changes and improvements in the train for which he or she is responsible. Of course, it's also true that the product line manager must be able to justify the cost of each of those improvements, which usually means being able to demonstrate that the change has resulted in more and happier passengers.

Service Manager

Every long-distance train operated by Amtrak also has several service managers assigned to it. These people are located at key stops along the route and deal with an almost limitless variety of operational problems that may occur as the train passes through their territory. Here are a couple of examples:

- The westbound *Sunset Limited* is scheduled to end its 2,700-mile, coast-to-coast journey with a 6:30 A.M. arrival in Los Angeles. If the train is running on time, the dining car doesn't open for breakfast that morning, but I rode that train recently and on that occasion it was almost five hours late, meaning breakfast would have to be served after all. The service manager had to make sure enough food to feed several hundred people was put aboard the train at one of the stops during the previous night.
- On another trip, a freight train derailed up ahead of the *California Zephyr.* We had to be diverted around the accident, which delayed us for several hours. That, in turn, meant our operating crew (the engineers and conductors) would reach their twelve-hour limit and "go dead" before we arrived in Denver, where the new crew would normally come aboard. It was the service manager's responsibility to anticipate the problem and arrange to transport the relief crew several hundred miles east where the *Zephyr* was waiting—all without adding to the delay we had already experienced.

Dispatcher

Wherever the train may be, its progress is controlled every inch of the way by a dispatcher. The airline equivalent is the air traffic controller, but there is an important difference: railroad dispatchers are employees of the individual railroads, while air traffic controllers are employed by the Federal Aviation Administration, an agency of the U.S. Department of Transportation. (One more hidden government subsidy of the airline industry not enjoyed by the railroads, by the way.) Dispatchers who control trains traveling in the Northeast Corridor between Washington, D.C., and Boston are Amtrak employees, because those tracks are owned by Amtrak. Elsewhere throughout the country, the movement of Amtrak trains is controlled by dispatchers employed by the host railroads—that is, the railroads over whose tracks the Amtrak train is traveling.

Like their aviation counterparts, dispatchers are critical to the safe operation of the nation's railroads. Typically, they work in darkened rooms, keeping track of trains on an illuminated display of the tracks for which they are responsible. The job requires complete concentration, and their fellow employees take pains not to interrupt or distract them.

Dispatchers communicate directly with the train's engineer by radio. They also control the signals seen by the engineer along the route. The dispatcher's main and constant concern is knowing exactly where each train is at all times. To assist the dispatcher, the engineer checks in by radio regularly—when the train passes specific checkpoints, when it leaves each station stop, and at other times along the way. Many engineers even "answer" the recorded voices of automated hot box detectors they pass, which is just one more way of letting the dispatcher know where they are. (See "Railroad Terms and Slang" for an explanation of "hot box.")

There is other, more specific communication between the train crew and dispatcher, of course. The dispatcher frequently directs the train to slow down, stop, or resume normal speed. The dispatcher may remind the engineer that workers are on the track at a certain location or instruct the engineer to reduce speed between two specific mileposts where new track has just been laid. When receiving such instructions, the engineer will acknowledge the call and carefully repeat the message so the dispatcher will be sure it was heard correctly. The engineer will often conclude the transmission by verbally noting the time and the train number and then identifying himself or herself by name. For important matters, the dispatcher is also the train's link to the rest of the world. If a passenger becomes seriously ill, for instance, the engineer can call the dispatcher and ask to arrange for paramedics to meet the train at the next station stop.

Station Agent

While not part of the onboard crew, station agents deserve at least some mention, since they're often the first Amtrak employees that passengers encounter. Depending on the size of the station, the station agent's job may or may not be full-time. Basic responsibilities include keeping the station clean, selling tickets, and handling baggage. They also direct you to the spot on the platform to wait so you'll be near your car when the train stops. Frequently, however, an agent is called on for other things. For instance, if the lounge car on an incoming train is running low on ice, the onboard chief may have a radio message sent, asking the station agent to have several bags of crushed ice waiting when the train pulls in.

Some Amtrak station agents really make their presence felt in a positive way. One of the best is Scott Hurd, who runs the Amtrak station in Portland, Oregon. A while back, Scott convinced Amtrak's management to let him create a comfortable lounge for first-class passengers out of some unused space in the station. Now, while waiting for their train to arrive, sleeping-car passengers can enjoy a complimentary soft drink and relax in quiet, comfortable surroundings. It's a wonderful amenity, and it came about because an enthusiastic, imaginative employee took the initiative to make it happen.

Yard Workers

As your train passes through major stations around the country, you'll see railroad employees in hard hats working around the trains—both freight and passenger. This is tough, dangerous work. They'll be hanging onto ladders on the sides of rolling cars and working between railcars for the coupling and uncoupling process. They talk with the engineer by radio and help direct the train when it is backing up to add more cars to the train. They do this by calling out car lengths ("two cars . . . one car . . . "), then switching to feet ("twenty feet . . . ten . . . five . . ."). Finally—and this is a curious railroad tradition—they will all call out, "That'll do!" just before the cars bump together.

CHAPTER 8

When Things Go Wrong

Every year, Amtrak carries more than twenty million passengers over more than 20,000 miles of track on trips ranging from short commuter runs to cross-country odysseys. To the company's credit, most train trips are an enjoyable experience from start to finish. Our national rail passenger system, however, is an immensely complex operation, and not surprisingly things can and do go wrong. Knowing what could happen can help head off problems in the first place or help you deal with situations if they do occur. Not knowing and being unprepared, mentally or otherwise, can turn a minor inconvenience into a major problem.

Whom Do You Turn to for Help?

When a problem occurs, the best advice is to ask for help calmly, politely, and early. Since areas of responsibility are divided, knowing which onboard crew member to talk to is also helpful.

- The car attendant has primary responsibility for your comfort and safety. See him or her about problems within your car.

- The chief of onboard services is responsible for the service you get anywhere on the train. (If there's no chief on your train, start with the car attendant. If he or she can't help, take your problem to the conductor.)
- The conductor is responsible for problems of an operational nature. Like the captain of a ship at sea, the conductor is the ultimate authority aboard a train.

There is a welcome trend at Amtrak to give more authority to onboard employees. Conductors can now waive penalties for passengers who purchase their tickets after they board the train, and both conductors and onboard chiefs can upgrade passengers into first-class accommodations if in their judgment the circumstances warrant it. Conductors and chiefs can also issue Amtrak travel vouchers on the spot in order to handle problems. The voucher amounts given are rather small, but everyone concerned applauds the management principle involved.

That being said, let's look at some typical problems that can crop up during your trip.

What If You Get Sick?

If you experience some kind of a health problem while on board, inform your car attendant right away. An unexpected illness can happen to anyone, so don't be embarrassed. And don't wait until you're in a real emergency situation before asking for assistance. For one thing, the sooner you notify the crew, the more time they'll have to consider the options and make the appropriate arrangements.

As with any problem, go to the car attendant first. Give him or her your best assessment of what's happening and, if it's something you've experienced before, what you think you'll need. The car attendant will probably alert the chief of onboard services or, if there is no chief on your train, the conductor.

Sometimes the crew will use the train's public address system to ask if a physician is on board who can take a look at you. The conductor may also decide to radio ahead and arrange for paramedics to meet the train at the next station stop. The paramedics can evaluate your condition and take the appropriate action. Sometimes that means providing medication; sometimes it means leaving the train and taking a trip to the local hospital. Whatever the circumstance, you can take some comfort in the knowledge that a sick passenger is not an unusual occurrence on Amtrak trains. You'll find crew members concerned, sympathetic, and capable.

Missed Connections: The Number One Problem

Trains running behind schedule are the single biggest headache Amtrak has to deal with—at least in terms of its day-to-day operations. When trains are late, passengers miss connections, and when those are "guaranteed connections," it's Amtrak's responsibility to make things right. Unfortunately, it's almost a certain lose-lose situation for Amtrak. Missed connections, or "misconnects" as they're called, cost the railroad a lot of money, and no matter what kind of a solution is worked out, the affected passengers will not be happy.

Regular riders and people who understand the unique complexities of running a long-distance railroad operation are usually more tolerant of delays than the infrequent or first-time traveler. Veteran rail travelers also take the likelihood of delays into consideration when they make their travel plans, allowing plenty of time between connecting trains even if that means spending the night in a hotel and continuing on the next day.

If you're on a train that's running late and have a connection to make up ahead, get a hold of the chief of on-board services even before you arrive to get advice on your options. Once you pull into the station (it will most likely be in New York, Washington, D.C., Chicago, or Los Angeles, since most scheduled connections take place in one of those four locations), go immediately to Amtrak's Passenger Service Desk in the station. Other passengers from your train will be in the same situation, so the object is to be one of the first people in the problem-solving line. The Amtrak employee at the desk will already be aware that a connection was missed and will probably have some tentative answers for you by the time you show up. If you don't get immediate help or if you're not satisfied with the alternative arrangements offered, ask to see the supervisor for station services.

The important thing is to let them know what you want. Be reasonable, however. Amtrak may be willing to meet your request but unable to because of the time of year, the weather, the time of day, the number of people involved, the availability of nearby hotel accommodations, and many other factors. Through it all, try to keep your cool. The person you're dealing with isn't the cause of the problem and is no doubt doing his or her best to help you.

Problems with Accommodations

Occasionally, passengers with first-class tickets find themselves in the wrong type of room or, more typically, think they are in the wrong room. Some first-time rail travelers (especially if traveling as a couple) take one look at an economy bedroom on a Superliner and are convinced they can't possibly spend two days in a room that small. These problems almost always occur because whoever booked the trip, either the passenger or a travel agent, wasn't familiar with Amtrak accommodations. Sometimes, of course, real mix-ups do indeed occur. Whatever the problem, if you want to change your sleeping car accommodations, start with the car attendant; if the car attendant can't help, ask to speak with the chief of onboard services or the conductor. Bedroom space is very tight, especially in the summer months, but sometimes a last-minute cancellation or no-show will enable the chief to take care of your problem.

Plan for a Late Arrival

If your train runs late, that can cause a real inconvenience for those who plan to meet you at your destination. When you make pickup arrangements, by all means instruct them to call Amtrak at 800-USA-RAIL to get the latest arrival time before they leave for the station. It's a basic precaution that could keep them from having to sit in a station parking lot—perhaps in the middle of the night—waiting for a train that's two or more hours late.

Poor Service

In any organization of 23,000-plus employees, there will be some bad apples. That certainly doesn't excuse poor service, but it should serve to remind us all that maintaining a high level of competent service is an ongoing effort. By the same token, it helps if your expectations are reasonable. For instance, if you're traveling in a sleeper and ask for a meal to be served in your room, remember that your car attendant can be looking after as many as forty other people. The attendant has to take your order to the dining car, wait until your meal is prepared, then bring it back to you. In the meantime, other passengers are asking to have their beds made up, one of the toilets isn't working, and there's a station stop coming up with a passenger who will need help getting off. Cut the attendant some slack if you can. Car attendants and serving personnel in the dining cars have a very tough job. Sometimes even the best of them will get cranky and let slip a brusque remark. Be understanding, try to keep things in perspective, and don't let one person who is having a bad day spoil your trip.

In the unlikely event that you run into a real problem employee, seek out the chief of onboard services or the conductor. If you're not satisfied with the action taken, note the employee's name and, after you get home, write to Amtrak about the problem. How can the company deal with problem employees if you don't? (See details of how and where to write at the end of this chapter.)

Rattles and Squeaks

As mentioned in an earlier chapter, the railcar in which you're riding may have been around a long time. The constant motion of the train can cause strange noises to develop and, if you're like me, they can drive you crazy when you're trying to sleep. Usually it's something easy to find and simple to fix (slamming a washcloth in a loose cabinet door, for instance), so at least make the effort. The next step is to call your car attendant, who will probably be able to locate the problem and take care of it quickly. On rare occasions, mysterious squeaks and rattles just can't be silenced. When that happens, it may be possible to change rooms. Otherwise, you'll just have to tough it out. Heck, if a rattle will bother you that much, you won't be sleeping much anyway.

Problem Passengers

Occasionally the stranger sitting next to you turns out to be something of a problem—a constant talker, for instance. When it happens on a plane, most of us just suffer through it for three or four hours. On a long-distance train, however, a chatterbox can become a forty-eight-hour ordeal. At the very least, you can get up and sit for a while in the lounge car.

If your seatmate or someone nearby turns out to be significantly more than just an annoyance—makes sexual advances or becomes drunk or quarrelsome, for instance—you can and should ask for help from your car attendant or the onboard chief. Amtrak personnel are more than willing to take firm action against the occasional serious troublemaker, to the point of putting that person off the train, bag and baggage.

The conductor is the ultimate authority in these matters. One told me with a smile, "Occasionally there'll be a group in the lounge car that gets rowdy from drinking too much. That keeps families from enjoying the lounge car, so I tell 'em pretty firmly to settle down. If they don't, I'll just put the ringleader off the train. When that happens, his pals are like little lambs the rest of the way."

In extreme cases, the local highway patrol is contacted by radio, and a police car meets the train where the tracks cross a major highway. I was once aboard the *Desert Wind* (since discontinued) when it stopped at a grade crossing somewhere near the Nevada-Utah state line. An obnoxious character who had come aboard the train in Las Vegas and had been drinking steadily ever since was suddenly confronted at his seat by two state troopers and hustled off the train—to the enthusiastic applause of several dozen fellow passengers. When last seen, he was twisted around and looking back at us through the rear window of the police car, on his way to at least one night in the jail at Caliente, Nevada. Incidentally, in order to avoid a loud argument or worse, a disorderly passenger who refuses to cooperate with train crew members is given no warning before being put off the train.

Equipment Failures

Mechanical breakdowns do occur and can be very disruptive, depending on how and when they happen. The most significant problem, as you might expect, occurs when a locomotive breaks down. Even a partial loss of power at the head end can disrupt an entire schedule. For instance, if you're on the *California Zephyr* heading west out of Denver and one of the three engines fails, it could be enough to delay the entire train until a replacement unit arrives. Two units might not be enough to haul that entire train over the Rockies as well as provide electricity to the rest of the train.

The most common problem is the breakdown of toilets in a Superliner or other new equipment. Sometimes the problem is mechanical and sometimes they're clogged, and in the winter they occasionally freeze. Whatever the reason, it's unpleasant, annoying, and inconvenient for passengers and crew alike. (The original toilets in the older cars simply emptied onto the tracks and, because they were so simple, almost never failed. This is yet another reason why the federal mandate to retrofit all the older Amtrak cars with self-contained toilets is an expensive and unnecessary idea.)

Electrical problems in the dining car can be bad news for the entire train. When the ovens or the grills go down, the kitchen crew has to improvise. Sometimes the only answer is a frantic phone call to a fast-food restaurant near the station at the next scheduled stop. One way or another, however, the crew makes sure folks get fed.

Follow Up on Your Complaint

There may be a certain amount of nostalgia attached to the image of the grizzled old railroad veteran brought up on steam and with railroading in his blood. Because the odds were against Amtrak in its early days, hard-nosed railroad people were necessary to make it all work and keep things running. The trouble is, many of those old-timers thought of passengers as a necessary evil, just a particularly bothersome type of freight. That attitude was felt by passengers.

With the passing years, the old-time railroad men are leaving Amtrak and a new crop of younger executives is taking their place. As a result, there is a much broader understanding that first and foremost Amtrak is in the service business. Should you follow up on complaints? You bet! How else can someone in a position of authority improve or correct things? Amtrak takes all complaints seriously. They're categorized, the source of the problem is tracked down, and (in my experience, anyway) a reasonable effort is made to take corrective action.

Here's how to pursue your complaint most effectively: Avoid the temptation to gripe about relatively trivial problems. Put your complaint in writing. Be specific, but be as brief as possible. Stick to the facts and try to express the issue unemotionally. Send your letter to Amtrak Customer Relations, 60 Massachusetts Avenue NE, Washington, D.C. 20002.

Try to remember that Amtrak is a very large organization performing a complex service for millions of people. Things are bound to go wrong from time to time. Give them a reasonable amount of time to investigate and make things right. Above all, don't just take your grievance home and bad-mouth the entire Amtrak system to all your friends. Outraged letters to the editor won't solve anything either, and complaining to your representatives in Washington could have a negative effect on what is already inadequate funding by the federal government. In other words, by all means go ahead and complain, but try to keep your complaint constructive.

CHAPTER 9

Passenger Train Equipment

As you will notice, both Amtrak across the United States and VIA Rail in Canada use quite a variety of equipment. We'll get into a few details in this chapter, but first let's focus on some basic standards that are common to all or most railcars.

Most passenger cars are about eighty feet long, give or take a foot or two, and no more than ten and a half feet wide. The traditional single-level railcar is about thirteen and a half feet high, but newer cars are taller. The bi-level Superliners, which Amtrak began adding to its fleet in the 1970s, measure sixteen feet, two inches, from the rails to the top of the car itself. The new Viewliners, which are single-level cars, are fourteen feet high. Dome cars, still in use on Canada's premier trains, have a glass viewing dome mounted on top of the standard railcar, which increases their height to nearly sixteen feet. Height is an important consideration when determining which type of railcar will be assigned to certain trains. For example, on a number of eastern routes, Superliners still can't be used, because they're just too tall for some of the bridges and tunnels along the way.

Each railcar has a total of eight wheels, four at each end. Those four wheels are part of a unit called a truck. The number of wheels on the locomotives vary, depending on what it's used for. Some have eight wheels, others twelve, and some of the really heavy-duty freight locomotives can have as many as sixteen wheels.

Locomotives

All told, Amtrak has over 300 passenger locomotives in its fleet. Most Amtrak trains are pulled by one of four basic types, but others are used for specialized service.

- A new generation of diesel-electric locomotive has been put into service over the past several years. Originally, they were called AMD-103s. Then, because it was the first locomotive in probably forty years to be specifically designed for passenger service, Amtrak began referring to them as the Genesis series. That was a bit too exotic for railroad folks, so today this locomotive is known simply as the P40. There are now about 120 of these locomotives in the Amtrak fleet, with more on order. Depending on who you ask, they're either the best-looking or the worst-looking locomotive ever to come along. One thing is for sure—you can't miss P40s. They look very big and very powerful, as indeed they are. Each produces 4,000 horsepower, meaning that two of these new units can haul a train that previously required three engines. To provide an example in another context, one P40 can produce enough electrical power for 700 homes. The P40 offers better acceleration and greater reliability. It's also modular in design, so a faulty component can be pulled out and replaced immediately, keeping the locomotive in operation.
- Although they're now being replaced by the P40s, the backbone of Amtrak's fleet for many years was the locomotive referred to as the F40 or, more completely, as an F40PH. The P stands for "passenger" and the H

Amtrak's new P40 locomotives are state of the art, have more horsepower than the venerable F40s, and can operate at speeds up to 105 miles per hour. The P40s also have enclosed, air-conditioned cabs, an unaccustomed luxury for head-end crews who have long been used to working conditions that were often hot or cold and always noisy. (Photo courtesy of Amtrak)

indicates that it's equipped to provide head-end power (electrical power) to the rest of the train. These diesel-electric locomotives were made by the Electro-Motive Division of General Motors—tough, reliable work-horses, each capable of producing 3,000 horsepower. They're easy to recognize, and you'll continue to see them for a while yet.

- Along the Northeast Corridor and between Philadelphia and Harrisburg in Pennsylvania, Amtrak trains are pulled by pure electric locomotives called AEM-7s. They draw their electric power directly from an over-head wire (a catenary) the way old-fashioned trolley cars did. Built from a European design, they can pull

For years, brawny F40PHs have been the locomotive of choice for both Amtrak and VIA Rail. The distinctive prow makes them easy to identify. These two, at the head of VIA's transcontinental train, the *Canadian,* were photographed in the heart of the Canadian Rockies during a servicing stop at Jasper, Alberta. Amtrak has been replacing its trains with the newer P40s, but these durable locomotives are still used exclusively for VIA's long-distance trains. (Photo by the author)

trains at much higher speeds than the F40s, and at 7,000 horsepower, they are a lot more powerful.

- Twenty diesel-electric locomotives, built by General Electric and called P32s, were put into service in 1992. Except for the distinctive red and blue Amtrak stripes, they look a lot like the locomotives you see hauling freight trains, and are primarily used on trains running out of Los Angeles.

- If you're traveling in the Pacific Northwest, you may see one of the new Talgo trainsets. These sleek, Spanish-built trains have been tested on the *Mount Adams* and

Currently the fastest and most powerful locomotive in Amtrak's fleet, the all-electric AEM-7 draws its power from an overhead wire, called a catenary. Most of these loco-motives are only used along the Northeast Corridor, between Washington, D.C., and New Haven, Connecticut, although the stretch from there to Boston is currently being "electrified." AEM-7s operate at speeds of up to 125 miles per hour. (Photo courtesy of Amtrak)

the *Cascadia* between Seattle and Portland for the past year or so. The roadbed won't yet permit them to oper-ate at the speeds they were designed for, but they have nevertheless proven to be very popular.

Information on how locomotives operate can be found in Chapter 10, "How It All Works." For a description of the engineer's job, see Chapter 7, "Who's in Charge Here?"

Mail Cars

Hauling the mail is big business for Amtrak. Most of what the company carries for the U.S. Postal Service is second-class mail (newspapers, magazines, and other dated material). Amtrak does carry first-class mail to some areas with spotty air service. Amtrak also offers an express service, carrying packages between cities throughout its system. All told, almost $60 million a year is generated for Amtrak from these services. Everything—express packages and mail—is carried in what Amtrak people refer to as MHCs, or materials handling cars. In lay terms, they're simply boxcars built to run at high speed. Amtrak's fleet includes almost 200 of these cars, and you'll probably see at least one and perhaps even two or three in every Amtrak consist, usually up front right behind the locomotives.

Very recently, in an effort to generate more revenue, Amtrak has made some tentative forays into the freight handling business. MHCs are used for this purpose, too. How can you tell if the car is carrying mail or boxes of lettuce? In the latter instance, the car will usually be at the rear of the train.

Baggage Cars

There's always at least one baggage car on every long-distance train, located right in front of the first coach. This is where Amtrak carries baggage checked by passengers, as well as other parcels shipped from one point to another along the route. Occasionally, these cars will carry mail, too.

Amfleet Equipment

You'll be able to spot these cars right away, because the exterior shape is more rounded than the classic passenger railcar. You may also notice that the windows are rather small compared to newer and older Amtrak equipment. When these cars were designed and built, air travel had become the way to go, and apparently the idea behind the small windows was to evoke the feeling that you were in an airliner. There may be something to that, since Amtrak uses these cars along the Northeast Corridor, where trains travel at speeds of up to 125 mph. Amfleet cars are primarily used on shorter routes around the country: Los Angeles–San Diego, Boston–New York–Washington, D.C., and Springfield–Hartford–New York City.

Standard Coach

These cars have two comfortable seats on each side of a center aisle. The seats recline and an airline-type tray folds down from the seat-back in front of you. There's an overhead reading light and a luggage rack above all seats. Each car has two lavatories, one of which is designed to accommodate a wheelchair. Coaches used on longer routes have more legroom, and each seat has a foldout leg rest.

Club Coach

This is where Amtrak provides first-class service on all-coach trains. It's often referred to as a "parlor car," although that's really a term from another era of railroading. Club coach seats are wider than those in the standard coach and therefore are placed in a one-two configuration, that is, two seats on one side of the center aisle and only one on the other side. These seats are really plush and recline wonderfully. There's a footrest, a service tray that folds down from the seat-back in front of you, and an overhead reading light. The club coach section occupies about a third of the railcar. In the middle of the car is a cafe service area from which complimentary meals and drinks are provided to club coach passengers. A lounge area serving all passengers is at the opposite end of the car. As you would expect, there is a surcharge for these accommodations. Frankly, if you make a strictly objective decision, the wider seat and free meal isn't worth the extra cost. If you can afford it, however, it's fun to take a what-the-hell attitude and treat yourself.

Lounge Car

These cars are found on medium- and long-distance trains. A very efficient service area is located in the middle of the car from which you can buy hot or cold sandwiches, a variety of snacks, and beverages, including soft drinks, beer, and some mixed drinks. An arrangement of tables and chairs is available where you can sit and relax, or you can take your food back to your seat.

Dinette Car

These cars (also found on medium- and long-distance trains in the east) are basically a step up from the lounge car. A compact food-service area turns out complete hot meals in addition to the fare provided in lounge cars. The seating area is set up in the more traditional dining car configuration: booths for four people on each side of the center aisle. Usually someone is there to provide table service. Don't mistake this for full dining-car service, however. The meals are prepackaged and heated in a microwave oven. Basically, it's big airline food.

Metroliners

This is Amtrak's designation for the high-speed trains that operate along the Northeast Corridor between Washington, D.C., and New York. The cars are really standard Amfleet coaches but have fewer seats. That translates to more legroom, and because of the extra space between seats, they also recline a bit more. Metroliner locomotives are the all-electric AEM-7s, the only type able to run at 125 mph. Metroliner consists are limited to either five or six cars, which is one way to identify those high-speed trains.

Heritage Equipment

These cars once belonged to one of the many former passenger railroads but were acquired and refurbished by Amtrak when it began operation. Most were built in the 1950s and 1960s; in contrast to the rounded shape of the Amfleet and Metroliner cars, they have the classic, boxier look of the traditional rail passenger car. Amtrak has been phasing these cars out for some time, and the *Adirondack* is the only train still using Heritage lounge cars, all of which have been refurbished.

Heritage sleepers are almost gone from Amtrak's fleet now, and I confess that I miss them. They were old, but they came from the golden age of rail travel and were built for comfort, which I appreciated at bedtime when I settled down on that nice, thick mattress. The only ones still used by Amtrak trains are dorm cars for crews on overnight eastern trains. VIA Rail in Canada still runs wonderfully refurbished versions of these grand old cars, which you can read about in Chapter 13, "Taking the Train in Canada."

Heritage diners, which can serve as many as fifty-six people at a time, are still used on overnight eastern trains. While some of the food is necessarily precooked, most is prepared on board and the quality is usually quite good. Dining is family-style in all Amtrak diners, which means you'll have fellow passengers at your table unless you happen to be traveling as a party of four. This is where you'll meet some very nice and interesting people—and some real characters, too.

Viewliners

Viewliners are the newest single-level cars in Amtrak's fleet and were really the first passenger cars that Amtrak was able to create from square one. After three prototypes were tested in service, fifty Viewliners were ordered and are now in service. The Viewliner sleeping cars (as yet there are no Viewliner coaches) were designed for long-

Floor plan of an Amtrack Viewliner sleeping car

distance overnight service in the eastern part of the country. The single-level Viewliners are not as tall as the Superliners but are significantly larger than the traditional Heritage-type cars.

The most obvious innovation in the Viewliner is the double row of windows, which provide additional viewing for passengers in the upper berths. The berths are larger than those in Superliners, too, and that combination should pretty well eliminate the claustrophobic feeling some passengers had when tucked away in an upper berth. Each sleeping car can accommodate a maximum of thirty people in fifteen different rooms.

Every Viewliner sleeping car includes three deluxe bedrooms, one of which has been designed to accommodate a disabled passenger and a companion. The other two can connect to form a large suite with plenty of room for four people. Each includes a washbasin, a toilet, and a shower. There's a temperature control and a call button if and when you need the car attendant. There is also a small clothes closet and space for storing two suitcases.

The twelve other standard bedrooms are smaller but will adequately accommodate two people. Because the room is much narrower than the deluxe bedroom, whoever draws the upper berth will especially appreciate that second window. Each compartment includes a washbasin and a toilet. There's room for a couple of suitcases, although it's a bit awkward to get at your suitcases if the upper berth is lowered. Passengers in these compartments will have access to a shower located at the end of the car. One other innovation (if indeed we can call it that) should

One of Amtrak's finest, car attendant John Turk, is ready to welcome passengers aboard a new Viewliner sleeping car on the *Crescent,* en route to New Orleans on a sunny day in May. Note the second row of windows, which are for passengers in upper berths. (Photo by the author)

be mentioned: Each Viewliner bedroom has a small video monitor on which you can see short features and movies.

Insider Tip: How to Get a Smoother Ride

Ask for a room near the middle of the car when you book. If you're traveling in a Viewliner sleeper, standard compartments 1–8 will be the better choice. Either of the two deluxe bedrooms, A and B, are fine, with A being closer to the middle of the car. The special bedroom, designated as bedroom H, is at the end of the car. All economy and deluxe bedrooms in Superliner sleepers are either not over the wheels or on the upper level, where it really doesn't matter.

Superliners

These bi-level cars are found on all of Amtrak's long-distance western trains, including the *Sunset Limited,* which extends to

Florida. Superliner equipment is also being used on several eastern trains: the *City of New Orleans,* the *Cardinal,* the *Capitol Limited,* and the *Auto Train.* Superliner cars are larger and heavier than the traditional single-level rail passenger car, so the ride is smoother and more comfortable. Passengers move between cars on the upper level only.

Coaches

There are minor variations based on the way the cars are laid out, but a typical Superliner coach can accommodate seventy or more passengers. Most of the seating is on the upper level, although many coaches include some seats on the lower level primarily for the use of disabled and elderly passengers who might have trouble climbing the narrow stairway. They have plenty of room for baggage. You should stash your suitcases in the large storage racks located near the lower-level entrance to the car. Don't worry about leaving your luggage in these racks. Just be sure that each of your bags is clearly and prominently identified so someone with a similar-looking suitcase doesn't take yours by mistake. There's also a luggage rack above the seats running the full length of each car,

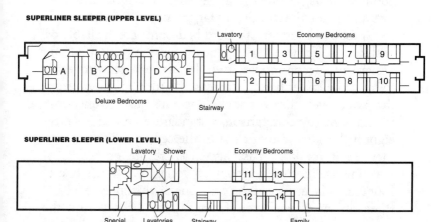

Floor plan of an Amtrak Superliner sleeping car

which is the best place for your shoulder bag and any other carry-on items you'll need while in your seat.

The coach seats are wide and comfortable. Most will recline as much as thirty-five degrees, and each is equipped with a foldout leg rest. If you have to sleep sitting up, this is definitely the way to do it. Don't pick a seat in the last row, however, because those seats are in front of a wall and won't recline as far as the others. And, because they face a wall, avoid the first row of seats, too. No big deal—but they have slightly less legroom there.

Sleeping Cars

When fully occupied, a standard Superliner sleeper will accommodate as many as forty-four people in four distinct types of accommodations. As do the coaches, sleeping cars have a large luggage rack located on the lower level of the car just as you enter. This is where you should keep all your luggage—everything except the few personal items you'll need in your compartment. These should be in a shoulder bag. You will have access to your luggage during the trip; it's just a lot easier to take the few necessities with you to your room. As already mentioned, don't worry about your bags, which will be perfectly safe in the rack. Just make sure they're clearly tagged with your name.

A total of fourteen standard bedrooms are available on both levels. They're very adequate for one person but are designed to accommodate two. Facing seats slide together to form the lower berth. The upper berth folds down from the wall over the window. Since it's just twenty-four inches wide (by comparison, a standard twin bed is thirty-eight inches) and rather close to the ceiling, I don't recommended it for large passengers. There are no toilets or washing facilities in the room, so you'll have to use one of four unisex lavatories in the car—one on the upper level and three on the lower level. There is also a shower on the lower level.

If two people are occupying the room, you'll have to leave your luggage in the storage racks on the lower level, bringing only a few toiletries and other bare essentials into the room. If you're traveling by yourself, there's a small shelf that will barely accommodate an airline-sized carry-on bag. There is room to hang two or three garments in a little closet. Yes, these rooms are small, but because you pay for your sleeping-car accommodations by the room and not per person, this is by far the most economical way for two people to enjoy the advantages that sleeping cars provide.

Insider Tip: A Room to Avoid

Although it's located on the upper level of a Superliner, avoid economy bedroom number 2, which is almost directly across the corridor from a lavatory. Every time it's flushed during the night—whoosh!—you will very likely wake up with a start. Bedroom number 1 is located right next to the lavatory, so that's even worse. Fortunately for us paying passengers, it's usually occupied by the car attendant, but not always. If there are any other empty rooms in the car, he or she will avoid room 1, too, and now you know why.

The five deluxe bedrooms are all located on the upper level and are very adequate for two adults. There's a long bench-type seat facing a comfortable chair. The seat flattens out to form the lower berth. It's three-quarters the width of a standard double bed and can accommodate an adult and a small child. Two adults will find it either crowded or cozy, depending I suppose on the couple's priorities at the time. The upper bunk folds down and is thirty-two inches wide—a good deal roomier than the upper bunk in economy bedrooms. The room includes a washbasin with lighted vanity mirror and a combination toilet/shower. (I say this again, too: When using the toilet, be sure to hit the flush button and not the button for the shower. It seems obvious, but

Deluxe bedrooms on the upper level of Superliner sleeping cars are larger than the standard bedrooms and include a small sink and vanity as well as private toilet and shower facilities. (Photo by the author)

someone does it on almost every trip.) A small closet allows space for two or three hanging garments. Theoretically, there is room for one or two suitcases, but you'll have to keep them on the seat or on the floor. They'll be in your way so, as with the economy bedrooms, it's better to have some essentials in a couple of shoulder bags and keep the luggage in racks on the lower level.

As with bedrooms in Viewliner cars, two pairs of these rooms have a folding partition between them that can be opened to form a rather large suite.

Insider Tip: All Bedrooms Are Not Created Equal

Ask for one of the standard bedrooms on the upper level in the Superliners. Lower-level rooms have a bit less of the side-to-side sway, but you get better viewing and a quieter ride up top. Bedrooms 1–10 are located on the upper level; numbers 11–14 are below. Given a choice, avoid deluxe bedroom A. It's at the very end of the car, and as you will see from the Superliner floorplan, the angle of the corridor outside gives this room a more cramped configuration than the others.

Each Superliner sleeping car has one family bedroom. These were designed for two adults and two small children and do the job quite well. Two of the berths are good-sized and will handle mom and dad very nicely. The other two—one upper and one lower—are definitely for kids, since each is just four feet, nine inches long. Family rooms include a washbasin, mirror, and a changing table for infants. There is no toilet in the room, but three lavatories and a shower are just a few feet from the door. If you need to have luggage in the room for the kids, it's less of a problem here simply because there's more floor and seating area on which to put the bags. As a practical matter, however, I suggest keeping all bags in the luggage racks, which are right outside in the corridor.

These family bedrooms offer two big advantages. One is that they extend the entire width of the car, providing a look at scenery on both sides of the train. I once sat in my standard bedroom for the better part of an hour with a rocky cliff passing by just a few feet outside the window, unaware that a beautiful vista was on the other side of the train. The other advantage is cost. Family bedrooms will sleep two adults and two kids, but Amtrak has priced them well below the deluxe bedrooms, which really accommodate only two adults. And all four people will get complimentary meals when traveling in a family bedroom. Just remember that there is only one such room in each car—another reason to make your reservations well ahead of time.

There is also one special bedroom in each sleeping car. This is really just a politically correct term meaning that these accommodations are for a passenger with disabilities and a companion. The room is well designed and handles a wheelchair very neatly. There are two beds, a toilet, a washbasin and mirror, a little closet, and—ta-da!—a storage rack for two suitcases. Like the family bedroom, the special bedroom runs the entire width of the car, and there is only one in each Superliner. These rooms will be sold to non-disabled passengers if the rest of the car is sold out or within seventy-two hours of a specific train's departure time.

All Superliner rooms include a small built-in, fold-down table for playing cards or games. Likewise, all rooms have a temperature control, and you can also adjust the flow of air through a vent in the ceiling.

You should know one other little quirky thing about Superliner sleepers. To summon the car attendant, pull, don't push, the call button. When the button is pulled, a bell rings and a small light goes on outside your door. *Don't push the button back in until the attendant arrives.* If you do, the light will go out and he or she won't know which passenger rang.

Remember to Buckle Up!

No matter what kind of sleeping car you're in, when anyone climbs up into that comfy upper berth, make sure you hook up the straps designed to keep the occupant from rolling out during the night. After all, he or she is four feet off the floor in a strange, narrow bed on a moving train.

Lounge Car

This is the place to be for the best look at passing scenery. The upper level features comfortable chairs and huge windows that wrap halfway up the roof of the car. Below is a snack bar where you can buy sandwiches, snacks, and a variety of beverages, nonalcoholic and otherwise. There is also a limited selection of souvenir items: playing cards, coffee mugs, postcards, and the like. The lounge car attendant opens up early in the morning and, except for several well-deserved breaks during the day, will serve passengers until midnight or close to it. The upper level of the lounge is open and available to all passengers all night.

Dining Car

These cars will accommodate seventy-two people at one sitting, although one table for four is usually reserved for members of the crew. The diner is located in the middle of the train next to the lounge car so that no one is too far from either car. The food is prepared in a gleaming stainless-steel kitchen on the lower level and sent up in a dumbwaiter. As noted elsewhere, the culinary offerings vary from train to train depending on its route, with one or two regional dishes featured on each menu.

Transition Sleeper

This is always the first bi-level car in the Superliner consist, located right behind the baggage car. Amtrak people call it simply the "dorm car," and as that name implies, it's for most of the onboard crew members. Sleeping-car attendants usually occupy economy bedroom number 1 in their cars, but other crew members sleep on the upper level of the dorm car, which is configured with economy bedrooms only. The lower level includes combination bedroom/offices for the conductors and the chief of onboard services, toilets, showers, and a crew lounge. Most of these cars originally came from the Santa Fe when Amtrak was created in 1971, but a few of them are newly built.

Insider Tip: How to Get a Better Night's Sleep

Most veteran rail travelers feel they sleep better if they're facing forward; that is, they prefer lying in the same direction the train is moving. In the Viewliners, you'll sleep facing forward in all standard compartments and across the width of the car in the deluxe bedrooms. In the Superliners, you'll sleep facing forward in all economy bedrooms, but across the width of the car in all the deluxe bedrooms. In the family bedrooms, adults sleep across the width of the car, kids in the two small berths sleep facing forward.

How It All Works

Hauling more than twenty million passengers all over the country is a complicated business. The Amtrak system includes a total of some 25,000 miles stretching from coast to coast. Amtrak itself owns only about 750 miles of that track, most of it along what is called the Northeast Corridor, the route running between Boston and Washington, D.C., by way of New York City. Almost everywhere else, Amtrak trains are operating over track owned and maintained by private freight railroads, referred to as "contract" or "host" railroads by Amtrak.

Passenger and freight operations have some distinct differences, but the basic technology and operating procedures are pretty much the same—whether we're talking about Amtrak throughout the United States, VIA Rail across Canada (Chapter 13), a luxury train traveling through Mexico's Copper Canyon (Chapter 14), or a freight railroad hauling a variety of commodities back and forth through just one section of the county.

The Track

When you stop and think about it, the track is what makes rail travel different from every other form of transportation.

Railroads spend a lot of time and money on the construction and maintenance of their track. It's important, too, because a poor track means trains must run at slower speeds, and that means reduced revenues for the railroad. Sometimes trains run slowly because the track has just been rebuilt. New track will settle a bit, and until it has stabilized, trains must travel over it at slow speed, usually about ten miles per hour.

The first step in laying track is to carve the path (called the *subgrade*) out of the terrain and, as much as possible, level it off. This is done by removing earth from the high spots and using it to fill in the low areas. Look for this as you travel. You'll immediately be aware of the terrain rising and falling as it passes your window, while the actual roadbed remains more or less level.

Once this subgrade has been prepared, two layers of ballast are added. The first is a coarse gravel; the second is crushed rock or crushed slag. These two layers of ballast can be as much as two and a half feet deep, depending on the condition of the subgrade.

Next come the cross ties—traditionally wood, but more and more are being made from concrete—which are embedded in the top ballast. Wooden ties are placed a foot apart, 3,000 to every mile of track; concrete ties are larger and heavier and are placed two feet apart. Concrete ties are used more in areas where there is heavy or high-speed train traffic. They last up to twenty-five years before needing to be replaced. Under the same conditions, a wooden tie, even when it has been chemically treated to resist rotting, will last for about seven years.

When wooden ties are used, heavy metal plates, called *tie plates,* are placed on the ties. The rails are laid over the tie plates, then both are fastened to the ties with track spikes—really just huge nails. Tie plates are embedded in the concrete ties when they're made, and the rails are fastened to the ties with heavy metal clips. There are minor variations, but generally that's the way all track is laid.

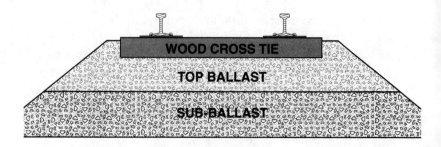

This is how most railroad track is laid: rails and wooden cross ties on top of two layers of gravel and crushed rock. On heavily traveled and high-speed runs, you will also see concrete cross ties, which last longer under those conditions.

The two rails are laid exactly four feet, eight and a half inches apart, which is known as *standard gauge*. The importance of establishing a standard width for track is obvious: It means an individual freight car can be hauled virtually anywhere in all of North and Central America. Parallel tracks are laid fourteen feet apart—that's the distance from the center of one track to the center of the adjacent track.

There are a number of *narrow-gauge* railroads in this country. The track is just three feet between the rails to accommodate smaller locomotives and cars designed to operate on steep grades and around tight curves in mountainous terrain. Most of these narrow-gauge railroads have become tourist attractions and provide excellent opportunities to experience railroad operations typical of another era, not to mention a chance to view spectacular scenery up close. (You'll find a list of scenic excursion trains in Appendix C.)

For years, individual rails have been thirty-nine feet long, which is not really a strange number, since they were originally hauled on standard forty-foot flatcars. They're laid end to end and bolted together at the joints. It's this joint that makes the clickety-clack when the car's wheels pass over it. Today, when track has to be replaced, quarter-mile lengths of welded rail are often used. It goes down much faster, and because the joints are some 1,300 feet apart and are welded together, the clickety-clack is gone. That, of course, is how you can tell when your train passes onto a stretch of welded rail.

The rails themselves vary in size, weighing anywhere from 112 to 145 pounds per yard. The size of the rail used depends on the amount, weight, and speed of traffic it's going to get. Heavy-duty rails are found on main lines, with lighter-weight track used for spurs and sidings.

You'll probably notice track work going on in several locations during your train trips. The equipment they use is fascinating to watch. One machine (actually, it's several machines mounted on a number of articulated cars) will remove the old wooden ties, level the ballast rock, put new concrete ties into position, and install welded rail—all in one operation. For years railroad workers laid track using only hand tools. Incidentally, back in the late 1800s, most of those tools were made by the Gandy Manufacturing Company. The word "Gandy" was stamped on the handle of every pick, shovel, and hammer. That's why even today, track workers are still called gandy dancers.

Every so often you may see one or more cross ties smeared with white paint. That means those ties have either been marked for replacement or for treatment with a chemical preservative. Occasionally you'll also see one cross tie painted yellow. That tells the engineer where to stop the train so it won't activate crossing lights and barricades at a grade crossing up ahead. No sense stopping all that automobile traffic if the train isn't ready to proceed across the intersection.

The Wheel

Every wheel on every railroad locomotive or car has a unique feature making it different from all other wheels: a *flange*. It's a one-inch ridge projecting from the inside edge of the wheel that, with the flange on the wheel at the other

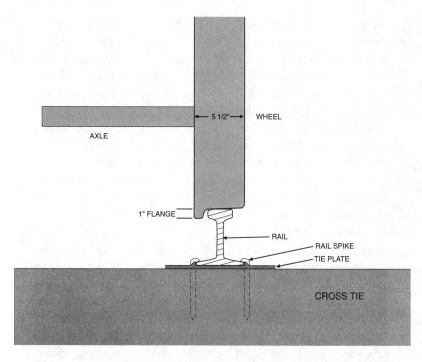

Two things make a railroad different from other forms of wheeled transportation: the flange on the inner edge of the wheel and the fact that the wheel is welded to the axle. Both are designed to make sure the train stays on the track. You can also see from this illustration how the rail fits into the tie plate and is fastened to the wooden cross tie with spikes.

end of the axle, keeps the wheel on the rail and the train on the track.

Here's something else unique about the way a train works: The wheels of a railcar are welded to the axles, and the entire unit turns. You'll notice it immediately if you look carefully at the wheels of a train rolling by at a slow speed. It's done that way to ensure that the wheels stay on the rails, and it provides better distribution of the immense weight of the railcar.

It All Starts with the Locomotive

The proper term for this monster is indeed *locomotive,* but railroad people also use the terms *engine* and *moto,* depending on the company. Like ships, a locomotive is always spoken of as though it were female.

When it rolls off the production line, every locomotive is assigned a number that is unique all across the country; no two have the same number, regardless of which railroad may own them.

When speaking about a modern railroad locomotive, most people refer to it as a "diesel." They're half right. Technically, it's a diesel-electric locomotive. Its diesel motors (there can be several) are not actually used to move the train, but they power electric alternators that generate DC current, which is sent to traction motors on each of the locomotive's axles. That's what makes the train go. In addition to powering the traction motors, a locomotive's generators run fans for removing heat and the air compressor for the braking system, and they provide electricity for the rest of the train.

There are also pure electric locomotives. Instead of producing their own electricity, they draw it directly from an overhead wire, called a catenary. These locomotives are much more powerful than the diesel-electrics. Faster, too.

In any discussion of railroad locomotives, *traction* is the key word. That's why locomotives are weighted—to provide as much traction as possible. Traditionally, traction motors have used DC (direct current), but that's changing. Some newer locomotives now have AC (alternating current) traction motors. AC uses less electricity and is therefore more fuel-efficient. AC locomotives also have more pulling power—three AC locomotives can replace five DCs—and they require less maintenance.

Unlike automobiles or airplanes, the engineer of a locomotive sits on the right side of the cab, with the assistant engineer occupying the left-hand seat. The assistant engineer is fully capable of operating the locomotive and in fact frequently relieves the engineer at the controls. Short-haul trains often have only one engineer.

The locomotive has a single set of controls on the right side of the cab in front of the engineer. There's a throttle to increase or reduce power to the traction motors, a control for the air brakes, and a little handle or button that blows the whistle. A number of gauges allow the engineer to monitor all the machinery, plus fuel reserves and the train's speed.

The whistle is blown as the train approaches grade crossings where automobile traffic crosses the tracks. On many locomotives, the loudness of the whistle can be adjusted to some degree according to how hard the handle is pulled. Engineers will often ease up a bit at night when passing through a residential area, when they can clearly see no traffic near the grade crossing or when the train is moving at slow speeds. Pull that handle all the way, however, and the whistle will make your ears ring!

A built-in device called an *alerter* is found in all locomotives. If the engineer doesn't adjust the throttle, apply the brakes, or blow the whistle for twenty to twenty-five seconds, a horn sounds and a bright light starts flashing in the cab. It pretty well guarantees that the engineer won't become distracted from his duties or fall asleep. If the engineer fails to respond after the horn and light have been activated for several seconds, the brakes will be applied automatically and the train will come to a safe stop. These devices are in place should the engineer become unable to operate the locomotive for any reason.

Head-End Power

Most of us take electricity for granted around the house and at work. Flip a switch, and the light goes on. That's true on a train, too, but making sure it happens every time is a bit more complicated. A fully loaded passenger train requires a lot of electric power. In the coaches and sleepers it powers the air-conditioning, the lights, the outlets for electric razors and hair dryers, and provides hot water for washing up and showering. In the lounge car, TV sets, VCRs, a microwave oven, and refrigerators are all run by electricity. The biggest user of electricity in the consist is, as you would expect, the dining car with its ovens, ranges, grills, freezers, refrigerators, dishwashers, and water heater. There's even a dumbwaiter in the Superliner diners, and it, too, is run by electricity.

We've already talked about how diesel motors in the locomotive run generators to produce the electricity that moves the train. The electric power to run all those lights and appliances comes from the same source—a special generator just for that purpose in the locomotive. It's referred to as *head-end power* by the crew, and you'll frequently see it abbreviated as HEP.

Long before passengers arrive, the service crew is on board preparing the train for departure. They all need to see what they're doing, of course. In particular, the dining-car crew needs to have all of the appliances working to store perishable food and to prepare meals. Before the locomotive is attached to the train, that electricity comes from a cable provided at the station. It's called *hotel power.*

Coupling

The coupling device that joins one car to another has two principal features: a drawbar with a knuckle on the end. The drawbar is attached to the car's frame and is constructed so it will slide forward or backward to provide slack. The knuckle looks like a cupped hand, which grips and locks with the knuckle on the other car. The cars are also connected by hoses to provide air pressure for the braking system and cables to carry electricity from the locomotive throughout the train. The knuckles hook together automatically when two cars are pushed firmly together, but the complete coupling process requires a railroad worker to manually connect the air hoses and electric cables. When uncoupling two railcars, the yard worker simply releases a lever on the knuckle, and a locomotive pulls the cars apart, the hoses and cables parting by themselves.

Train Orders

Immediately before departing at the train's point of origin, or wherever boarding the train en route, the engineer is given a set of train orders. This is a sheaf of papers that authorizes that specific trip and notifies the operating crew of any changes from normal track conditions along the way. These could include specific locations where crews are working on the track and *slow orders* for other sections of track. Trains operate at slow speeds over new track until it has had a chance to stabilize. Train orders can also be called *track warrants.*

Starting

Smooth starts are a lot easier with a passenger train, because there are a lot fewer cars and little or no slack between them. Engineers pride themselves on smooth starts, which, with practice, can be done consistently.

Starting a freight train of 100-plus cars is quite another matter. In fact, theoretically it's just not possible for a locomotive to move all that weight. It does, though, and the secret is in the freight car's coupling mechanism. There's roughly a foot of slack between each car in the train. When starting the train, the freight engineer first gets rid of all the slack by backing up enough to compress the entire train. When the locomotive starts moving forward, the slack is taken up and the train starts moving, one car at a time. Once all the cars are moving, the locomotive can keep them rolling, even speeding up and slowing down. But it was the slack that got them all started.

Stopping

Being able to stop a train is critically important but not an easy thing to do. It is, after all, a massive amount of weight moving at high speed. For example, an eight-car passenger train traveling at 80 miles per hour requires a minimum of three-quarters of a mile to stop, even under emergency braking conditions. Much greater weights are involved with freights, and as would be expected, they are that much more difficult to stop. A 100-car freight train can weigh more then 10,000 tons and, even at 30 mph, will simply not be able to stop in less than one mile.

There's really only one way to stop any rolling vehicle— by applying pressure against the wheels. That's the way we stop cars, and it's the way trains are stopped, too. There is a brake on every wheel of every car on every train.

Braking was done manually on the earliest trains, but it wasn't until about 1900 that air brakes became standard equipment on all railroad cars, whether freight or passenger. Although the air brakes on every car in the train are controlled by the engineer from the locomotive cab, in an emergency the conductor can activate the brakes from anywhere on the train.

The brakes are operated by using compressed air, which is carried throughout the train by hoses that are connected when any two cars are coupled. The first air brakes used the compressed air to force the brake shoes against the wheels. That method worked well as long as nothing went wrong. However, if the air compressor failed or if a hose broke anywhere along the train, the resulting loss of air pressure meant the entire braking system failed—

leading rather quickly to very unpleasant consequences. In 1887, in Burlington, Iowa, George Westinghouse had a simple but very bright idea: Instead of using the air pressure to force the brake shoes against the wheels, use it to hold them away from the wheels. In that manner, the brakes would automatically be applied if the system failed for any reason—and the train would stop. There have been frequent changes and improvements ever since, but the basic principle behind the air brake still applies, and it's still the way trains are stopped.

Another braking system is worth mentioning. *Dynamic braking* is used to gradually slow the train without applying the air brakes. In the simplest terms, instead of sending electricity to the traction motors to move the train, the whole process is reversed. The turning wheels are used to power the traction motors and generate electricity. The resulting "drag" causes the train to slow gradually. That electricity has to be used in some way, so it's put to work operating blowers that cool the traction motors. Any excess produces heat, which is dissipated through giant grids on the roof of the locomotive, like the coils on top of your electric stove. A very rough equivalent is slowing your family car by putting it into second gear.

As a passenger, you can frequently tell whether the engineer is using the dynamic brakes or the air brakes. For one thing, air brakes slow the train much more rapidly and you can hear them quite clearly—not the escaping air pressure, but the sound of the brake shoes being applied to the wheels under your car. There's no noticeable sound when the dynamic brakes are applied, but you can usually feel a slight bump just before the train begins losing speed—the slack between the engine and the baggage cars being compressed.

"Spotting" the Train

When a passenger train pulls into a station, the tricky part to stopping is more the where than the how. The object is to stop the train at just the right spot so passengers on the platform can step right into their cars and boxes, crates, and heavy suitcases can be handed right out of the baggage car onto the waiting carts. The engineer often gets some help in *spotting* the train by radio—from the conductor, the baggage man, or the station agent. If the train is longer than the platform (which is often the case in small-town stations), the engineer will have to *double-spot* the train, meaning the train will stop to unload and board passengers, then pull ahead to repeat the process for passengers in the rear cars.

Hills and Curves

When it comes to railroading, flatter is better. (That's why railroad tracks were often built along the banks of rivers.) Hills, referred to as *grades,* can be a problem. Because of the train's immense weight, the steeper the grade, the more difficult it is to negotiate. The engineer's main concern is to keep the locomotive's wheels from slipping, causing a sudden loss of traction. To keep that from happening, the engineer must apply just enough power to do the job, reducing speed gradually if necessary. Driving your family car up a slope in icy conditions is a pretty good comparison. Speaking of ice, poor weather conditions just make the job that much tougher. Most locomotives are equipped with sanders, operated by the engineer, which sprinkle sand on the rails just ahead of the locomotive's driving wheels to give them better traction.

Railroad people measure the steepness of a grade in terms of percentage. For example, a 1 percent grade means that the track rises (or falls) one foot in altitude for every 100 feet of rail. For a typical Amtrak passenger train, grades of 2 percent can be handled without any particular problem. Operating a freight train up such a grade is more complicated because they are a lot heavier and a lot longer. The steepest grade on any mainline track in the United States is 4.7 percent—crossing the Blue Ridge

Mountains near Melrose, North Carolina. How steep is that? Well, railroaders consider anything more than 1.8 percent to be *mountain grade.*

With a train, down can often be a much bigger problem than up. The whole principle of a steel wheel on a steel rail is to reduce friction to a minimum in order to move those massive weights. That's well and good, but the result is called a lack of rolling resistance, and it simply means that once a train gets rolling, it can be hard to stop. If it's coming downhill—even a hill that would be unnoticed by the driver of an automobile—a train can react like a roller coaster and accelerate. As mentioned elsewhere, an engineer can be at the head of a long train that's actually going downhill and uphill, part pushing and part pulling, at the same time. How does a freight engineer handle a train? The same way a porcupine makes love—very carefully.

Keep to the Right

Where there is double track (two tracks running parallel with each other), trains usually stay to the right. There are exceptions, as you will probably notice, but they are usually caused by track work of some kind.

Speed Limits

In most parts of the country, the maximum speed allowed for Amtrak trains is 79 mph. Why 79 and not 80, you ask? Well, federal regulations require that any train operating at 80 mph or faster must have a device in the locomotive cab that picks up and visually displays trackside signals for the engineer. Since most standard Amtrak locomotives are not so equipped, they hold their top speed to 79 mph.

This is certainly not to say that many trains don't go faster than 79 mph. Along the Northeast Corridor between

New York City and Washington, D.C., Amtrak's Metroliners travel at speeds of up to 125 mph. In parts of Missouri, Pennsylvania, and a few other areas, passenger
trains travel at 90 mph and higher. Apart from the speed
limits, how fast the train goes depends on several factors,
including track conditions, the weight of the train (meaning the number of cars), the type and number of locomotives pulling the train, and, as mentioned, whether or not
that automatic signaling device has been installed in the
engine cab.

Communication

In the old days, members of the train crew communicated
among themselves with visual signals, waving their hands,
or, at night, lanterns. Today it's all done by handheld radios,
linking the conductors with the crew in the head end. The
most powerful radio on the train is in the locomotive cab,
and with it the engineer can communicate with the dispatcher, who may be hundreds of miles away. The engineer
can also receive radio messages from crews of other trains,
from Amtrak personnel at stations passed, and from other
official sources using the railroad frequency.

When the need to communicate comes up among
members of the service crew, they will either use the inter-
com (a mini onboard telephone) or the train's public address system.

Trackside Signs

During your railroad journey you'll see a lot of signs beside
the track, obviously meant to communicate information to
the crew in the head end. Once explained, the meanings are
pretty obvious. I found that knowing what those signs
mean added to the interest and enjoyment of my train trips.

While all railroads use signs to convey the same information to the engineer, the appearance of those signs differs somewhat from one railroad to another (just another reason why engineers have to qualify on each route). Here is a rundown on the most common railroad signs.

Mileposts

Mileposts are the most common of all the railroad signs and in many ways are the most important. Look for three-foot-high white posts with black numerals located every mile along each route. They're positioned right next to the track, so you'll need to get close up to the window to see them. Sometimes they're not posts at all but signs on

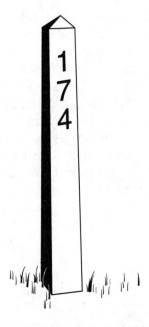

Mileposts like this—sometimes they are small signs mounted on metal poles—are placed one mile apart beside the track. The numbers indicate the distance either to or from a major rail center and are used to pinpoint the train's location as it travels along its route. You can use mileposts to compute the train's exact speed (see page 97).

metal poles next to the track. Some are even attached to the electric poles running parallel to the tracks. In any event, you'll quickly be able to identify them because they're numbered in sequence, indicating the number of miles from that spot to a major terminus. Depending on which direction you're traveling, the numbers will get larger or smaller, one mile at a time.

Mileposts are important because they enable the railroad to pinpoint a location along a route. For example, before starting out on the day's run, the engineer will be given train orders in which it may be noted that he or she can expect to find work crews on the track between mileposts 745 and 749. It works the other way, too. If the engineer notices any kind of problem en route, he or she can radio the dispatcher and refer to a specific milepost.

You can make use of the mileposts to figure out how fast the train is moving. There's a simple formula for that in Chapter 6, "Life on Board." In some areas, curves in the track may have been straightened to permit higher speeds, and when that happens, the old mileposts might not be exactly one mile apart. So if you want to be really accurate, check the speed several times over any given stretch of track.

Whistle Posts

You'll notice these right away, because there are a lot of them—a black "W" on a small white sign right at trackside. They tell the engineer to blow the whistle because a grade crossing is ahead—that is, a place where automobile traffic crosses over the tracks. These signs are placed at varying distances from the grade crossing so that trains traveling at the maximum speed limit for that stretch of track will give adequate advance warning of its approach. Slower trains will either wait a few seconds after they pass the whistle post before sounding the whistle or whistle several times.

In some parts of the country, mostly in the South, whistle posts are white paddle-shaped signs with two black bars, a black circle, and another black bar—a graphic depiction of the long-long-short-long whistle pattern traditionally used at grade crossings.

Flags

These come in four colors: red, yellow, green, and blue. Originally, flags were used as warning signals. Three of the colors mean exactly what you would think: red for "stop," yellow for "slow," and green for "resume normal speed." They're used to alert the engineer to something ahead on or near the track. Usually a work crew is involved, perhaps clearing a rock slide from the track or simply doing normal track maintenance. Whatever the reason, these flags are a visual warning to the engineer. Blue flags are placed at the front and rear of a single car, several cars, or an entire train, and they alert all concerned that people are working around or under the cars. Although still called flags by railroad people, these signs are usually colored squares of metal attached to a little metal pole. (They still look like flags.) At night, electric lanterns in the appropriate color are used. It's easy to miss these flags. They're pretty small, perhaps eight inches square. Usually you'll see them stuck into the ballast rock alongside the track just a foot or so from the rail.

Speed Limit Signs

These are quite common, and as the name implies, they tell the engineer how fast the train is allowed to travel. Most of the time two numbers are posted. The top number is the speed limit for passenger trains; the bottom number applies to freight trains. As an exact equivalent, on many of our highways two speed limits are posted—one for passenger cars and another for trucks. The principal difference is that signs along a highway tell drivers what the speed limit is between that exact spot and the next sign, while most speed limit signs on a railroad tell the engineer how fast the train can be traveling two miles ahead. The

This speed limit sign (often called a *speed board* by railroad crews) indicates that the speed limit for passenger trains is seventy miles per hour, while freight trains may not exceed fifty miles per hour.

reason for that difference, of course, is that it can take that distance for the engineer to reduce speed gradually from, say, seventy to forty miles per hour.

If the number shown on the sign means the engineer can increase the speed of the train, he or she may do so as soon as the entire train passes the sign. Train crews often refer to these signs as *speed boards.* Just to confuse you, on some railroads there are two kinds of speed limit signs: Black numbers on yellow signs mounted diagonally on the pole indicate the speed limit two miles ahead; black numerals on white signs mounted level indicate the speed limit at that spot.

Exceeding the posted speed limit is a big no-no in railroading. Inspectors from the Federal Railway Administration are responsible for enforcing speed limits and other safety rules and do so by checking train speeds with radar guns. One or two speeding offenses by an engineer, even a few miles an hour over the limit, and he or she will be looking for a new career.

Crossing Ahead

A simple black X on a white sign tells the engineer that the tracks will be crossing another set of tracks up ahead. It does not mean that a road crosses the tracks.

Derail Signs

You'll often see these little derail signs, usually black letters on yellow or orange signs, along sidings as your train enters or leaves rail yards or stations. Near these signs, a metal device, often painted bright yellow or orange, is attached to a rail. It's designed to deliberately derail a freight car that might otherwise roll out onto the main line and become an obvious safety hazard.

Other Signage

Unfortunately, there is some variation in signage from one railroad to another. For instance, in some parts of the east you may see signs shaped like small yellow pyramids. These simply tell the head-end crew that there's a break in the rail ahead, meaning a switch or another track crossing. In Canada, you'll see a lot of small black signs with two white dots. These tell the engineer to pay attention—something is just ahead of which he or she should be aware. Most of the other signs you'll occasionally see along rail routes let the head-end crew know when the method used by dispatchers to control their progress has changed. For instance, "Begin CTC" tells the engineer that the train is now under Centralized Traffic Control; "Begin ABS" means an Automatic Block Signal system is in use from that point on.

Signals

You can see a lot of these during any train ride, but you have to be looking for them, because they're either placed right alongside or directly over the tracks. There are a number of different kinds, but whatever the shape, almost all use green, yellow, and red lights to communicate with the engineer. These signals are used to keep trains running on the same track properly spaced and, in almost all cases, now operate automatically.

The track over which your train is running is divided into sections, called *blocks*. A signal located at the beginning of each block controls the rail traffic moving through it. Sometimes the distance between signals can be a number of miles, while other times it will be just a matter of a few hundred yards. How frequently the signals appear depends on how far ahead the engineer can see, where another track joins the main line, the location of a switch, and other factors. Generally, signals are set to keep a following train at least two blocks apart from the train up ahead.

For many years, signal lights were operated by electricity carried through wires strung on utility poles running alongside the track. You can still see those poles passing by outside the train window. More recently, especially since welded rail has become more commonly used, the electric impulses used to operate the signals are actually carried to them through the rails themselves.

In most cases it's pretty obvious, but here's what those signals mean:

Green: Proceed at normal speed (also called a *clear* signal).
Yellow: Approach (meaning pass) and be prepared to stop at the next signal.
Red: Stop and proceed at slow speed (usually 15 mph).
Absolute red: Stop and do not proceed.

There are a number of ways to distinguish an absolute red from a normal red signal—for instance, a second red light will be illuminated as well.

Whistle Signals

If you're sitting close enough to the engine to hear the whistle, you'll soon notice that several different whistle patterns are used. Here's what they mean:

Long, long, short, long: This signal is used when approaching a grade crossing and is used when the locomotive passes a whistle post. (I've asked several engineers about the origin of this particular pattern, but none have known. The consensus seems to be that it's railroad tradition.)

Short, short: The train is about to move forward.

Short, short, short: The train is about to back up.

Long: This means the engineer is going to set (meaning test) the brakes. This is done when the train is stopped and members of the train crew are outside to visually inspect the brakes once applied.

A series of long blasts: This indicates a serious emergency of some kind. Chances are extremely rare that you'll ever hear this signal.

By the way, "whistle"—both as a verb and as a noun— is still used, even though the term comes from the days of steam locomotives. Technically, it's an air horn.

Hot Box Detectors

These remarkable electronic gadgets are an important safety feature for our modern railroads. They're located in metal cases on either side of the track and are equipped with sensors that look for overheated journal bearings, referred to as hot boxes by railroad people. Potentially, a hot box is big trouble. A bad bearing means steel in contact with steel at high speed. The axle and wheel become red hot and, left undetected, can fracture and cause an instant derailment. (Refer to "Railroad Terms and Slang" for more information about hot boxes and journal bearings.)

As soon as the train passes over one of these detectors, an automated message is broadcast on the train's radio frequency, then is picked up by the crew in the locomotive and by the conductors. Here's a transmission from one of these detectors, which I recorded on a recent trip:

> *SP detector, Pasco. Temperature, eighty-seven. Speed, sixty-four. Track one. Number of axles, fifty-two. No defects. Repeat: No defects. Detector out.*

As you can see, the engineer can glean a lot of important information from those few words.

SP detector: The detector belongs to Southern Pacific.

Pasco: We're in or near Pasco, Washington.

Temperature, eighty-seven: It's a warm day out there . . . but not hot enough to worry about heat kinks in the rails.

Speed, sixty-four: We're traveling within the 65-mph speed limit.

Track one: Where there's double track, this eliminates any confusion in case there's another train passing us on track two at the same time.

Number of axles, fifty-two: Yes, it's talking about us; and furthermore we're now sure the detector is functioning properly.

No defects: Good! Our train has no hot boxes and nothing is dragging on the track.

Repeat: No defects: Just making sure we got the critical information.

Detector out: So we know the message is over.

Sometimes the detector will conclude its message by saying "Over," requiring the engineer to verbally acknowledge. That's so the dispatcher listening will know where we are and that we received the detector's message. Often there's another check: The conductor will radio the engineer following a detector's report just to be sure the message was heard in the head end. The following exchange is typical:

"Good report, Number 7": This is the conductor telling the engineer that the detector reported no defects. The reference to the train number is to be certain the engineer knows the message is directed at him or her.

"Highball, 7": The engineer acknowledges the conductor's message and reports that the train is proceeding at track speed, the maximum permissible.

Although it's rare that a detector discovers a hot box on a passenger train, the electronic voice will leave little doubt about what to do: *"You have a defect. Stop your train! Stop your train!"*

If this does occur, there is almost always a *set out track*—you and I would call it a siding—near most hot box detectors where the train can be diverted while the crew assesses the problem. The car with the hot box is usually cut out and left on the siding while the rest of the train continues on its way. This is a minor inconvenience in the case of freight trains, but it clearly is a much bigger problem for a passenger car full of people. In that case, Amtrak people really earn their pay. The onboard crew tries to accommodate the displaced people throughout the rest of the train. If that's not possible (and frequently it isn't), they'll arrange for alternate transportation and, if necessary, pick up the cost of meals and overnight lodging, too. But, let me emphasize that this is an extremely rare occurrence with passenger equipment, especially on a long-distance train, which is carefully inspected after each trip and periodically along the way.

High-Tech Equipment

Every so often, while passing through a rail yard, you may notice a pair of posts on each side of a track with what appear to be floodlights mounted on each. This is a good example of modern technology being used in the railroad industry. These lights are actually a scanner—pretty much like the one you're familiar with in the checkout line at the supermarket. As a freight train passes slowly between these posts, the scanner is used to identify, count, and sort specific freight cars from coded numbers on their sides.

Delays—Why They Happen

Unlike most of the railroads in Europe, passenger trains in North America are required to operate within a system primarily designed to handle freight trains. When an Amtrak train is running on track owned by another railroad, that company and not Amtrak becomes responsible for the train's progress. Amtrak has incentive contracts with many of these host railroads, paying bonuses to the railroad for keeping Amtrak trains on time and withholding those payments for a poor record. In spite of these arrangements, Amtrak trains can be delayed when dispatchers for these host railroads give priority to their own freight trains. Unfortunately, that still happens and with some railroads more than others.

The long-distance trains are more likely to experience delays than those on the shorter runs, and that's simply because there's more time for something to interfere with the train's progress. A Metroliner running between New York City and Washington, D.C., is on 225 miles of track owned and controlled by Amtrak. It's far more likely to run on time than the *California Zephyr,* which travels the 2,400 miles between Chicago and Oakland over tracks controlled by three different railroads—Burlington Northern Santa Fe, Southern Pacific, and Union Pacific.

Delays are a fact of life in rail travel, but it will ease the aggravation if you know something about why they occur.

Amtrak makes a distinction between in-bound delays (late arrival) and out-bound delays (late departure), but they're closely related. In fact, the most common cause of an out-bound delay is the late arrival of an in-bound train. Amtrak will often hold up a departure if there are passengers on the arriving train who are expecting to make that connection. (You can see how this puts Amtrak in a no-win situation: Passengers on the *California Zephyr* will be unhappy if their departure from Chicago is delayed waiting for the *Lake Shore Limited* to arrive; but if Amtrak doesn't hold the *Zephyr,* forty or fifty passengers on the *Lake Shore* will miss their connection and then they will be unhappy.)

In-bound delays can cause other problems for Amtrak, too. Arriving trains must be "turned" for the return trip, and if they're significantly late, Amtrak crews have less time than they need for that process, and there's a lot to do. The train has to be cleaned, of course, and a mind-boggling variety of supplies have to be checked and restocked: food, fresh linen, and clean tableware for the dining car; ice, snacks, and drinks for the lounge car; fresh pillows for the coaches; clean sheets, pillowcases, and towels for the sleepers. Most of those beds have to be made up, too. There's also a lot going on outside the train, because every arriving train must be inspected before it can go out again. Of course this will no doubt be a day when the U.S. Postal Service shows up with an extra heavy volume of mail, which means at the last minute another mail car will have to be brought in and added to the consist.

Once en route, trains can be delayed for any number of reasons. An engine can break down with the closest replacement unit hours away. Perhaps there's an electrical problem in the dining car, and an Amtrak electrician has to come aboard somewhere along the way to fix it. If it's unusually hot outside, perhaps there are heat kinks in the rail caused by the steel expanding. Under those conditions, the train could be poking along under a slow order. Maybe it's nothing more than unusually heavy freight traffic that slows the train's progress. Causes for delays seem to come in an endless variety. Here are just a few I've personally experienced over the past few years while gathering material for this book:

- Westbound *California Zephyr* is delayed three hours when a freight ahead of us breaks a wheel and the track has to be repaired.
- Northbound *Silver Meteor* is delayed thirty minutes in Savannah, Georgia, while paramedics come aboard to examine a sick passenger. (He's finally removed from the train and driven off in an ambulance.)
- Southbound *Silver Meteor*'s departure from Washington is delayed for four hours when a flash flood washes out a section of track south of the city.
- Eastbound *Empire Builder* is delayed a total of two hours and forty minutes after waiting on sidings to allow four other trains to pass (three freights and the westbound *Builder*).
- Northbound *Montrealer* is delayed forty-five minutes while the train crew removes an old refrigerator and a mattress placed on the track by vandals. (This train has since been replaced by the *Vermonter*.)
- Westbound *Broadway Limited* is delayed ninety minutes just outside Philadelphia when the train loses head-end power from the locomotive. (This train has since been eliminated, alas!)

- Northbound *Coast Starlight* is delayed twenty minutes in Oakland, where the tracks run down the middle of a main street fronting Jack London Square. Someone has parked a car on the tracks, locked it, and gone off shopping. (Yes, of course it's true. No one could make up something like that!)

It's interesting to note that of those seven delays, only one—the equipment failure near Philadelphia—could be laid at Amtrak's door. The others were caused by weather, equipment failure on another railroad, or quirky human beings. The delays experienced by the *Empire Builder* occurred because the host railroad's dispatcher gave priority to the other trains.

By the way, if the train is delayed for more than just a few minutes, the conductor should provide an explanation over the P.A. system. Unfortunately, not all of them do, which is a pet peeve of all regular rail travelers. Don't bother asking one of the service crew (your car attendant or one of the servers in the dining car)—they're usually too busy with their duties and almost certainly won't know why the train has stopped.

Hard-core railfans traveling with their scanners (see Chapter 6, "Life on Board") can usually find out why the train has stopped by eavesdropping while the engineer and the conductor discuss the delay on their radios. Passengers without such electronic gizmos can still make educated guesses. Take a look out each side of the train. If there's another track out there, odds are the train is on a siding waiting for a train coming from the other direction; if on a single track, your train probably has a red signal—most likely because it has caught up to a slower train ahead of it.

Even when a train is late, it can still be considered on time. Most airlines record a flight as having left on time if the plane pushes away from the gate within fifteen minutes of its scheduled departure time. In much the same way, Amtrak determines if a train has arrived on time by establishing what are called on-time tolerances. They vary somewhat according to the length of the trip, but if a train's arrival falls within this grace period, it's still considered to be on time. Overall, about 80 percent of Amtrak trains arrive at their destinations within on-time tolerances.

Amtrak On-Time Tolerances

Length of Trip	Grace Period
0–250 miles	10 minutes
251–350 miles	15 minutes
351–450 miles	20 minutes
451–500 miles	25 minutes
551+ miles	30 minutes

Making Up Time

Contrary to popular belief, it isn't possible to make up lost time by increasing the speed of the train, since the schedule assumes the train will be running right at the posted speeds. Exceeding those speeds is just not done. For one thing, it's too easy to get caught, and the penalties are severe.

Once a train falls behind schedule, there are only two ways to make up the time. The first is by hurrying up the loading and unloading of passengers and baggage at station stops along the way; the second is through padding in the schedule itself.

Padding is extra time built into the schedule. It's like having a little emergency stash in a savings account to cover unexpected expenses. So, if a train is delayed for twenty minutes because of track work somewhere along the route, a little padding here and there helps get it back on schedule.

For example, take a look at this excerpt from a recent Amtrak timetable:

Train 3	Mile	Southwest Chief	Train 4
10:22P	317	Marceline, MO	9:19A
12:35A	421	Kansas City, MO	7:38A

Reading down, you see that Train 3, the westbound *Southwest Chief* en route from Chicago to Los Angeles, is scheduled to leave Marceline, Missouri, at 10:22 P.M. and arrive in Kansas City at 12:35 A.M. That's two hours and thirteen minutes to cover a distance of 104 miles. Now, reading up, look at the schedule for Train 4, the eastbound *Southwest Chief.* According to the same timetable, it requires only one hour and thirty-one minutes to travel the exact same distance. That extra forty-two minutes is padding to cover any delays that Train 3 might have encountered between Chicago and Kansas City.

Backing into the Station

Most of the time, trains simply pass through a station—pulling in on a specific track, stopping to load and unload passengers, then continuing on their run. At several of the major stops, however, trains will back into the stations as a matter of normal procedure. This is done for two reasons.

First, to facilitate the train's departure, especially when the station is also a major junction. The train approaches from one direction, backs into the station, and departs in another direction. Look at a capital letter Y and imagine the station at the bottom. The train backs down the left branch to the station, then departs out the right branch. In fact, the arrangement of tracks that permits this maneuver is called—Surprise!—a *wye.*

Second, there may be environmental and safety reasons for backing into a station. This is the case at Chicago's Union Station, for example, where the platforms are on a lower level under the streets. Trains back in to keep the diesel-powered locomotives and their fumes as far from the terminal as possible. There's another consideration: In an enclosed area, those big locomotives are loud!

Weather Problems

Trains are usually bothered less by weather conditions than are cars or planes, but rain, snow, or cold can and do cause problems for railroads. Heavy rain can wash out track or, more precisely, the roadbed on which the rails and cross ties have been laid. Drifting snow in mountain passes can slow or even stop a train. Steel rails contract and occasionally break in cold weather. Prolonged periods of subzero temperatures can freeze switches. Fog sometimes causes delays because it can severely reduce visibility for the head-end crew.

Whatever the cause, and whether the train carries passenger or freight, railroads will go to great extremes to keep rolling or, failing that, to resume service as quickly as possible. Washed-out track can usually be repaired in relatively short time, but not always. The summer of 1993, for instance, brought such severe and widespread flooding throughout the Midwest that service on Amtrak's western trains was disrupted for several weeks. In winter, special locomotives equipped with snowplows or snow-blowers are constantly on alert for use in the mountain passes.

There are also safety procedures that automatically go into effect. For instance, it's pretty much standard procedure for crews to reduce speeds once the temperature drops below zero degrees Fahrenheit for more than a few hours. Preventative measures are also taken. If you're traveling on a mountain route or in areas that are very cold in the winter, look for cylindrical propane tanks located next to switches. The propane is used to feed gas burners— very similar to the burners on the top of a gas stove—

which heat the switches and prevent them from freezing in bitter cold weather. In some areas, kerosene is used for the same purpose.

Delays or interruption in train service can also be caused by other natural events. Earthquakes can twist rails out of alignment, and in mountainous areas, rock or snowslides can obstruct tracks. Look for *slide fences* in many mountain passes. These are rather flimsy looking wire fences located beside the tracks in slide-prone areas. Their function is not to be a barrier for the rocks. When one or more of the wires is broken by a rock slide, a signal is automatically sent to the operating railroad. Trains are warned by radio about a possible obstruction at that location, and a crew is dispatched to clear the track.

Courtesy

The headlights of a locomotive, which are very bright as you might expect, can be dimmed in much the same way you dim the lights on your family car. Depending on circumstances, most engineers will dim their headlights when meeting or overtaking another train. Many will even dim their lights if they're directed into the eyes of motorists on a highway running parallel to the track.

Train crews help each other out and will look carefully at a passing train for any sign of a problem—smoke coming from a truck under one of the cars or a shifting load on one of the flatcars. If a freight train is waiting on a siding as your train goes by, the engineer of the freight will usually radio your train's crew to say something like, "Good run-by, Amtrak." The foreman of a track repair crew will do the same.

Split Trains

Some trains separate into two or more trains partway through their route. For instance, the *Lake Shore Limited* leaves Chicago and heads east as one train. In Albany, New York, several cars are cut out of the original consist, coupled to a new engine, and taken off through the Berkshire Mountains to Boston. The original train turns south and heads down the Hudson River to New York City. The entire process is reversed when the train is westbound, starting as two separate trains in Boston and New York City, joining in Albany, and ultimately arriving in Chicago as two trains in one.

Passenger Manifest

A few hours before a train's departure time, Amtrak's computer prints out a list of all passengers booked on that trip. The printout provides the conductor and car attendants with the names of all passengers, the station where each will be boarding, their destination, and, in the case of sleeping-car passengers, their car and room number. The manifest will also note if a particular passenger is elderly, disabled, or might need special service.

Clean Windows . . . Please!

Before each trip, most long-distance trains are taken through an automatic wash, a super-sized version of the one around the corner where you take the family car. Some long-distance trains get their windows washed a second time at service stops along the way—the *Southwest Chief* gets this treatment in Albuquerque, the *California Zephyr* in Denver.

Keeping the windows clean is not easy, however. A brief rain squall followed by a dusty stretch of track can undo all those good efforts pretty quickly. So can passing through a lot of tunnels. You'll see a lot of blackened freight locomotives operating on the *California Zephyr*'s route west of Denver. That's the result of the heat and smoke from the diesel motors in all those mountain tunnels. Finally, if a train is late arriving at its destination, there just may not be time to wash the consist before it gets serviced and sent off on its return trip.

Whatever the problems, clean windows should be a priority on all passenger trains. Amtrak justifiably sells itself as the best way to see America, but who wants to see the country through dirty windows? In recent years, Amtrak has started paying much closer attention to what had long been a nagging problem.

Private Railcars

Occasionally you'll find that a private railcar has been added to the rear of your Amtrak train. Most have been lovingly restored and refurbished by wealthy individuals who use them as land-going yachts. Others belong to railroads and other corporations that use them as rolling conference rooms. Traveling in a private railcar falls into the everyone-should-do-it-once category, and it may not be as far-fetched as you might think. A few travel companies that own this kind of equipment charter it for special excursions to individuals, groups, and organizations. On at least several occasions, inventive companies have used private railcars as the venue for new business presentations to potential clients. The railroad expression for these cars is *private varnish,* a reference to the luxurious wood trim once commonly found in such equipment.

Amtrak charges $1.80 a mile for hauling these cars around the country, and there may be additional costs depending on how many times the private car has to be handled along the way. Furthermore, Amtrak will not haul a private railcar until it has been inspected and certified as meeting all of Amtrak's standards.

For information on private railcar travel, call 202-547-5696 or write to AAPRCO Charter Group, 106 North Carolina SE, Washington, D.C. 20003.

Railfans

Finally, a word about the folks who have turned their fascination for trains into a hobby—sometimes a consuming one. They call themselves *railfans* but are often referred to as *foamers* by railroad employees, meaning that they begin to foam at the mouth whenever they see a train. For some, the interest is broad and general; for others, it gets pretty narrow. There are people who collect old railroad timetables, for example, or dining car menus, tickets, posters, or other memorabilia.

During almost any train ride, you'll see photographer/railfans by the tracks taking your picture as you roll past. Others are train spotters and spend their free time checking off locomotive numbers in notebooks. The object is to have spotted every locomotive of a certain series or owned by a certain railroad.

As with any group of hobbyists, a few railfans allow their passion to get in the way of their good judgment. Some can be found wandering around in areas of rail yards that are restricted to railroad employees only. Some "collect" objects, which they acquire under dubious if not dishonest circumstances. A good example are the builders' plates attached to every railcar by the manufacturer. The sad fact is, very few passenger railcars still have the original plates in place. Most have been—let's use the right word—*stolen* by overenthusiastic collectors.

Largely because of these illegal or unauthorized activities of the very few, railfans occasionally run into open hostility from railroad people. More typically, though, they're treated with friendly, if maybe a bit weary, tolerance. After all, as one veteran Amtrak road foreman pointed out, it's the railfans who write all those impassioned letters to their congressperson supporting rail travel in general and Amtrak in particular. For that, they are justifiably appreciated.

CHAPTER 11

What About All Those Freight Trains?

At last count, there were 541 railroad companies in the United States, although the vast majority—a total of 500 in 1996—serves very specific and usually very small geographical areas. In fact, these local railroads only operate an average of just over fifty miles of track. At the other end of the spectrum, we have what are called the Class 1 railroads. There are only ten of them, but their trains run over more than 125,000 miles of track and employ more than 185,000 people. Class 1 railroads rang up some $31 billion in revenues for the freight they carried in 1995. Here's a list of those companies (you'll see their identifying logos on locomotives and freight cars everywhere as you ride around the country):

Burlington Northern Santa Fe (because the Burlington Northern Railroad and the Atchison, Topeka & Santa Fe merged in 1995, most of the locomotives and freight cars you see will still be displaying the logos of those two railroads)

Canadian National Railway (CN)

Canadian Pacific Railway (CPR) (also includes the Soo Line)

Consolidated Rail Corporation (Conrail)

CSX Transportation

Illinois Central
Kansas City Southern
Norfolk Southern
Southern Pacific (including the Denver & Rio Grande Western)
Union Pacific (including the Chicago and North Western)

It really takes a cross-country train trip before most of us realize how extensive the country's system of freight railroads really is. Freight trains haul every conceivable type of commodity, but coal is still number one, accounting for almost 22 percent of all freight revenues. From just one huge mine in Wyoming, a train pulling 110 cars loaded with coal to run Midwestern power plants travels east to the Chicago area every single day of the year. You'll also begin to appreciate the immense capacity of the grain-producing areas of this continent when you pass one train after another, each pulling a hundred or more hopper cars filled with wheat or corn. Then there are the trains hauling chemicals, frozen food, fresh vegetables, motor vehicles, petroleum, minerals, lumber, paper, scrap metal, and . . . well, you name it, and it moves by rail.

Freight Locomotives

Pulling all those freight cars are some 19,000 diesel-electric locomotives. That may sound like a lot, and of course it is, but back in 1929 more than 57,500 locomotives were in service. (All but 600 of those were steam engines.)

The appearance and design of freight locomotives varies tremendously—by weight, horsepower, number of axles, AC or DC traction motors, air-brake configuration, with or without dynamic brakes, and so forth. They're all fundamentally the same underneath: big, powerful diesel motors mounted on a rolling platform. (A more detailed description of how a locomotive operates can be found in Chapter 10, "How It All Works.")

Two factors determine the type of job for which any given locomotive is best suited: *horsepower* and *tractive force*. Horsepower is simply the common way of measuring how powerful the locomotive is—exactly the way we do with the family car. Another term for tractive force, certainly more familiar to the layman, would be traction. Whether a car or a locomotive, all that power can become almost useless if the wheels start slipping. That's what tractive force is all about, and that's why railroad locomotives are so heavy—to increase the tractive force and keep the wheels from slipping on the rails.

Depending on the gross weight of a train, additional *helper* locomotives may be added to provide more horsepower and more tractive force. The train's weight is determined by the number of cars in the consist and what's in those cars. Obviously, 100 cars loaded with coal will weigh much more than 100 cars loaded with wood chips, but the average capacity of a freight car is about eighty-nine tons.

Passenger trains weigh much less than freight trains but need to go faster, and that's why passenger locomotives can afford to sacrifice tractive force in favor of more horsepower. It's an oversimplification, but generally speaking freight locomotives are designed to pull very heavy weights at relatively slow speeds while passenger locomotives are designed to pull less weight but go faster. Until Amtrak's new Genesis series, now called the P40, most of the locomotives used to pull passenger trains were freight engines that had been modified to operate at higher speeds.

Freight Cars

More than 1.2 million freight cars of all types travel back and forth across the country. Almost exactly half of them are owned by the Class 1 railroads, the rest by independent railroad car companies, the shippers themselves, and the small regional and local railroads.

As you might expect, railroad equipment can be expensive. The average price tag for all freight cars is now about $51,000, and some cars, designed for carrying specific kinds of equipment or machinery, can be four times that amount. Every year, the Class 1 railroads in the U.S. and the two major Canadian railroads buy about 60,000 new freight cars to either add to their fleets or replace worn-out equipment.

The average freight train is 66 cars long, and many will have well over 100 cars in the consist. In terms of the physics involved, there is almost no limit to how long a freight train might be given an adequate number of locomotives. There are a number of practical considerations, however. Probably the most obvious is how much of a train's capacity has been sold by the railroad's sales department. Very long freight trains, however, can block busy city intersections for very long times and generate serious public relations problems. Extra-long trains can even cause the railroad problems if they block important switches in the rail yard.

You'll see thousands of freight cars from the window of your train. Part of what's interesting about a train ride is knowing what all those cars are for and what's inside them. There is an almost infinite variety of sizes and designs, but it all starts to take shape if we break them down into a few simple categories.

Boxcars

This is what most of us mean when we say "freight car." It's an enclosed car with a roof and sliding doors in the sides. It's used to carry a whole variety of general merchandise, particularly items that must be protected from the weather. If your local hardware store orders 200 power lawn mowers from a manufacturer, chances are those mowers rode across the country in one of these railroad cars.

The boxcar is the most basic of all freight cars. This one happens to be insulated to help minimize the effects of either cold or heat on whatever it is carrying. Numbers indicating the capacity of the car are stenciled on its side. Fully loaded, this car will carry almost seventy tons of cargo. (Photo courtesy of Burlington Northern Santa Fe)

A lot of boxcars are specially equipped in one way or another. For example, many are used to carry fresh produce from California all over the country. These refrigerator cars have to be equipped to maintain a constant, cool temperature so the fruits and vegetables inside won't spoil in the summer. In the winter, when shippers have the opposite problem, fresh produce crosses the country in heater cars to keep it from freezing.

Gondola Cars

Take a common boxcar and cut it in half horizontally and—*voila!*—you have a gondola car, or "gonnie," as the train crews call them. Gondola cars have low sides and ends, a solid floor (meaning the contents can't be unloaded

Gondola cars loaded with coal make up this train's consist. It is hard to tell because the camera's telephoto lens has "squeezed" the length of the train, but just the part we can see in this picture is a half-mile long. In all, there are 110 "gonnies" being hauled by three AC Traction locomotives. (Photo courtesy of Burlington Northern Santa Fe)

through a trap door in the bottom), and no top. Depending on the weight of the material they were designed to carry, some gondola cars have higher sides than others. You'll see all sorts of things being hauled in these cars—scrap metal for recycling, iron and steel products, and almost anything else that's heavy and doesn't need protection from the weather.

Hopper Cars

These look a lot like gondola cars, except they all have high sides and many are covered. All hopper cars have one thing in common: The interior walls slope toward three or four trapdoors in the bottom of the car (clearly visible if you look for them) through which the contents are

Covered hopper cars are used to haul bulk products that need protection from the weather: wheat, for instance, or potash, which is used to make fertilizer, glass, enamels, and soaps. The material is loaded from the top and unloaded through three trapdoors in the bottom of the car. (Photo courtesy of Burlington Northern Santa Fe)

unloaded. These cars are used to carry such things as coal and grain in bulk.

Tanker Cars

You can identify these cars very easily, because they're basically long cylinders with a dome on top through which they are filled. Tanker cars are used for carrying liquids ranging all the way from milk to petroleum to some pretty dangerous materials—primarily chemicals. Many of these cars are pressurized to carry such things as carbon dioxide, which we think of as gas (providing the bubbles in soft drinks, for example), but which turns into a liquid when it's compressed.

Tanker cars are used to haul liquids of all kinds, from highly toxic chemicals to milk. Each of these cars will hold almost 21,000 gallons. (Photo courtesy of Burlington Northern Santa Fe)

Flatcars

As the name implies, these cars are really nothing more than rolling platforms with no sides or top. The basic flatcar traditionally has been used to carry things such as logs (to a sawmill), lumber (from a sawmill), and other commodities that can be stacked flat and don't need to be covered from the weather. Some flatcars have high reinforced panels at each end, designed to keep loads—lumber, for example—from shifting either forward or backward with the movement of the train. The military uses flatcars to move tanks, trucks, and other heavy vehicles; and you'll often see very large pieces of machinery being carried in this manner.

Intermodal Flatcars

These cars were first designed to carry truck trailers, which are hauled to the railroad yard by truck, unhooked,

Double-stacked, intermodal flatcars are the most cost-effective way to move goods across the country. Two shipping containers are stacked on each railcar; after the train reaches its destination, each container is placed on a flatbed truck and delivered to the consignee's door. (Photo courtesy of Burlington Northern Santa Fe)

and simply swung aboard this special flatcar. At its destination, the trailer is lifted off the flatcar, hooked to the cab portion of a semitrailer truck, and driven straight to its destination. Railroad people refer to this arrangement as TOFC (trailer on flatcar) or piggyback, and to the everlasting confusion of the general population, the trains themselves are called pig trains.

Double-Stack Cars

These are a fairly recent innovation—actually a modified flatcar that features a sunken bed, which permits two shipping containers to be stacked, one on top of the other, yet still remain under the normal height limit of about twenty feet. The benefits to these stack trains are obvious: Trains that could formerly haul 120 trailers in a piggyback configuration can now carry up to 240 containers without adding

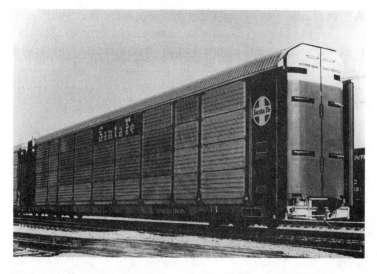

You will see a lot of these auto rack cars on any cross-country train ride. They are also called "autoveyors" and are used for transporting cars and small trucks, which are carried on two or three levels inside. (Photo courtesy of Burlington Northern Santa Fe)

to the length of the train. These cars are certainly easy to spot, and you'll see them almost exclusively on western routes. When these cars are loaded with two nine-foot-high containers, they're too tall to run on many eastern routes, which have low bridges and tunnels. Many of these flatcars are now articulated (permanently linked together) so that each set of wheels actually serves two flatcars. The net effect of this ingenious arrangement is to reduce the number of wheels touching the track by 50 percent, meaning there is a corresponding reduction in drag. That, in turn, translates into a significant savings in fuel costs.

Auto Rack Cars

You soon recognize auto rack cars. First of all, they're high—fully sixteen feet. Automobiles and small trucks are driven inside and tied down into position on one of the two or three levels. The sides of these railcars are very distinctive, too. They're made from panels of lightweight aluminum, which are designed to protect the cars and trucks inside from being damaged by material swirling up from the roadbed or—more common, I'm sorry to say—from stones thrown by youngsters from trackside.

Specialty Cars

If you want to ship some strange kind of cargo by rail, there will either be a specially built car that can accommodate it, or if you're going to ship a lot of these things, someone will build a car just for you. For instance, Boeing has some special high-wide cars to transport airplane fuselages. There are even special rails inside these cars to make loading and unloading easier.

Etcetera, Etcetera

You'll see many different subtypes of railcars during your rail travels, but most are variations of these basic types, modified in some way to meet a specific need. It almost doesn't matter what it is—a head of lettuce or the Army's latest tank—it's probably transported by train in or on a railcar that's uniquely suited to that purpose.

It should be noted that Canada's two largest freight railroads account for some very impressive numbers, too. Between them, CN Rail and CP Rail System (originally called Canadian National and Canadian Pacific respectively) operate over 36,000 miles of road with 3,568 locomotives and more than 112,000 freight cars. The combined revenue for the two companies is about $5.8 billion annually.

Finally, I'm sure my friends with the various railroads who helped provide information for this and other sections of the book would like you to know that America's Class 1 railroads pay out somewhere between four and five billion dollars in taxes every year.

CHAPTER 12

Safety—Priority Number One

If you spend any time around railroad people, you'll soon become aware that safety is constantly on everyone's mind. And with good reason. With massive weights moving at high speeds, railroading is an inherently dangerous business. The consequences of poor safety practices can mean wrecks, which are hugely expensive—millions of dollars in damage to equipment and freight, not to mention additional millions when people are hurt or killed. The fact is, safety gets top priority because safety pays.

Every railroad employee is responsible for safe operations and is empowered to override orders from superiors if necessary. For example, an engineer receiving confusing or garbled radio instructions from a dispatcher can refuse to move the train until satisfied that he or she clearly understands what needs to be done.

Maintenance

Regular maintenance is just as important to a railroad as it is to an airline. Amtrak has several maintenance yards around the country, usually located in or near major terminals. The

Sunnyside Yard in New York City, formerly the principal repair and maintenance facility for the Pennsylvania Railroad, is one of Amtrak's busiest, servicing some seventy trains and as many as 250 cars every day. Other facilities are located at Wilmington and Bear, Delaware, at Beach Grove, Indiana, and in Chicago, New Orleans, and Los Angeles. Every locomotive is inspected every day to make sure it's functioning properly; as with airplanes, locomotives are pulled out of service for preventive maintenance at regular intervals. The cars themselves go through similar checks and overhauls, although not as often as the locomotives.

Safety Procedures

Whether running a railroad or an airline or a steel mill, the key to safety lies in establishing and rigidly sticking to prescribed systems and procedures. For every function or task in railroad operations, there is one right way to perform it. Railroad workers, regardless of their job, know that to deviate from proper procedures is to court disaster.

Speed limits Individual railroads set the speed limits that apply to their tracks. How fast a train is permitted to go is determined by the "level of sophistication in the track," meaning the quality of the roadbed and the "super elevation" (that's what we would call the banking or tilting of the track, which counteracts centrifugal force and permits higher speeds around corners). Once set by the railroads, speed limits are actually enforced by Federal Railroad Administration inspectors who monitor randomly selected areas of track with radar guns to make sure limits are observed. There are circumstances when a train might exceed the maximum authorized speed (going downhill, for example), but a horn will sound in the locomotive cab, and if the engineer doesn't use the brakes, they are automatically applied. In railroad lingo, that's called a *penalty application.*

Time off   Every member of the operating crew—the engineer, assistant engineer, and conductors—has a limit to the number of on-duty hours he or she is permitted to work. These crew members are not allowed to work for more than twelve hours without a break of at least eight hours. That rule is strictly enforced. Once that limit is reached, engineers or conductors "go dead" and cannot continue to operate their train. That's true even if bad weather or mechanical problems have delayed the train so much that their time runs out before they reach a station. They must stop the train wherever they are and wait for a new operating crew to be put aboard. Amtrak will have been alerted to the problem in advance by radio and will arrange for a fresh crew to meet the train somewhere en route.

Drugs and alcohol   Railroads have always had strict rules against the use of alcohol or drugs, but they were always self-policed. That all changed a number of years ago when an accident occurred in Chase, Maryland. A Conrail engineer, Ricky Gates, ran his locomotive onto the main line and into an Amtrak train, killing a number of people. Gates tested positive for marijuana, and as a direct result, the federal government pressed for a universal policy of random drug testing. Those tests are now administered by the railroads to their conductors, engineers, assistant engineers, and dispatchers.

An additional and somewhat ironic benefit came from the accident that railroad people refer to now simply as "Chase, Maryland." The railroad unions and the various companies realized they if they didn't work together closely and productively to find an acceptable and meaningful drug testing policy, the federal government would probably do it for them. From this improved relationship between the two traditional adversaries has come Operation Red Block, an anti–drug and alcohol program. It's run by the unions, supported by management, and considered effective by all concerned.

Another result of that accident is that every American railroad now meets specific federal guidelines for the certification of engineers. Prior to the accident, each company had its own standards and requirements for training, knowledge of rules, and physical exams. Today, however, minimum standards are constant throughout the industry and engineers are recertified every three years.

Here are a few examples of railroad safety procedures to illustrate their variety and depth:

- When preparing to move a locomotive, the engineer will (1) start the bell ringing to indicate the locomotive is about to move, and (2) blow the whistle to indicate direction of movement: two toots, forward; three toots, back.
- A road foreman must be present whenever a "civilian"—meaning you or me—rides in the cab of an Amtrak locomotive to minimize possible distractions for the engineer.
- Radio messages from dispatcher to engineer are acknowledged and carefully repeated to be certain that every detail of the message was understood.
- When a blue flag (or light) is placed at the end of a train to indicate that people are working under or around the train, the only person permitted to remove the flag is the one who put it there.
- When backing into a station, the train will come to a "safety stop" 50 to 100 feet from the bumper post, then continue backing slowly before coming to a final stop.
- The assistant engineer calls out passing signals to be certain they have been seen and noted by the engineer.
- A train may not depart without train orders, which provide the engineer with the latest information about track conditions and contain formal permission to depart.

Safety Equipment

Railroading is still very much a hands-on business, but more and more automation is being introduced, particularly in the area of safety devices. Again, it's impossible to list all of these gadgets, but a good sampling should give you the idea.

- As mentioned in Chapter 10, in every locomotive cab there's something called an *alerter*, which is designed to make sure the engineer is always in command of the train. If the engineer doesn't change the throttle position, touch the brakes, or blow the whistle (on some locomotives, a special button must be pushed) for a period of twenty to twenty-five seconds, a strobe light will begin to flash in the cab and a horn will sound. At that point, the engineer has just a few seconds to perform one of those tasks (to demonstrate "Yes, I'm still here and still in control"). If the engineer doesn't do this, the brakes will be applied automatically and the train will come to a complete stop.
- Electronic detectors are located beside the tracks that broadcast warnings to the train crew if they sense overheated journal bearings (called hot boxes) or any kind of dragging gear. For more information about these devices, see Chapter 10, "How It All Works."
- Every locomotive is equipped with an *event recorder* just like the "black box" carried in airplanes. It records the motion and speed of the train and the use of controls by the engineer throughout the trip. In the event of an accident, the information from this device will be used to help determine the cause.
- Where trains traveling through mountain passes run close to canyon walls, wire fences are installed along sections where rock slides could obstruct the tracks. When you spot one you'll realize immediately that these flimsy *slide fences* couldn't hold back any falling

rocks. On the contrary, they're intended to break, and when that happens a warning signal is triggered. The railroad's dispatcher is immediately alerted and will notify the engineer of any train that may be approaching the area.

- Supplementing direct voice communication between the locomotive engineer and the railroad's dispatcher is an entire sophisticated and complex system of signals to control the movement and location of every train. A key element in all these systems is that each signal is automatically activated by the train itself, not by an individual at a distant location who may not be certain of the exact location of the train.

Grade-Crossing Accidents

This is without doubt the single biggest safety problem facing America's railroads. On city streets, main highways, and dirt roads, cars cross over train tracks at thousands of locations from one end of the country to the other. Every one is the site of a potential tragedy. Motor vehicles of all kinds are hit by trains with a frequency that is astounding—about one every ninety minutes! The circumstances vary, but the outcome doesn't: The train always wins. You want a comparison? A train hitting a car is roughly comparable to a car running over a mailbox.

Every year, somewhere around 600 people are killed and 2,000 are seriously hurt in grade-crossing accidents. Most of these accidents occur during broad daylight, with good visibility, and with the warning signals working perfectly. Furthermore, most of the time the driver of the car involved is sober.

In about a third of all the car/train collisions occurring at night, the car drives smack into the side of a moving train! Speed is almost always the critical factor in these accidents, because the driver of the car is overdriving his headlights—that is, by the time his headlights reveal the train, he's unable to stop before reaching the crossing.

It's sad but true that an unknown percentage of these incidents are actually suicides or attempts at suicide. Even so, I think we would agree that those deaths and injuries are all equally unnecessary.

It's rare to find a railroad engineer who hasn't been involved in a grade-crossing accident. Some handle it philosophically, realizing that they can't feel responsible for the death of someone who drove around a gate and into their path. For others, that's easier said than done. Recognizing that, most railroads make professional counseling available to crews involved in fatal accidents. For a few engineers, however, the experience is enough to force them out of their chosen profession. (More on this very serious problem and how it affects head-end crews can be found in Chapter 7, "Who's in Charge Here?")

Several years ago, the nation's railroads joined other organizations to form Operation Lifesaver, a program of information and education aimed at reducing the number of these awful accidents. It has been working, although some of the credit goes to the railroads for installing warning lights and gates at more and more crossings.

Here are a few commonsense rules for drivers approaching train tracks:

- Always assume a train is coming, in the same way you would anticipate a car if you were crossing another road.
- Slow down, roll down the window, and listen. You can't hear the train if your car is closed in winter weather or the radio is blaring.
- Never *ever* ignore active warning signals or drive around lowered gates. (This isn't as obvious as it sounds. A driver may see a switch engine parked a hundred yards down the track to the left and assume that's what brought the gate down. Wrong. Another train is approaching at high speed from the right.)

- Where there's more than one track, watch out for a second train coming from the opposite direction behind the first one.
- Don't be tempted to race a train to the crossing, even if it looks like a safe bet. Because of their enormous size, trains appear to be traveling much slower than they really are. Ever watched a Boeing 747 on its final approach? It looks like it's floating lazily along when, in actuality, the plane is moving at 170 miles per hour.
- Don't ever stop your car on a track. If traffic is backed up, wait until there's room on the other side before you cross over. If your car happens to stall on the track, get everyone out immediately and call the police. They'll contact the railroad's dispatcher, who will alert the engineer of any approaching train by radio.

Amazingly, in addition to grade-crossing accidents, more than 500 people are struck and killed by trains every year while trespassing on railroad property. (Technically, that includes railroad track wherever it might be—multiple tracks in a busy rail yard or a single track passing through Midwest farmland.) Again, a few of these are probably suicides, but most often it's just a combination of curiosity and carelessness. No matter. Whether it's an auto/train collision or someone is hit while walking too near the track, they're all tough on the train crews.

Derailments

Technically, and as the term implies, a derailment occurs when the wheels of one or more cars come off the track. A number of things can cause derailments. If an overheated journal bearing (called a hot box, remember?) goes undetected long enough, the wheel and axle will get red hot and finally break. Sometimes very hot weather can cause *sun kinks,* which push the rails out of alignment. Sometimes an obstruction on the track causes the train to slip off the rails. Whatever the reason, derailments are a major headache for railroads. When they do occur, particularly if it happens at high speed, there can be a lot of damage to track and equipment. Railcars are very heavy, and it takes special know-how and equipment to get them back on the track. There could also be several hundred yards of track to repair. All of this could be happening many miles from the nearest available manpower or equipment.

The chances of a rail passenger ever experiencing a derailment are remote. In freight operations, however, derailments are not so uncommon. Because they interrupt the flow of freight, derailments can mean big-time loss of revenue to a railroad. It's essential, therefore, that operations get back to normal as quickly as possible. Some railroads have their own crews and equipment on standby for this purpose. Others use one of several companies that are on call around the clock and specialize in handling derailments.

Safety Rules for You

Some of these warnings may not have occurred to you, and others may seem obvious, but you would be amazed at some of the dumb things people do around trains.

- When crossing tracks, step over the rails, not on them. They're slippery, particularly if wet, so it's a very easy way to twist or break an ankle.
- Don't walk right next to the locomotive, especially if it's off the station platform. Every so often an automatic "blow down" clears the air brake reservoir with 140 pounds of pressure. Accumulated water, sometimes mixed with just a tad of fuel oil, can spray on anyone who happens to be standing too close at the time. All that pressure can also cause small ballast rocks to fly. Please note that a blow down is an automatic function

and is not controlled by the head-end crew. People standing close to the engine are startled when a blow down occurs, and sometimes when they see an engineer laughing mistakenly think it was done deliberately as a practical joke. Not so.

- Don't try to get to the other side of the train by crawling under it. (Yes, people really do.) The train could move unexpectedly or another train could be passing on the adjacent track. In either case, you're history. Don't walk around behind the train for the same reason.

- Once on board, don't leave your seat without shoes on, and for heaven's sake, don't let your kids run around without shoes. Amtrak makes an announcement about this, but in my opinion it isn't given enough emphasis. The principal danger is the moving, overlapping metal plates that passengers walk across when passing between cars. Get one of your tootsies caught in there, and the next thing you know the conductor will be calling ahead for an ambulance to meet the train at the next station.

- Even with their shoes on, kids running around loose, whether on board or on the station platform, cause real heartburn for Amtrak people. A lot can happen to an uncontrolled youngster, and none of it is good. If you're traveling with kids, keep them on a tight leash. (See Chapter 6, "Life on Board," for some ideas on how to keep them occupied.)

- If you find yourself in the upper berth in a sleeping car, hook up the restraining straps designed to keep you from falling out. After all, you're sleeping in an unfamiliar bed four feet off the ground on a moving train.

- Most people don't think so, but it really can be dangerous to open the hinged window in a vestibule door to look out of the train or to take pictures—particularly at high speeds. Dust and debris from the track often fly up into the vacuum created by the moving train, and there can be very little clearance between the train and objects it passes.

- As you should do on a plane or when spending the night in a hotel, be sure you know how to get out of the rail-car in a hurry if you should have to do so. A number of windows in every car serve as emergency exits. Each is clearly marked and will have a red handle on it. Pull on that handle to remove the rubber gasket holding the window in place, then push the glass out.

The bottom line for all this talk about safety: The rail-roads have their act together pretty well. All it takes for the rest of us is common sense.

CHAPTER 13

Taking the Train in Canada

Several years ago, a two-hour television documentary called *Last Train Across Canada* was carried on PBS throughout the United States. It's about an inquisitive older gentleman who travels clear across Canada by train. It's an absolutely delightful presentation, and for that very reason it has been rebroadcast periodically several times since. Most unfortunately, however, the program has given millions of viewers the mistaken impression that transcontinental train service in Canada no longer exists. Happily, that is not true. VIA Rail, Canada's equivalent to Amtrak, can still take you all the way from Halifax, Nova Scotia, in the east to Vancouver on the Pacific Coast in the west.

Although Canada is a huge country covering millions and millions of square miles, 90 percent of the country's population lives within 200 miles of its border with the United States. For that reason, Canada's passenger rail system is strung out more or less through the middle of this populated area—roughly 4,000 miles long and just 200 miles wide.

VIA Rail Canada, Inc. is the company responsible for operating Canada's system of nationwide passenger trains. In some ways, its job is a lot less complicated than Amtrak's. Because of the long, narrow area it serves and the much smaller population, VIA operates fewer trains. Amtrak lists more than 100 trains in its timetables, of which nearly twenty run overnight and offer sleeping-car service. VIA Rail, on the other hand, operates some thirty-three trains, most running along sections of the 725-mile corridor between Windsor and Quebec City, where the population density is located. Of those, just five are overnight trains with sleeping-car accommodations. Don't let those comparisons give you the idea that VIA trains don't have something special to offer, however. To the contrary, they will take you through some of the most varied and magnificent scenery anywhere in the world.

The Canadian Rail Epic

The story of Canada's transcontinental railway has grown to something of epic proportions in that country, and not

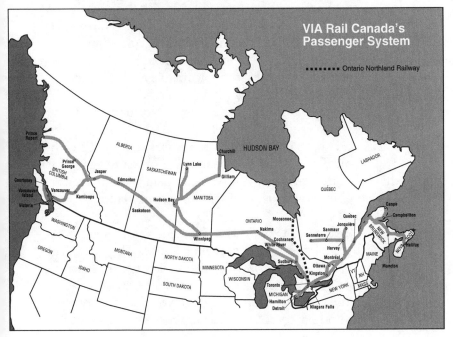

without good reason. There are many obvious similarities with the American railroad, with one very significant difference. In America, people settled the West and the railroad followed; in Canada, the train came first. The idea was to link settlements on the far-off Pacific Coast with the growing cities of the east and, by doing so, encourage people to settle in the vast areas in between. Actually, British Columbia forced the issue by refusing to join the Canadian Federation until, in 1872, its leaders had secured the promise that a transcontinental railroad would be built within ten years.

So indeed it was. In 1881, the Canadian Pacific Railway (CPR) began construction of the railroad, which was finished just four years later—a tribute to the honest and able people who financed, designed, and built it. It passed through some extremely difficult terrain, in particular an area known as the Canadian Shield north of the Great Lakes, where engineers had to blast their way through hundreds of miles of some of the oldest and hardest rock on earth. Then it was across the prairies, through the Rockies, into the dense forests of the Pacific Northwest, and finally to the sea. In terms of the difficulties involved, the Canadian Pacific overcame natural barriers and weather conditions at least as formidable as those encountered by the Americans twenty years earlier.

Two other railroads, the Great Northern and the Grand Trunk Pacific, came a few years later, and by the 1920s had completed another route farther to the north. The Grand Trunk struggled financially for many years; for this and other reasons, the two companies were eventually combined and became the Canadian National (CN) Railway.

As had been expected, cities and towns sprang up along both of the transcontinental routes. The Canadian Pacific, in particular, took a decidedly paternal approach to the communities it had literally created. In fact, after deciding that the CPR's western terminus would be the town of Coal Harbour, a company official, who evidently felt the name was uninspired and dreary, decreed that the community should instead be named for the British seaman who first explored the area, George Vancouver. And so it was. By 1924, the Canadian Pacific was claiming to have settled 55,000 families on thirty million acres of land between the Great Lakes and the Pacific. While it's possible to argue those numbers, it is considered a fact that the CPR created some 800 cities and towns in three provinces along its route. Farther to the north, the Canadian National laid claim to 132 towns, although for many the word "town" was probably an exaggeration.

For many years, the CPR and the CN competed vigorously for passengers as well as freight. The CPR took the additional step of building what are to this day some of the finest hotels in the world in major cities along its route. Each railroad ran its "name" trains, many of which reached into the United States for business by terminating in major American cities such as New York, Chicago, and Detroit. Canadian Pacific's best included the *Mountaineer*, which ran during warmer months from St. Paul, Minnesota, through the famous resort town of Banff in the Canadian Rockies, to Vancouver. Another CPR train out of St. Paul was the *Soo-Dominion* to Calgary. The Canadian National focused on Chicago, with trains from there to Toronto and Montreal, among other cities. Both railroads ran transcontinental trains within their own country.

Along Comes VIA Rail

Canadian railroads struggled against many of the same problems that beset American trains in the decades after World War II, but they held out a bit longer. Finally, in 1978, the Canadian Pacific and Canadian National merged their passenger operations. The result was VIA Rail Canada, a Crown Corporation wholly owned by the Canadian government. VIA Rail now provides passenger train service on a 9,000-mile system. It stretches from coast to coast and extends more than a thousand miles north to the town of Churchill on the shores of Hudson Bay. A number of VIA Rail's trains—the one to Churchill is a good example—provide the only link to the rest of the country for hundreds of isolated communities across the northern part of the country. Although operated at a loss, those trains are mandated by the Canadian government. As is the case with Amtrak, VIA Rail owns almost no track of its own, mostly operating instead over tracks belonging to the CN.

Also like Amtrak, VIA has not had an easy existence, waging a constant battle against those in the Canadian government who cannot or will not see the necessity if not the wisdom of a national rail transportation system. There have been periodic reductions in both personnel and service—the vogue term is downsizing—but still the system remains more or less intact. Furthermore, you'll find the equipment to be modern, the service good, and, all things considered, the food really first-rate.

What You Should Know About Canada's Trains

Basically, there isn't a great deal of difference between VIA Rail's operation and Amtrak's, so there's no reason you can't include a trip on a Canadian train in a rail itinerary. Again, I would suggest you try putting together your own schedule as much as possible, turning everything over to a knowledgeable travel agent to double-check what you've done and then handle the actual ticketing.

Most of the information contained elsewhere in this book will apply equally to either Amtrak or VIA Rail. A few things deserve mention, however, either because VIA does it a bit differently or because it bears repeating.

Reservations   Book as far in advance as possible, especially if your itinerary includes VIA's transcontinental train, the *Canadian,* during the summer months. For a few weeks every year, the *Hudson Bay* is often sold out, too. That train runs way up north to Churchill on the shores of Hudson Bay. Churchill becomes a tourist attraction toward the end of each September when polar bears come wandering into town. Whatever the train, if you choose to make reservations yourself, you can call VIA Rail toll free from anywhere in the U.S. The number is 800-561-3949. From Canada, call the VIA number listed in the local telephone book.

Timetables   Contact a knowledgeable travel agent, call VIA Rail's toll-free number, or go to VIA's interactive web site on the Internet (*www.viarail.ca*) for a free copy.

Discount fares   There are quite a few opportunities to cash in on special low fares. In fact, there are so many special rates, this is one area where a knowledgeable travel agent can be a big help. Generally speaking, discounts from 25 to 40 percent are available if you travel during off-peak times. That can mean certain periods during the year (winter months except over the Christmas holidays), on certain days of the week, or on travel to remote areas. There are other discounts, too:

- Seniors (aged sixty and over) get a 10 percent discount.
- Full-time students and youths aged sixteen and seventeen get a 40 percent discount in economy class and an additional 10 percent in VIA1 or sleeping cars. Note that students must present an International Student Identity Card (ISIC) in order to receive the discounts. An ID issued by a school or college will not suffice. To obtain an ISIC, call 800-GET-AN-ID (438-2643).
- Children aged two through fifteen get a 50 percent discount in economy class and 25 percent off in VIA1 or the sleepers.
- Infants under two years of age travel free as long as they don't occupy a seat.

Frequent Traveler Program   This is a good deal, especially if you're Canadian and have easy access to VIA trains. U.S. citizens may also join, and as you will see, even an occasional traveler can benefit. Members of VIA Preference, which is the name of the program, get one point for every dollar spent on train travel. In addition, new members will receive 1,000 bonus points upon joining. It doesn't take that long to accumulate enough points for a free ticket: for instance, 1,500 points will get you a free trip along the high-speed Windsor–Quebec City corridor. To join, call VIA's toll-free number (800-561-3949) or go to its web site (*www.viarail.ca*).

CANRAILPASS   This pass is only valid for travel on the VIA Rail system and is a good deal if you plan to do a fair amount of travel. Basically you get unlimited travel for a total of twelve days within a thirty-day period. You can also arrange for additional days on a pass by paying a supplementary charge. The pass is good for coach travel, but you can still upgrade to VIA1 class or into sleeping-car accommodations by paying a supplement. A limited number of seats on every train is set aside for people using these passes, which means it's possible you won't be able to travel on a particular train even though you have already bought your CANRAIL-PASS. Note that you must have a ticket in addition to the pass, so make your travel plans, get your pass, then buy your tickets.

North American Rail Pass   If your rail itinerary is extensive and includes travel in both the U.S. and Canada, by all means consider this recent innovation. It provides significant savings and unlimited coach travel in both countries during a thirty-day period. (See page 43 for more details.)

Is the train on time?   Maybe, but maybe not. If you're planning to board a VIA Rail train at a stop other than its point of origin, your best bet for correct information is to call the VIA phone number listed in the local telephone directory.

Parlez-vous français?   No? Well, if you don't speak French, that's a pity, but don't worry about it. VIA employees (indeed, most people you'll meet in the French-speaking parts of Canada) are quite fluent in English.

Baggage   As in Europe, you'll find free baggage carts in many stations. The Montreal and Toronto stations are two exceptions, but redcap service is available there. You may check heavy baggage if you wish, but be sure to find out in advance if that service is available at both ends of your trip.

Classes of service   It's pretty much the same as Amtrak, but VIA just gives different names to their various levels of service. Sleeper class refers to the private accommodations in sleeping cars on overnight trains, with two notable exceptions: To add some additional luster to what is already a first-rate experience, sleeper class on the *Canadian* (Toronto to Vancouver) is referred to as Silver & Blue class, and, as in Amtrak sleeping cars, all your dining car meals are included in the price of the ticket; you will have to pay for any alcoholic beverages. The equivalent class of service on the *Ocean* (Montreal to Halifax) is Easterly class. Within the Windsor to Quebec corridor, you can opt for VIA1, a first-class coach service provided on the shorter trips. If you board in Toronto, Montreal, or Ottawa, you'll get to wait for your train in a fancy lounge, and you'll be preboarded ahead of the regular coach passengers. The VIA1 cars are spiffy, and you get quite a good complimentary meal served to you at your seat. VIA1 includes specific seat assignments, so you can reserve either a window or aisle seat when you book. (I'm always disappointed if I can't sit by a window, so this one feature alone makes VIA1 a very attractive option for me.) There is, of course, an extra charge for this service. Coach class, as on Amtrak trains, means you'll be in a standard railcar with rows of two seats on each side of a center aisle.

Paying for things   Cash, personal check (for exact amount and with two proper IDs), and the usual credit cards will be accepted either in railroad stations or on board. You may also use your American money, but don't let that lull you into thinking you can get by without having to exchange your dollars for Canadian currency. Once off the train or away from the major hotels, Canadian dollars are the coin of the realm, and you'll need them.

What to wear?   Comfortable clothing is the standard for both VIA Rail and Amtrak. However, if you're traveling in Silver & Blue class on the *Canadian* or Easterly class on the *Ocean,* you will probably feel more at ease if you dress up a bit for meals in the dining car—especially for dinner. Because the service and the ambiance in the dining cars on those trains is very nice, a sport coat and tie is just more appropriate. Of course, you will not be tossed out into a passing snow bank if you show up in a polo shirt.

Tipping   Basically, it's just about the same as Amtrak—not necessary in coach unless your attendant provides some special service for you; $3 to $5 (Canadian) per night, per person in sleepers; and 12–15 percent of your tab in the dining car. Remember that if you're part of a package tour, tips are usually included in the cost of the tour.

Smoking policy   There's no smoking in any of the meal-service cars at any time. Nor is smoking permitted on any of the corridor trains running between Windsor and Quebec. On all other trains, smoking is allowed only in certain cars, both coaches and sleepers, so be sure to note your preference either way when making reservations.

Special needs   There are provisions on all VIA Rail trains to accommodate passengers in wheelchairs or who may have some other special needs. VIA Rail's only requirement, and it's a reasonable one, is that a passenger who will need special care during the journey (feeding, bathing, medication, and so forth) must travel with an escort. The good news is that VIA will permit the escort to travel at no charge—an enlightened policy. Whatever your special requirements, please give VIA at least forty-eight hours advance notice.

What about pets? VIA is more flexible than Amtrak, but only seeing-eye and other service dogs are permitted to actually ride with their owners. Other pets, from parakeets to St. Bernards, ride in the baggage car where you, not the VIA people, are responsible for looking after them. On longer trips, you are permitted to take Rover for a "stroll" when the train reaches servicing stops.

Complaints or compliments   If you run into problems and can't get things straightened out on the spot, by all means pursue the matter later with a letter. Be concise, be unemotional, be polite. Write to: Customer Relations, VIA Rail Canada, P.O. Box 8116, Station Centre-Ville, Montreal, Quebec H3C 3N3. Or you can communicate by e-mail: *vialog@viarail.ca*. And hey, if you get some really excellent, genuinely friendly service along the way, as I rather suspect you will, send an "Atta-boy" to that same address, specifying the date, train number, and employee by name.

Railfans   Yes, Canada has its proportionate share of folks who are fascinated by trains, too. As noted elsewhere, these people are referred to as foamers by professional railroaders in the U.S., implying that they foam at the mouth upon catching sight of a train. That word is known north of the U.S. border, but, with a tact and gentility rather typical of the Canadians, the preferred term in that country seems to be DRF, for Demented Rail Fan.

Onboard Crews

Crew responsibilities are divided in almost exactly the same manner on VIA Rail trains as on Amtrak's. The only difference of note is that the person in charge of the crew on VIA's long-distance trains, comparable to Amtrak's chief of onboard services, is called a service manager.

Another point of possible interest: Compared to Amtrak, you'll see far fewer female conductors on VIA trains. In the past few years the company has made an effort to hire more women in nontraditional jobs. Unfortunately, when mandatory cutbacks came, the most recent hires were the first to be let go and that meant most of the women.

Passenger Equipment

When it got started almost twenty years ago, a lack of quality rolling stock was one of VIA's biggest problems. Like Amtrak, VIA Rail went through a make-do period with the older traditional railcars it inherited from both Canadian Pacific and Canadian National. Also included in that collection of equipment were 200 classic stainless-steel cars originally built in the 1950s. Some sainted soul at VIA Rail decided these vintage cars were worth saving, and more than $200 million was spent to rebuild the fleet completely from the wheels up. A number of structural and mechanical improvements were made in the cars, but the most important of these did away with the old steam heating systems in each individual car.

Today the cars are all heated with head-end power, meaning with electricity supplied by a powerful generator in one of the diesel locomotives pulling the train. It's a far more reliable system, and if you're traveling across Canada in the winter, a reliable source of heat is a very good thing indeed! More about these wonderful cars a bit further on. As to the boxy old traditional cars, the last of them have been phased out within the past couple of years and replaced with refurbished stainless-steel cars.

The trains operating in the Windsor-to-Quebec corridor are designated as LRC (light, rapid, comfortable) equipment, and indeed they are. These matched trainsets are quite sophisticated. A computer system actually tilts both the locomotive and the cars as the train rounds curves, helping to neutralize the effects of centrifugal force on passengers and permitting higher average speeds. In fact, these LRC trains cover the 320 miles between Montreal and Toronto in a minute or two under four hours flat—the fastest time in the world for conventional trains over that much distance. Furthermore, with modified technology and some track improvements, VIA expects to further reduce traveling time between those two major cities to three hours, fifteen minutes, which will be averaging close to 100 miles per hour.

Locomotives

All of VIA Rail's locomotives are diesel-electrics. The formal designation for the engines that haul the LRC corridor trains is GPA27, but VIA people refer to them simply as LRC locomotives. They're fast and powerful, capable of running at 125 miles per hour, although they won't be able to do so until all of the track in that stretch has been upgraded. For their long-distance trains, VIA uses good old F40s—the same locomotive that has been the bulwark of Amtrak's fleet for years. They're tough, durable, and reliable. They had better be, because as you will hopefully see for yourself, all of those trains pass through long stretches of wilderness areas. Not a good place for breakdowns. (Don't worry, VIA uses twin locomotives on those trains . . . just in case.)

The Stainless-Steel Fleet

Even if you're not a true-blue train fan, the renovated and redecorated interiors of these cars—especially the sleepers—will make you think you've died and gone to heaven. They're neat, clean, are decorated in a very attractive color scheme, but still somehow haven't lost the feel of the 1950s when the cars were built. Both coaches and sleepers are now in use on five of VIA's trains: the *Canadian,* the *Skeena,* and the *Hudson Bay* in the west, and the *Ocean* and the *Chaleur* in the eastern part of the country. Here are some details on these wonderful cars.

Coaches

The layout is standard for most rail coaches—rows of seats, two on each side of a center aisle. There are seats for sixty-two passengers plus room for a wheelchair. Chairs recline and include leg rests. VIA provides both a pillow and a blanket for all coach passengers. There is a lavatory at each end of the car. There's space overhead for one or two small to medium-sized bags, so plan to check anything more than that. (Better yet, leave all that extra stuff at home.)

Skyline Cafes

These cars are for coach passengers and include a food service area where a variety of sandwiches, hot meals, and drinks are available. Food may be taken back to your seat, or you can eat in a large lounge area with tables and chairs. There is a panoramic dome with twenty-four seats on the upper level.

Sleepers

There are two lavatories and a real, honest-to-goodness shower in each of these stainless-steel sleeping cars. You can choose from three different types of accommodations, but all provide a call button, a reading light, and, in roomettes and bedrooms, controls for heat and air-conditioning. Sections are two facing seats, which convert into a lower berth at night; an upper berth folds down from the wall above the window. Heavy zippered curtains are pulled across each section for privacy. (Remember the sleeping car scenes in the Jack Lemmon/Tony Curtis/Marilyn Monroe film *Some Like It Hot*? That's what a section looks like with the curtains pulled at night.)

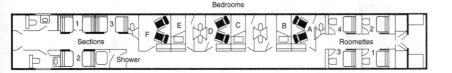

Floor plan of a sleeping car from VIA Rail's refurbished stainless-steel fleet

Roomettes are designed for one person and include a comfortable seat, a sink, a toilet, and a small closet where a few garments may be hung. At night, the bed folds down from the wall. It covers the toilet, however; so if you need to use the facilities during the night either get some instruction from the car attendant on how to raise the bed or be prepared to don a bathrobe and tip-toe to the lavatory at the end of the car. There are six bedrooms, each of which will accommodate two people and includes either a bench-type sofa or two chairs, a toilet, and a sink. The seating converts into two beds at night, a lower and an upper berth. Some sleepers and Park cars also have drawing rooms, which provide a sofa and two armchairs by day and three berths at night.

Insider Tip: Choosing the Best Room
- Bedroom F is about a foot larger than the others, and on a three-night trip you will appreciate the extra space. Try to get this particular room when you book.
- Bedrooms A, C, and E are configured so that your seats are facing toward the rear of the train. Some people don't care, but I much prefer to ride facing forward. (Just to complicate things, these sleepers come in two slightly different configurations so, if these variables matter to you, double check with the VIA Rail reservations agent when the booking is made.)
- The best arrangement for a family of four traveling together would be to reserve Sections 1 and 2. They're located directly across from each other, so you'll be able

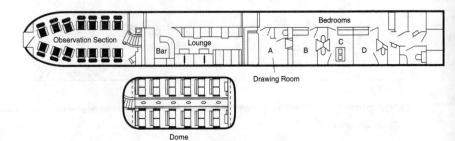

Floor plan of a Park car, which is always the last car on VIA Rail's two premier trains, the *Canadian* and the *Ocean*

to see out of both sides of the train during the day. The downside might be having other passengers walking by your seats as they pass through the car; but you'll quickly get used to that, and the reasonable cost of these accommodations should more than make up for it.

Park Cars

Several cars are named for Canada's national parks. They're certainly easy to spot, always being the last car of each train and with the distinctive bullet-shaped end. Park cars are reserved for use by sleeping-car passengers only. There's a comfortable observation area at the end of the car, a lounge toward the middle where passengers can get coffee and other beverages, and a dome on the upper level with two dozen seats. These cars also include sleeping accommodations: one drawing room with three beds and three bedrooms with two beds apiece.

LRC Fleet

VIA's LRC cars are found in the Windsor–Toronto–Ottawa–Montreal–Quebec corridor. Trains operating along this route run quietly and smoothly at speeds up to 100 miles per hour. The cars are well designed with large windows and are tastefully decorated. Two types of service are offered in this central corridor.

Coaches

The standard LRC coach will accommodate seventy-four passengers in rows of seats, two on each side of the aisle, and includes room for a wheelchair. Two lavatories are at the rear end of the car. A small food-service area is located at the opposite end, although passengers may purchase food and beverages right from their seats. Coffee, tea, and soft drinks are complimentary.

VIA1 Cars

These upgraded coaches have twenty fewer seats than the standard coach, which means more legroom. There are two lavatories at one end of the car and a fairly extensive food-service area at the opposite end from which the complimentary meals are served. The food in VIA1 class is quite good, rivaling first-class meals served by the airlines. Apéritifs, wine, and after-dinner drinks are all complimentary. No doubt about it, this is a very pleasant way to travel and, in my opinion, is definitely worth the extra fare.

Bottom Line

Generally speaking, no matter which train you ride, you'll find VIA Rail's equipment modern, clean, and comfortable—especially those stainless-steel beauties. If you really want a taste of the golden age, ride the *Canadian,* the *Skeena,* or the *Ocean.* You'll find a description of their routes, along with routes of most other VIA trains, in Chapter 15, "Now, Where Would You Like to Go?"

CHAPTER 14

Traveling by Train in Mexico

As this edition of *All Aboard!* went to press, the Mexican government was in the process of privatizing much of the rail service in that country, leaving the status of first-class train service very much up in the air. Despite this uncertainty, there is still at least one truly extraordinary train ride readily available for visitors to that interesting and colorful country: the Copper Canyon route, running between Chihuahua City in north-central Mexico and Los Mochis on the Sea of Cortez. Because there are both public and private train options available to those wishing to take this trip, I can still recommend it—and I do so enthusiastically.

An American-Mexican Rail Link

In the 1860s, about the same time entrepreneurs were starting to push for transcontinental railways in the United States and Canada, an American named Albert K. Owen began looking for a way to link the American Midwest with a Pacific seaport by running a rail line through Mexico. Owen, an engineer by training, tried to sell his idea to a number of governors of U.S. states and to Congress, without success.

Nevertheless, the idea had some serious economic potential, at least on paper, and other eager would-be railroaders came after Owen. In 1897, Foster Higgens, also an American, formed a company called the Rio Grande, Sierra Madre y Pacifico, which began building a rail line south from Juarez for 160 miles to Corralitos. In that same year, a Mexican entrepreneur, Enrique Creel, formed a rail company called the Chihuahua al Pacifico and started laying 125 miles of track between Chihuahua and Miñaca.

The first really serious effort to construct a railroad to the Pacific through Mexico was driven by a visionary American businessman named Arthur Stillwell, who saw it as a way to open up trade between the eastern part of the United States and Asian markets. His plan called for the rail line to originate in Kansas City, head south through Texas and into Mexico, then swing southwest and terminate at one of North America's great natural deep-water harbors, Topolobampo, on the Sea of Cortez. Stillwell saw limitless potential in the future of trade between North America and the Far East and calculated that a rail line through Mexico would reduce the time it took to ship goods between Kansas City and the Pacific by four days—a major economic incentive. (By the way, Port Arthur, Texas, was named for Stillwell.)

Work on the rail line sputtered on and off over the next several decades, with several companies being formed and building various segments of the line. The Mexican Revolution was a major interruption, with Pancho Villa and his troops staging periodic attacks on railroad facilities and construction crews. Nevertheless, several different railway companies continued working during that period, and by 1914, Juarez on the Texas border was linked to Chihuahua. From Chihuahua the line had also been extended to the little logging town of Creel.

The Copper Canyon Route Is Completed

In 1940, the Mexican government took over several of the small railway companies and formed the Chihuahua al Pacifico, which remains to this day as a division of the Ferrocarriles Nacionales de Mexico (Mexican National Railway). Most of the construction that had occurred prior to that time had been relatively easy. The really difficult terrain—some 160 miles across the Sierra Occidental range—had yet to be tackled. That work began in the early 1950s; by the time it was completed, the cost had run into the billions of pesos. No wonder: The route goes through some of most rugged country anywhere in North America.

The entire line was finally finished in 1961 and is without a doubt an engineering marvel. In the 357 miles between Creel and Los Mochis, there are eighty-eight tunnels. The longest is 5,996 feet, and all together their combined length is almost fourteen miles. One tunnel makes a 180-degree turn and descends 100 feet—all inside a mountain. Then there are the bridges, more than 220 of them. If joined together, their combined length would be over five miles. One, the Chinipas Bridge, is 1,000 feet long and more than 300 feet high.

The real attraction of this rail journey is, of course, the terrain it traverses. As the train heads southwest from Chihuahua en route to the Pacific, there are fields and farms. They soon give way to pine forests and then, for miles and miles, the train winds through gorges and hugs canyon walls, burrows into mountains, and crosses rivers—either placid or rushing, according to the time of year.

Whatever the problems a visitor to Mexico might encounter when traveling by train in other parts of the country, the ride along the Copper Canyon route is a once-in-a-lifetime experience. Because this route is traveled by both public trains and private excursion trains, it's an experience that is available to almost anyone.

Ferrocarriles Nacionales de Mexico

From its real beginnings in the late 1940s, the Ferrocarriles Nacionales de Mexico (FNM) grew into a railroad of significant size and scope. By the end of 1997, there were about 1,800 locomotives in its fleet, of which all but a handful were diesel-electric. A great deal of the rail traffic in Mexico is devoted to freight—mostly grain, coal, a variety of minerals, petroleum, fertilizers, and auto parts. All this cargo is hauled in a total of some 50,000 freight cars, many of which are privately owned by companies that produce the oil, dig the coal, build the automobiles, and so on. In all, Mexican freight trains haul about sixty-five million tons of cargo every year.

As of late 1997, the FNM had about 800 passenger cars, of which three-quarters were being used for second-class service. Frankly, on most of the rail lines, the equipment is pretty run down. Over the last few years, Mexico's struggle to stabilize its economy has taken a toll on a number of institutions. One casualty has been the country's rail passenger service; overall, the national system has deteriorated. For example, although overnight trains are still running, there are no longer any sleepers or dining cars in use.

The reasons for the unfortunate state of rail service are many and complex, but they include budget cuts, a shortage of usable equipment leading to "deferred maintenance," plus the uncertainty brought about by privatization. That's a shame, because in the same tradition of railroads in the United States and Canada, the FNM has a proud history and has offered some first-rate rail experiences to visitors over the years. Today, however, it's just not clear how soon Mexico's national rail system will be able to offer a quality of service that would be acceptable to most international visitors.

A Bold Experiment

In early 1997, the Mexican government took formal steps to privatize its national rail system, meaning that private companies were invited to bid for the rights to operate both freight and passenger service throughout the country.

The first route to be privatized connects Mexico City with Laredo, Texas, and it was awarded to a joint Mexican-American consortium, Transportacion Ferroviaria Mexicana (TFM), of which 49 percent is owned by the parent company of Kansas City Southern Railway.

Another consortium, Grupo Ferroviario Mexicano (GFM), was the successful bidder for both the Pacific-North route and the Chihuahua al Pacifico line—some 3,800 miles of track in all. GFM is made up of Mexican mining and construction interests, and in addition the Union Pacific Railroad is a minority shareholder.

By late summer of 1997, negotiations were under way for the privatization of two other major rail lines and several smaller ones, too. While the picture is still unclear, here's how it all looked as this edition of *All Aboard!* was going to press:

- In return for agreed-upon fees paid to the Mexican government, the new operators will have the exclusive right to provide freight service over their respective routes.
- They may also provide some first-class passenger service, but *only if they wish to do so.* First indications were that GFM might and TFM would not.
- Meanwhile, the Ferrocarriles Nacionales de Mexico will continue to operate second-class trains on some fifteen rail lines throughout the country in order to provide basic passenger service for the Mexican people. One of those will be the Copper Canyon route between Chihuahua and Los Mochis. There is also the possibility that the FNM will continue to operate the first-class train on the Copper Canyon route.

The bottom line is this: For some time to come, travel within Mexico on what are referred to as the "normal" (or public) trains will probably not be an attractive option for all but the most adventuresome visitors.

A Few Details You Need to Know

Many Americans seem to be uneasy at the thought of travel to Mexico. It's really no more "foreign" than Canada and a visit across either border can be equally enjoyable. As with any trip abroad, however, you can enhance your Mexican travel experience and reduce the possibility of any problems along the way with a bit of study and some commonsense preparation ahead of time.

Crossing the border   Assuming you're in Mexico as a visitor and are staying less than six months, you won't need a visa but you will need a tourist card—an FMT, or Foletto de Migración Turística. You can get one where you cross the border or, if you're flying into Mexico, at the airline counter before you leave. You'll also need some proof of citizenship. A passport is best, of course, but an original birth certificate or voter registration card along with a photo ID will work, too. (Whatever proof of citizenship you choose, you'll need to have it with you in Mexico, too.) The best thing to do, especially if you don't have a passport or if there's anything at all unusual about your status, is to get your tourist card ahead of time from a Mexican embassy, consulate, or tourist office.

I've said this elsewhere, but it bears repeating here: Make photocopies of all your travel documents before you leave home—that means passport, tickets, and itinerary. Keep one set of copies with you when you travel, and leave another set with someone back home.

¿Habla usted Español?   It's always great to be able to speak another language when traveling, and if you do speak some Spanish, you'll enhance your enjoyment of your travels through Mexico. However, if you don't speak Spanish,

don't let that deter you from experiencing this wonderful train ride. Get a simple Spanish phrase book and work on the basics, and I mean the real basics. (The first phrase I learned was *Lo siento, no hablo español* . . . "I'm sorry, I don't speak Spanish.") Don't worry! You'll find everyone friendly and more than willing to deal with you in rudimentary English or simple sign language. If you're traveling on either of the deluxe excursion trains operating over the Copper Canyon route (the *South Orient Express* or the *Sierra Madre Express*), there will be any number of people on board who are fluent in both languages.

Paying for things   Be sure to buy traveler's checks! Change most of your American dollars into pesos before you cross the border, and when you do, make sure you get plenty of bills in small denominations. Large notes can be hard to change, even in some hotels. You'll be able to use credit cards in virtually all of the hotels and in most (but not all) restaurants.

What to wear   Dress comfortably by all means, but be prepared for real swings in temperature along the Copper Canyon route. After all, Chihuahua is located in a desert environment at some 4,000 feet in elevation, the highest point of the trip is over 8,000 feet, and you'll end up in Los Mochis at sea level. The "layered look" is definitely the way to go.

Health and safety   The best advice I can give—and it applies almost anywhere in the world you may be traveling—is to use common sense when it comes to where you go and what you do. That's true for the United States or Europe as well as Mexico. You wouldn't venture alone into strange areas of New York or Los Angeles at night, would you? Don't do it anywhere else!

When it comes to health issues, there are some basic precautions you should take, not so much because you're at any kind of serious risk, but because these few precautions are easy to take and could possibly save you a great deal of discomfort and inconvenience.

- Be sure to pack whatever medicines you need or might need.
- It can be very hot, so take and wear a hat and use a very strong sunscreen.
- Although it's very unlikely that you'll have a problem, there are some serious diseases lurking in some parts of the country. Most are transmitted by mosquitoes, so do the logical and sensible thing: Bring a good insect repellent—and use it!
- The local water is the most common source of the ever-popular *la turista,* or traveler's diarrhea. So don't drink it! Avoid the tap water, even in hotels where they tell you the water is okay. Plenty of bottled water is available. Drink it, brush your teeth with it, and wash your face with it. Shower with your mouth closed. Don't eat any vegetables that may have been washed. Fresh fruits and vegetables you peel yourself are fine. It's also a good idea to wash your hands before you eat.

Look, I know all this sounds very ominous, but don't let what are really routine and commonsense precautions put you off. The chances that you will get sick are small anyway, and you can reduce them to virtually nil with what amounts to very minor inconveniences. Makes sense, doesn't it?

Traveling by Bus

As a rail enthusiast I hate to say this, but unless you have a rental car, your own car, or an RV, the best way to travel within Mexico these days is by bus. Most major cities and towns now have clean, modern bus terminals with frequent departures to a wide variety of destinations. So, until the passenger train situation in Mexico is resolved one way or another, first-class travel on a bus will usually be a preferable option.

On a recent trip, I had to begin my rail journey through the Copper Canyon from Chihuahua City. To get there from El Paso, I taxied across the Rio Grande to the spacious new bus terminal in Juarez, where buses for Chihuahua leave every thirty minutes or so. My bus was a brand-new Mercedes, air-conditioned and equipped with a restroom. During the five-and-a-half-hour trip, two movies were shown. The fare was $16. Now that's pretty hard to beat!

Traveling by Train

Train travel within Mexico is certainly not impossible, although, as noted previously, the level of service is mostly designed to provide basic transportation for the local population. It's also unpredictable—more so now, because by the time you read this, privatization could have eliminated many routes.

Traditionally, there are usually two kinds of trains available—the *estrella,* which is supposedly the fast train, and the *burro,* which is slower—a lot slower. Take the *estrella* if you do travel by train, and ask if there is a first-class service offered. It will cost more, but it's still inexpensive.

How to Make Reservations

You can book specific dates for the *Sierra Madre Express* or the *South Orient Express* by calling either company directly or by working through a travel agent. As far as booking any of the "public" trains is concerned, I'd be astonished if you could find a travel agent who would even be willing to try—there's just too much uncertainty. If the Ferrocarriles Nacionales de Mexico is still operating a first-class train on the Copper Canyon route, you will have to make reservations once you arrive in either Los Mochis or Chihuahua. Reservations for the FNM's second-class train? Surely, you jest!

Fares

Train and bus fares in Mexico, even when traveling first class, are very reasonable. For example, the five-and-a-half-hour bus ride between Juarez and Chihuahua is about $16; the fourteen-hour train ride between Chihuahua and Los Mochis is less than $60. However—here comes the same disclaimer again—remember that everything about rail travel in Mexico is changing dramatically, so expect the unexpected. Of course, if you opt for one of the deluxe excursion trains plying the Copper Canyon route, almost any travel agent will be able to quote the latest costs. Or you can call those companies direct (see the phone numbers in the "Rail Travel Information Sources" section).

Is the Train on Time?

If you've booked one of the private excursion trains, they will be responsible for keeping you informed of all departure times. If you're traveling on an FNM train, it may be on time, but probably not. Furthermore, there's no 800 number to call to find out. The only alternative is to assume the train will be on time, then wait it out.

While on Board

Bring your own food and plenty to drink with you. Be prepared to handle your own baggage. Dress casually and comfortably, because the weather is likely to be hot and the odds are there won't be any air-conditioning, or if there is, it might not be working.

The Copper Canyon Trip

As I've already noted, there is one train ride in Mexico that I can enthusiastically recommend to anyone, and that is the rail line running from Chihuahua to Los Mochis. Though this is commonly referred to as the Copper Canyon route, it

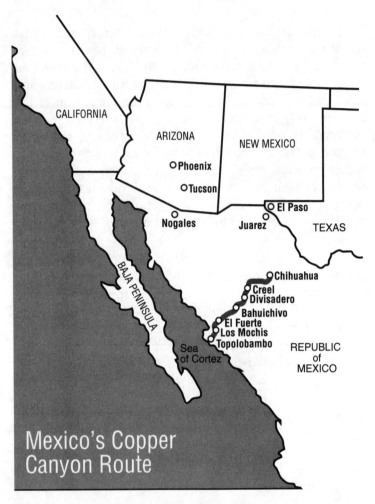

Mexico's Copper
Canyon Route

actually runs along and through a series of interlocking
canyons, of which the Copper Canyon, or Barrancas del
Cobre, is but one. Together, though, they offer an incredible
experience. These canyons are more than four times larger
and, in several areas, a full mile deeper than the Grand
Canyon in Arizona.

You can take this trip pretty much year-round, but the
best time is in September. The weather should be sunny
but not too hot, and because it's just after the rainy season,

you'll see some spectacular waterfalls. The foliage will be at its best, too.

How you choose to make this trip depends in large measure on your sense of adventure and your budget. In theory, you can take FNM trains almost from the minute you cross into Mexico. The first leg is from Juarez, just across the Rio Grande from El Paso, to Chihuahua. From Chihuahua, you take the Copper Canyon route to El Fuerte. The last segment would be from El Fuerte north to Nogales. From there, it's just over an hour by bus across the border to Tucson. Of course, you can follow that same route in reverse, too.

However, I would recommend the all-train option for only the truly adventurous and/or the doggedly committed rail traveler. For example, the westbound train through the Copper Canyon is scheduled to arrive at Sufragio Station near El Fuerte at about 7:15 P.M. The connecting northbound train to Nogales isn't due to arrive until around midnight but is often as much as four hours late! That could leave you waiting in what can best be described as marginal circumstances for as much as nine hours. Besides (you're probably sick of reading this by now), with privatization there's no guarantee which trains will still be running.

A reasonable alternative—and I'm quite comfortable recommending this to almost anyone—is to fly or take the bus to Chihuahua. After an overnight stay, take the FNM first-class train, *El Nuevo,* through to Los Mochis, with overnight stops in Creel and Divisadero at least. Then fly back to the U.S. from Los Mochis. (You can make this trip in the opposite direction, but because the bus ride between Tucson and Los Mochis is much longer, I suggest flying in both directions.)

If you prefer to have all the arrangements handled for you, by all means opt for one of the two deluxe excursion trains that regularly travel the Copper Canyon route: the *South Orient Express* and the *Sierra Madre Express.* In addition to having someone else worry about all the details, you'll have the added bonus of traveling in style and comfort aboard beautifully refurbished vintage rail-cars. Either train will provide you with an unforgettable experience. Although the heart of that experience is the ride between Chihuahua and Los Mochis, the two companies offer somewhat different itineraries, so it's best to call for their latest brochures.

A Variety of Rail Options

When choosing a train for traveling the Copper Canyon route between Chihuahua and Los Mochis, your choices can range from the ultra-basic to the super-deluxe. (You'll find a detailed description of the trip itself in Chapter 15, "Now, Where Would You Like to Go?")

El Nuevo

This is the daily train operated by the Ferrocarriles Nacionales de Mexico. The westbound train leaves Chihuahua

El Nuevo, the first-class train operated by the Ferrocarriles Nacionales de Mexico, arrives at Divisadero. From here, the train heads southwest along what is arguably one of the top three or four scenic rail trips in the world. (Photo by the author)

at 7:00 in the morning, arriving in Los Mochis some fourteen hours later. The eastbound train leaves Los Mochis at 6:00 A.M., arriving in Chihuahua at about 9:00 P.M. The coaches are not new, and while some are in disrepair, most used on this train are reasonably clean and quite comfortable. There is no diner or lounge car on the train, but the onboard crew will serve sandwiches and drinks at your seat. I was impressed by the service when I took this train. The car attendants were impeccably dressed, and most spoke enough English so that in combination with my very basic Spanish, there was no communication problem.

El Pollero

If you're really adventurous, you might consider taking the second-class train that departs daily from each terminus an hour after *El Nuevo*. It's slower and makes many more stops, but if it's color and a real taste of the country you're after, then this is surely the way to go. Some basic Spanish will be helpful, although it's not a necessity. The locals have given this train its nickname (*El Pollero*), which they will tell you with a good-natured smile is loosely translated as "the Chicken Train." Any additional description is probably unnecessary.

South Orient Express

This company operates a deluxe excursion train several times a year on a prearranged schedule. Depending on the number of people booking each of these trips, the train's consist can include as many as eight passenger cars, all from the golden age of train travel—that is, from the late 1940s to mid-1950s—and all beautifully and lovingly restored.

The *South Orient Express* operates with a variety of itineraries, which change according to the time of year, so call for the latest schedule.

In addition to the excursion train, the company operates what it calls the *Copper Canyon Limited*, a restored luxury coach pulled by the regular FNM train three days

In Nogales, the *Sierra Madre Express* gets spiffed up for a trip through Mexico's incredible Copper Canyon. (Photo by the author)

each week in each direction. This car is often booked by tour groups, but assuming it's operating on a day when you're traveling, individual passages are also sold. It's equipped with a small galley from which sandwiches and drinks are prepared and served to passengers at their seats. There's also a tour guide in the car to talk about points of interest along the way.

The *Copper Canyon Limited* coach is detached from the regular FNM train at Divisadero, with passengers spending the night in a hotel that's perched right on the canyon rim. The following day, the car is once again coupled to the daily FNM train for the remainder of the journey to Los Mochis.

For information, write to the Mexican American Railway Company, 16800 Greenspoint Park Drive, Suite 245 N, Houston, Texas 77060. Or call 800-659-7602.

Sierra Madre Express

This company has been operating a deluxe excursion train through the Copper Canyon since 1987. The usual consist is made up of refurbished classic railcars and includes several sleepers, a dome car, and a bullet-shaped observation car that brings up the rear of the train. One of the cars also has a unique open-air observation area. In my opinion, that's the place to be for most of the trip—except for mealtime, that is! It's hard to top the experience of enjoying a gourmet meal high in a vista dome car while gliding along one of the most spectacular rail trips in the world.

The *Sierra Madre Express* operates according to a published schedule, with most trips lasting seven nights and eight days. The trip starts with a get-together in Tucson the night before departure. The next morning, passengers are bused across the border to Nogales, just an hour's drive south of Tucson, where the train itself is located. Once everyone is boarded, the train heads south to Hermosilla and Sufragio, where passengers sleep overnight on board in private bedrooms. Next morning, it's off for the run through the canyons, with overnight stops along the way in some excellent and very picturesque hotels in Divisadero, Creel, and Chihuahua.

For information, write to the Sierra Madre Express, P.O. Box 26381, Tucson, Arizona 85726. Or call 800-666-0346.

RV Trains

If you own an RV or a motor home, here's an idea for you. There are several private U.S. companies that regularly contract with the FNM to put together trains of flatcars on which RVs and motor homes are loaded for the run through the Copper Canyon. In order to avoid the hot weather and the rainy season, most of these special trains operate between January and April, with a few in October, November, and December. One of the most common itineraries is for the group to assemble in the U.S. and caravan

Campers and RVs are loaded on special trains for the leisurely (and quite unforgettable) trip through Mexico's Copper Canyon. The trip begins in Chihuahua City, with Los Mochis on the Sea of Cortez as the final destination. En route, as shown here, the train stops at some of the particularly scenic points. (Photo courtesy of Tracks to Adventure, El Paso)

to La Junta, where the RVs are loaded aboard flatcars for the ride through to Los Mochis. These trains travel slowly and stop often—smack in the middle of some of the more spectacular bridges, for example. It's certainly a good way to experience this extraordinary rail route.

Three companies specialize in these RV tours through the Copper Canyon and elsewhere in Mexico. By the way, if you call to ask for their brochures, you should be aware that they also arrange RV rail trips in the U.S. and Canada. The oldest and largest of these firms is Tracks to Adventure, located in El Paso, Texas (800-351-6053). However, there's also Point South in Moreno Valley, California (909-247-1222) and Carnival Caravans of Sumas, Washington (800-556-5652).

If You Still Have Concerns...

Put them aside! Along with VIA Rail's *Canadian* and Amtrak's *California Zephyr,* I would rate the train ride through the Cooper Canyon one of the rail "musts" in North America. The scenery is incredibly rugged and beautiful, the culture is fascinating and colorful, and you don't have to be a structural engineer to be awed by the difficulties that were overcome to build this rail line. So with a few basic, commonsense precautions, you can travel on your own, taking the FNM train. Or leave all the worry and details to experienced, competent tour guides and book the trip on either the *Sierra Madre Express* or the *South Orient Express.* But go. You'll thank me.

CHAPTER 15

Now, Where Would You Like to Go?

This chapter contains information about many of the long-distance trains operated by Amtrak in the United States and VIA Rail in Canada. A few of the shorter routes are also mentioned, either because of their high ridership or because the scenery along the way is particularly note-worthy. (Because for a number of reasons it's really the only Mexican train trip I'm currently recommending, you'll find details about the justly famous rail route along the Copper Canyon in Chapter 14.)

In most cases, I've provided both the name and number for each train. There will usually be two numbers—odd numbers for trains headed south and west, even numbers for those headed north or east. A third number given to a train probably means it operates at a different time on weekends. I've given you a few of the major stops along the route but did not list them all. You can get that information by checking an Amtrak or VIA Rail timetable or by going to their web pages on the Internet (*www.amtrak.com* or *www.viarail.ca*).

Also shown is mileage from each train's point of origin to its ultimate destination and the approximate time it takes to cover that distance. You may notice that some trains take longer to travel in one direction than they do on their return trip, even though they cover exactly the same route. There are several explanations for that apparent discrepancy: a long grade that takes more time on the uphill run, more freight traffic encountered on one of the trips because it operates at a different time of day, or padding in the schedule. For details about specific arrival and departure times at all station stops en route, refer to current timetables or call Amtrak at 800-USA-RAIL or VIA Rail at 800-561-3949 or 800-561-9181.

In the comments that follow each listing, I've tried to tell you something about the scenery along the way and whatever else might make that trip different or interesting. In some cases, I tell you whether you'll see more or better scenery when traveling in one direction on a certain route as opposed to the other. This can indeed be the case, since a train may pass through a particularly scenic area during daylight hours when traveling one direction but through that same stretch during the night on its return trip. Occasionally I note from which side of the train you can best see special points of interest or particularly scenic areas. Between New York City and Albany, for instance, the westbound *Lake Shore Limited* travels for more than two hours along the east bank of the Hudson River, but if you're enclosed in a roomette on the right side of the train, you might never realize this. Of course, if you're traveling in the opposite direction (eastbound toward New York City), the river will be on the right side. If you're riding in coach, you'll be able to see out of both sides of the train but would probably prefer to grab a seat on the side where the great scenery will be.

But—please!—remember that both Amtrak and VIA issue new timetables regularly, and there are always changes. Always. Not just in the minor details, either. For example, just weeks before sending the final manuscript for this book to the publisher, I got a phone call from an Amtrak official in Washington alerting me that two trains I had included in this listing had been eliminated. So by all means, use the following information to help you plan a wonderful, scenic rail journey, but check all details with an Amtrak or VIA Rail reservations agent or a knowledgeable travel agent before your plans are set in concrete.

Insider Tip: Crossing the Border

Many Americans mistakenly think they can enter Canada with a wave of the hand. That's often true when traveling by car but not so if you're on the train. You'll need proof of identity, such as a passport, a birth certificate, a citizenship certificate, or naturalization certificate. A driver's license is not acceptable. If there's anything out of the ordinary about your status, check carefully ahead of time to be sure you have the documentation you'll need. There are no trains available to the general public that cross the U.S.–Mexico border, but you must be prepared to present essentially the same proof of citizenship to Mexican authorities when you enter that country. And you will need clear documentation when returning to the U.S.

Amtrak—United States

Eastern Trains

Adirondack (68, 69, 70, 71)

Between:	New York City and Montreal
Via:	Poughkeepsie, Albany, Saratoga Springs, Ticonderoga, Lake Placid
Operates:	Daily
Distance:	381 miles
Duration:	9½ hours
Equipment:	Amfleet coaches, cafe car

This is really a pretty trip. The train runs along the eastern bank of the Hudson River for almost two and a half hours between New York City and Albany, passing some magnificent old homes, the Military Academy at West Point, and Vassar College in Poughkeepsie. Northbound, the river will be on your left. Mondays through Saturdays, this train operates during daylight hours in both directions. On Sundays, however, the southbound train has a later departure from Montreal, and consequently most of the scenic trip down the Hudson will be after dark unless you're traveling in the summer months.

Ethan Allen Express (290, 291, 293, 294, 296)

Between:	New York City and Rutland (VT)
Via:	Poughkeepsie, Albany, Saratoga Springs
Operates:	Daily
Distance:	266 miles
Duration:	$5^1/_4$ hours
Equipment:	Amfleet coaches, cafe car

The *Ethan Allen* follows the same route as the *Adirondack* between New York City and Glens Falls, New York. From there it veers off to the northeast, enters the state of Vermont, and terminates in Rutland. This is a very scenic trip most all the way. However, the northbound trains leave Penn Station in the afternoon, so unless you're traveling in the summertime, much of the pretty stuff in upper New York State and Vermont will show up after dark. Southbound, that shouldn't be a problem if you're traveling Monday through Saturday; on Sunday, the southbound train also has a late-afternoon departure, which means the last hour or so (that lovely run down the Hudson River) will be after dark. The river will be on your right heading toward New York City.

Maple Leaf (63, 64)

Between:	New York City and Toronto
Via:	Poughkeepsie, Albany, Syracuse, Buffalo, Niagara Falls
Operates:	Daily
Distance:	544 miles
Duration:	12 hours
Equipment:	Amfleet coaches, cafe car

For the first three hours out of New York City, the northbound *Maple Leaf* follows the same route as the *Adirondack*—along the Hudson River (on the left) to Albany. At Schenectady, the train swings westward toward Lake Ontario. If you've never seen Niagara Falls, it is definitely worth a stopover. I recommend the northbound trip, which offers more daylight hours, especially in the summer.

Vermonter (55, 56)

Between:	(Montreal)/St. Albans (VT) and Washington, D.C.
Via:	Montpelier, White River Junction, Claremont (NH), Springfield, Hartford, New York City, Philadelphia
Operates:	Daily
Distance:	606 miles
Duration:	13½ hours
Equipment:	Amfleet coaches, cafe car, baggage car specially equipped to accommodate bicycles, skis, and snowboards

This train travels through some of the loveliest parts of Vermont and Massachusetts, mostly wooded hills and farmland, and you'll also see one of the longest covered bridges in the country. Heading south, the bridge is on your left as you cross the Connecticut River just before getting to Claremont, New Hampshire. Do opt for the southbound train if you have a choice, because the last few hours of the trip will be in the dark, especially during the fall and winter months. It is far better to have night fall on the industrialized corridor south of New York than on that lovely New England countryside. Southbound passengers can board an Amtrak bus in Montreal and, ninety minutes later, be delivered to the St. Albans station, where the *Vermonter* will be waiting. Likewise, a connecting bus will take northbound passengers over the border to Montreal.

Northeast Direct, Metroliner, and Clocker Services

There are a lot of these trains, and they run from early morning until later in the evening, although the weekend schedule is somewhat less frequent. Northeast Direct service refers to trains running between either Springfield or Boston, Massachusetts, to Washington, D.C. A few of those trains continue on past Washington through Richmond to Newport News, Virginia. The Metroliners are confined to the high-speed run between New York City and Washington, D.C. The Clocker trains (the name comes from the old Pennsylvania Railroad, because it was said you could set your clocks by their trains) run on weekdays only and essentially carry commuters between New York City and Philadelphia.

Bankers, Nutmeg State, Charter Oak, Bay State, Vermonter, Patriot, Senator

Between:	Springfield (MA) and New York City
Via:	Hartford, New Haven, Bridgeport, Stamford
Operates:	Several times daily
Distance:	133 miles
Duration:	3½ hours
Equipment:	Amfleet coaches, cafe car

This is a busy route, with trains operating fairly often during the day. Southbound, the train crosses the Connecticut River after leaving Springfield and runs through some very attractive areas of rural Connecticut. In the summertime, you'll see entire fields of tobacco covered by something that looks like white cheesecloth. The tobacco is a special variety used for cigar wrappers. Hartford's railroad station has had a facelift and now looks much the way it did around the turn of the century. The gold-domed State Capitol is on the left just as you leave the station. You'll get a new locomotive in New Haven, since only electric engines are permitted into the underground areas of New

York City. (Headed north, that's where you'll swap your all-electric locomotive for a diesel-electric.)

New Haven is the home of Yale University, and from here to New York you are sometimes within sight of the ocean (actually, Long Island Sound). Once you reach Bridgeport, you'll be passing through communities from which lots of people commute to work into New York City. You cross the Hellgate Bridge into Manhattan and, after passing some pretty depressing areas, dip underground and below the streets. These trains used to end up in wonderful old Grand Central Terminal (the commuter trains still do), but Amtrak now uses a bypass and goes straight to Pennsylvania Station. Some of these trains continue right on to Washington, D.C.

Mayflower, Old Dominion, Virginian, Potomac, Yankee Clipper, Bay State, Minute Man, Patriot, Narragansett, Senator, Merchants Limited

Between: Boston (MA) and New York City
Via: Providence, Mystic, New London, New
             Haven, Bridgeport, Stamford
Operates: Several times daily
Distance: 231 miles
Duration: 4^1/$_2$ hours
Equipment: Amfleet coaches, cafe car

This is really a nice ride. The southbound train passes through some typically New England areas after leaving Boston, coming within sight of the Atlantic Ocean soon after Providence, Rhode Island. For the next two hours, the ocean is frequently visible on the left. Also on the left, look for submarines as you cross the Thames River at New London. I'm not kidding—that's where they're built by the Electric Boat division of General Dynamics. The Merchant Marine Academy is also there. Along the Connecticut shore, you'll see some wonderful old homes built early in the century and pleasure boats by the hundreds. Approaching New York City, you get a good view of the city skyline.

Twilight Shoreliner (66, 67)

Between: Boston and Newport News (VA)
Via: New London, New Haven, New York City, Philadelphia, Baltimore, Washington, D.C., Richmond
Operates: Daily
Distance: 644 miles
Duration: $13\frac{1}{2}$ hours
Equipment: Amfleet coaches, custom class coaches, lounge car, Viewliner sleeper

Are you traveling between Boston and either Washington or Richmond for a business meeting? Go ahead and fly if you want, but this is surely the way I'd go. Board the *Twilight Shoreliner* in Boston in the evening, have a beverage, read or do some work, then crawl into a comfortable berth for a good night's sleep. You'll arrive in Washington bright and early the next morning, all rested and ready to do battle with a bureaucrat. If your business is in Richmond, you'll still be there in plenty of time for a midmorning meeting. The schedule is almost exactly the same in the opposite direction.

Veteran rail travelers should know that this train has recently replaced the venerable *Night Owl,* which ran overnight between Boston and Washington for more than twenty-five years. If you should book this train, remember that there's always a fair amount of tinkering with the schedule of any new train. Be sure and double-check arrival and departure times just before your departure date.

Metroliner Service

Between: New York City and Washington, D.C.
Via: Newark, Philadelphia, Wilmington, Baltimore
Operates: Daily
Distance: 226 miles

Duration: 3 hours
Equipment: Amfleet coaches, cafe car, club coach

This is Amtrak's much-touted high-speed service. Several things differentiate Metroliners from conventional Amtrak trains running along the same route. Obviously they're faster, but in order to reach and sustain their top speed of 125 miles per hour, the consists are limited to five or six cars. In order to cover the distance between New York and Washington in under three hours (the schedule says two hours and fifty-five minutes), these trains make fewer stops. All seats on the Metroliners are reserved, so you are assured of a seat even if the train is full.

You pay a hefty premium for choosing a Metroliner, however—as much as double the lowest possible fare for a conventional train. A good way to try out the Metroliner at a lower fare is to ride it on a weekend when the fares are quite a bit less. My suggestion is to take a Metroliner once for the experience, and after that, ride the conventional trains. They take a half hour or so longer but still run at well over 100 miles an hour.

International (364, 365, 367)

Between: Chicago and Toronto
Via: Kalamazoo, East Lansing, Flint, Port Huron
    (MI), London, Kitchener (ON)
Operates: Daily
Duration: 12 hours
Distance: 501 miles
Equipment: Amfleet coaches, cafe car

The *International* runs every day, passing through quite a number of rather small towns, with some very attractive farms and wooded areas in between. I suggest avoiding the westbound Sunday train (367) if you have a choice. That one train has a later departure than any of the others, and as a result, the last part of the trip—a full four or five hours in winter months—is made after dark. This train is a joint operation between Amtrak and VIA Rail, with American and Canadian crews taking the train up to their own borders. As noted earlier, you will have to present proof of citizenship at the border in either direction.

Lake Shore Limited (48, 49)

Between: Chicago and Boston or New York City
Via: Cleveland, Buffalo, Albany
Operates: Daily
Distance: Chicago–Boston, 1,017 miles;
             Chicago–NYC, 959 miles
Duration: Chicago–Boston, 21 hours;
             Chicago–NYC, 18¹/₂ hours
Equipment: Amfleet coaches, Viewliner sleepers, dining
             car, lounge car

The *Lake Shore* follows the same route as the New York Central's famous *Twentieth Century Limited,* skirting three of the Great Lakes: Michigan, Erie, and Ontario. The scenery will be quite different, however, depending on which direction you travel. The westbound train runs in daylight roughly from Cleveland to Chicago, while the sun follows the eastbound Lake Shore from Buffalo to either of its final destinations, Boston or New York City. In my opinion, the eastbound train is the more scenic trip. Off and on between Buffalo and Schenectady, you'll be following the old Erie Canal and can see a number of the canal locks from the right side of the train. When it was finished in 1825, the canal connected Buffalo on Lake Erie with the Hudson River at Albany, allowing people and goods to travel by water all the way from the Great Lakes to the Atlantic Ocean.

The *Lake Shore* splits into two trains at Albany. The New York section runs due south along the Hudson River for several hours before reaching New York City, but only the eastbound train passes this way during daylight hours—one more reason why it's the more scenic of the two. Best viewing is on the right. After leaving Albany, the other section heads east to Pittsfield in the middle of the Berkshire Mountains, one of the choice skiing areas in the entire eastern area. From there, you pass through Springfield and Worcester as well as a great many charming little New England towns, before reaching Boston in the late afternoon.

Capitol Limited (29, 30)

Between: Chicago and Washington, D.C.
Via: Toledo, Cleveland, Pittsburgh,
             Harpers Ferry (WV)
Operates: Daily
Distance: 780 miles
Duration: Eastbound, 17 hours; westbound, 18 hours
Equipment: Superliner coaches, sleepers, dining car,
             lounge car

The eastbound trip is, I think, the more scenic of the two. The train leaves Chicago in the early evening and, by dawn, has reached Pittsburgh. You'll have daylight from there all the way into Washington, and it's a very pretty run—across the Allegheny Mountains in West Virginia, a stop at Harpers Ferry, into Maryland farm country, finally arriving in Washington, D.C., by early afternoon. The westbound trip is very nice, too—but you'll pass through that stretch around Pittsburgh in darkness.

Pennsylvanian (43, 44)

Between: New York City and Pittsburgh
Via: Philadelphia, Harrisburg
Operates: Daily
Distance: 444 miles
Duration: 9½ hours
Equipment: Amfleet coaches, cafe car

Amtrak's *Three Rivers* climbs through the famous horseshoe curve near Altoona, Pennsylvania, on its way over the Allegheny Mountains. (Photo courtesy of Amtrak)

The *Pennsylvanian* passes through some very beautiful eastern scenery, particularly in the stretch between Philadelphia and Pittsburgh through Pennsylvania Dutch country, along the Susquehanna River and over the Allegheny Mountains. The ride also includes one of the best-known spots in the country for railroad fans: the famous horseshoe curve near Altoona, Pennsylvania. If you have a choice, the westbound train is the better one, since it operates entirely during daylight hours. The last part of the eastbound trip will be after dark, especially in the winter months. You'll see the horseshoe curve just fine either way, however. For the best view, be on the left side of the train heading west.

Three Rivers (40, 41)
Between: New York City and Pittsburgh
Via: Philadelphia, Harrisburg
Operates: Daily
Distance: 444 miles

Duration: $9^1/_2$ hours
Equipment: Amfleet coaches, cafe car

This train follows the same route as the *Pennsylvanian*. Because of the westbound train's schedule, however, some of the prettiest countryside, including the horse-shoe curve near Altoona, Pennsylvania, will be after dark through the winter months. So, if you're going to travel between New York and Pittsburgh and want to take full advantage of the best scenery (not to mention the horse-shoe curve), I suggest opting for the *Three Rivers* eastbound and the *Pennsylvanian* westbound.

Cardinal (50, 51)

Between: Washington, D.C., and Chicago
Via: White Sulphur Springs (WV), Cincinnati, Indianapolis
Operates: From Washington: Sunday, Wednesday, Friday; from Chicago: Tuesday, Thursday, Saturday
Distance: 929 miles
Duration: 23 hours
Equipment: Superliner coaches, sleepers, dining car, lounge car

The eastbound *Cardinal* is one of my favorite trips. It will be dark or close to it when you leave Chicago, but the real scenery happens the next day almost from the moment you wake up and lasts all the way into Washington. Probably the best part of the trip occurs as the train winds its way through the New River Gorge in West Virginia. About twenty-five minutes after leaving Montgomery, West Virginia, you see the New River Gorge Bridge from the right side. It's 1,700 feet long and almost 900 feet above the river. Remember the TV commercial in which a Chevy Blazer is hooked to a king-sized bungee cord and shoved off a very high bridge? This is the spot! The *Cardi-nal* crosses the river more than once, but most of the time the river will be on the right side. This is a lovely ride any time of the year, but it will really be something if you can manage to have your trip coincide with the fall colors.

Florida Trains

Silver Meteor (97, 98)

Between:	New York City and Miami
Via:	Philadelphia, Washington, D.C., Richmond, Charleston, Savannah, Jacksonville, Orlando
Operates:	Daily
Distance:	1,391 miles
Duration:	26½ hours
Equipment:	Amfleet coaches, Viewliner sleepers, dining car, lounge car

You pretty much see it all on this trip: big cities and small towns, industry and agriculture, temperate and tropical. Heading south, you'll leave New York's Pennsylvania Station in the early evening, so much of the high-speed part of the run will be after dark. Because they're so long, none of the Florida trains can reach the 125-mph speed of a Metroliner, but you'll still be moving over 100 mph en route to Washington. If you're breaking your trip in Washington—and I certainly recommend it—be sure to spend some time right there in Union Station. It has been restored to its original grandeur and then some!

Virginia and much of the Carolinas come and go during the night, but about the time you're enjoying breakfast in the diner you'll be in Charleston and not quite two hours later Savannah, Georgia—certainly two of the South's most charming cities. Jacksonville arrives just after noon, and from here, the *Meteor* takes you through Orlando and Kissimmee, both stops for Disney World. Then it's on down the eastern coast of Florida to Ft. Lauderdale and Miami for an evening arrival.

Silver Star (91, 92)

Between:	New York City and Miami
Via:	Philadelphia, Washington, D.C., Richmond, Columbia (SC), Savannah, Jacksonville, Orlando
Operates:	Daily
Distance:	1,433 miles
Duration:	29 hours
Equipment:	Amfleet coaches, Viewliner sleepers, dining car, lounge car

This train covers mostly the same route as the *Silver Meteor,* but because of different departure times, it provides somewhat more in the way of scenery in either direction. For example, its late-morning departure from New York means you'll still have some daylight left for the very pretty countryside south of Washington. At Rocky Mount, North Carolina, the *Silver Star* heads inland for a stop in the wee hours at Columbia, the capital of South Carolina, then rejoins the *Silver Meteor's* route in Savannah just before dawn. The southbound train runs about five hours earlier than the *Meteor,* which means Jacksonville for breakfast, Orlando for lunch, and Miami in time for dinner—perhaps at one of that city's great seafood restaurants. Heading north, this train leaves Miami before noon and reaches New York in the late afternoon the next day.

Silver Palm (89, 90)

Between:	New York City and Miami
Via:	Philadelphia, Washington, D.C., Richmond, Charleston, Savannah, Jacksonville, Tampa, Lakeland
Operates:	Daily
Distance:	1,446 miles
Duration:	28 hours
Equipment:	Amfleet coaches, Viewliner sleepers, dining car, lounge car

This is a fairly new train and follows the route of the *Silver Meteor,* leaving New York City in the early morning and reaching Jacksonville just about twenty-four hours later. At that point, however, the *Silver Palm* heads off through orange groves to Tampa on Florida's west coast. An Amtrak bus will be waiting there to take passengers farther down the Gulf Coast to Bradenton, Sarasota, and Fort Myers. After leaving Tampa, the *Silver Palm* turns east across the central part of Florida, passes through Lakeland, and rejoins the *Meteor*'s route in Winter Haven for the rest of the run to Miami and a midday arrival. It's important to note, however, that this train does not take you to either Orlando or Kissimmee, the two stops closest to Disney World.

Auto Train (52, 53)

Between:	Lorton (VA) and Sanford (FL)
Via:	This train makes no intermediate stops.
Operates:	Daily
Distance:	861 miles
Duration:	$17^{1}/_{4}$ hours
Equipment:	Superliner coaches, sleepers, dining car, lounge car; bi-level cars for transporting automobiles

The *Auto Train*'s northern terminus, Lorton, Virginia, is a suburb of Washington, D.C. At the other end, Sanford, Florida, is just a few miles from Orlando and Disney World. This is really a classic case of finding a need and filling it. The train operates for people who want to have their personal automobiles with them in Florida. Perhaps they just don't want to make the long drive south, or maybe they'll be spending enough time in Florida to make renting a car an expensive proposition. Either way, the *Auto Train* is the perfect answer. Note that there are no intermediate stops—you board in Lorton and end up in Sanford, or the reverse. That's because special facilities are

Automobiles are loaded aboard Amtrak's _Auto Train_ in Lorton, Virginia, for the overnight trip to Florida. (Photo courtesy of Amtrak)

required to load and unload the cars—this is a fascinating operation to watch, by the way.

Automobiles are carried in specially designed bi-level railcars while their owners ride up front in either coach or sleeping-car accommodations. Only passengers with cars can ride the _Auto Train_ (if you're heading for Florida without a car, the other Florida trains will be faster and more convenient anyway).

This is by far the longest train Amtrak operates, frequently consisting of as many as forty-four cars; because about half of those are basically freight cars, operationally that's the way this train performs—as a freight train. That just means you'll be traveling at somewhat slower speeds. Almost by definition, people who ride the _Auto Train_ travel in both directions, but for what it's worth, the southbound trip will be the more scenic, through Virginia and much of the Carolinas during daylight hours.

Southern Trains

Carolinian (79, 80)

Between: New York City and Charlotte (NC)
Via: Philadelphia, Washington, D.C.,
              Richmond, Raleigh
Operates: Daily
Distance: 702 miles
Duration: 14 hours
Equipment: Amfleet coaches, dinette car

Depending on the time of year, the last few hours of this trip will be in the dark, whichever direction you're traveling. So, if you have a choice, travel northbound on this train, which means you'll miss some of the industrial areas south of New York City. For as far as it goes, the *Carolinian* follows the same route as the Florida trains.

City of New Orleans (58, 59)

Between: Chicago and New Orleans
Via: Urbana (IL), Memphis, Jackson (MS)
Operates: Daily
Distance: 934 miles
Duration: Southbound, $19^{1}/_{4}$ hours; northbound, 19 hours
Equipment: Superliner coaches, sleepers, dining car,
              lounge car

I think I prefer the southbound trip because it offers a bit more daylight—although it may be because that's the direction Willie Nelson was headed. (If you don't get that reference, you're musically deprived. Buy his recording of "The City of New Orleans," very possibly the best railroad song ever written.) Anyway, it's dark or close to it when the train leaves Chicago, so you won't see much of all that Illinois farmland as you head south to Cairo. That's where you cross the Ohio River into Kentucky, although it happens in the early morning hours. About dawn, and just before you stop in Memphis, you'll see the thirty-two-story Great American Pyramid. It's on the right and, believe me, you can't miss it.

You continue on through the Mississippi delta to the capital city of Jackson. By now, the river itself is well to the west. Another eighty miles or so, after passing through the town of—I wouldn't make this up—Magnolia, Mississippi, the train crosses into Louisiana. This is low country . . . okay, swamp country. You can almost see the alligators and snakes out there, but it's very picturesque nevertheless. After a stop in Hammond, the train skirts around Lake Ponchartrain along the longest continuous railway curve in the world and into New Orleans. Let the fun begin!

Crescent (19, 20)

Between:	New York City and New Orleans
Via:	Philadelphia, Washington, D.C., Greenville (SC), Atlanta, Birmingham
Operates:	Daily
Distance:	1,380 miles
Duration:	32 hours
Equipment:	Amfleet coaches, Viewliner sleepers, dining car, lounge car

This train, which was the pride of Southern Railway for years, still follows the same route, passing through all the major cities along Amtrak's northeast corridor to Washington, then swinging down through Virginia farm country before running along the edge of the Blue Ridge Mountains for several hours. Stay alert for the impressive Wells Viaduct after you leave Toccoa, Georgia. (Depending on the time of year, you may cross it after dark on the northbound trip.) After Atlanta, you'll travel west through impressive pine forests and evidence of an active logging industry, then along the southern end of the Appalachian Mountains. Before arriving in Birmingham, you'll pass the Anniston Army Depot on the right side of the train. A good deal of military hardware, including quite a number of tanks and other armored vehicles, will be parked neatly on display as you roll by.

From there, the *Crescent* crosses into Mississippi, then turns and runs straight south. Much of this run is through some very swampy areas on both sides of the train, and you just know there are big, hungry gators lurking out there! A few minutes after a stop at Slidell, Louisiana, you cross Lake Ponchartrain on a six-mile-long causeway. It's just one track wide, and neither land nor any part of the causeway can be seen from either side of the train, creating the sensation that you're rolling right along on the water itself.

Once you're off the causeway, you'll pass quite a number of old fishing houses built out on the end of long piers and visible on the right side of the train. For environmental reasons, owners of these structures are prohibited from rebuilding or even making any repairs, so all are pretty ramshackle and many have already been abandoned. From there, you're just a half hour or so from arriving in New Orleans, where the train will back into the station. If the *Crescent* is even close to being on schedule, you'll be there in plenty of time to enjoy some Creole cooking and maybe catch a set by the jazz band at Preservation Hall. What a town!

Western Trains

California Zephyr (5, 6)

Between:	Chicago and Oakland
Via:	Omaha, Denver, Salt Lake City, Reno, Sacramento
Operates:	Daily
Distance:	2,425 miles
Duration:	Westbound, 52½ hours; eastbound, 53¼ hours
Equipment:	Superliner coaches, sleepers, dining car, lounge car

This is arguably Amtrak's most scenic trip. It's spectacular in either direction, although if the eastbound train should be running more than an hour or so late (and it often does), you could miss some of the more impressive views coming out of the Rockies and into the Denver area.

Westbound out of Chicago, you have corn and soybeans and more corn, then a dinnertime crossing of the Mississippi River at Burlington, Iowa. Omaha comes about midnight, and you wake up in cattle country just east of Denver. Things start getting spectacular shortly after leaving Denver, as the *Zephyr* begins its climb into the Rockies, with best viewing from the right side of the train. In the next two hours, you'll pass through twenty-seven tunnels, the last of which is the six-mile-long Moffatt Tunnel. Before it was completed in 1928, the ten-minute trip you just took over Rollins Pass took five hours. For the rest of the day, you follow the Colorado River through a series of canyons. The train crosses the river several times, but along this stretch most of the best viewing will be from the left side. You should see lots of rafters, although it's not the real white-water stuff.

You cross Utah and enter Nevada during the night, getting to Winnemucca bright and early. Butch Cassidy once robbed a bank here. Following a midmorning stop in Reno, the *Zephyr* starts its climb into the foothills of the Sierra Nevadas. After a stop at Truckee—you're in California now—get a seat on the right side of the train for the ride along mountain ridges and past Donner Lake. It was named for eighty-seven settlers, led by George Donner, who were trapped by snow in the winter of 1846–47. Next comes the American River Canyon on the left side. The California Gold Rush took place in the 1850s and 1860s all through this area. After leaving the mountains and stopping at Roseville, you'll pass McClellan Air Force Base and enter the Sacramento Valley, known for producing almonds and rice. Next stop is Sacramento, capital of California and home of the very-much-worth-seeing California State

Railroad Museum, followed by Davis, then Travis Air Force Base on the left.

After passing through some of the justly famous vineyards of Napa Valley, the train finally reaches the Pacific shore, where you'll see the Navy's "mothball fleet" in Suisun Bay on your left. After Martinez and Richmond, the *Zephyr* stops in Emeryville, where an Amtrak bus will be at trainside to take passengers across the bay to San Francisco. The *Zephyr's* final stop, Jack London Square in Oakland, is just a few minutes later.

Texas Eagle (21, 22)

Between:	Chicago and San Antonio (connecting for Los Angeles)
Via:	St. Louis, Little Rock, Dallas
Operates:	From Chicago: Sunday, Tuesday, Friday; from San Antonio: Sunday, Tuesday, Thursday
Distance:	1,308 miles
Duration:	Chicago–San Antonio, 29½ hours; San Antonio–Chicago, 30¼ hours
Equipment:	Superliner coaches, sleepers, dining car, lounge car

Southbound out of Chicago, you'll cross quite a number of rivers. There's the Chicago River first, followed by the Des Plaines and the Kankakee. You cross the Vermillion River just before a stop at Pontiac (Illinois, not Michigan, although both are named for the same Native American chief), followed by a number of other stops. It will be close to midnight when you reach St. Louis, but stay awake if you can, because the grand finale is the Mississippi, which you'll reach about twenty minutes after leaving Alton, Illinois. There's a great view of the city skyline on the left and, several minutes later, the Gateway Arch on the right. Okay, now you can go to sleep.

You wake up in Arkansas, probably about the time the *Eagle* crosses the Arkansas River and pulls into Little Rock. You can see the dome of the State Capitol on the left. About midmorning, you'll stop in Texarkana. The Arkansas/Texas state line runs right through the town. In fact, it runs right through the railroad station, and depending on whether you're sitting toward the front or the rear of the train, you'll be either in Texas or still in Arkansas.

By the time the train reaches Longview, you're in the middle of oil country. Then, as you follow along the Sabine River, you see cattle and horses. Dallas comes toward the middle of the afternoon, and after a stop in Austin, the state capital, the train crosses the Colorado River, reaching San Antonio about midnight. In San Antonio, cars from the *Texas Eagle* are coupled to the westbound *Sunset Limited* and continue on to Los Angeles. (If your trip began in Los Angeles, your car will be detached from the *Sunset Limited* in San Antonio and become part of the northbound *Texas Eagle*.) Either way, the train will be stopped in San Antonio for several hours. Not to worry, however. Whether traveling north or south, the stop will occur in the middle of the night, and without any train motion to disturb you, you'll sleep like a baby!

Southwest Chief (3, 4)

Between:	Chicago and Los Angeles
Via:	Kansas City, Dodge City, Trinidad (CO), Santa Fe, Albuquerque, Flagstaff, San Bernardino
Operates:	Daily
Distance:	2,230 miles
Duration:	41 1/4 hours
Equipment:	Superliner coaches, sleepers, dining car, lounge car

This is another of my favorite trips, because it passes through some truly beautiful parts of the country. After a

Passengers riding in a Superliner sleeping car stretch their legs while the *Southwest Chief* is serviced in Albuquerque, New Mexico. (Photo by the author)

late-afternoon departure from Chicago, you head west across Illinois farmland for several hours, finally reaching and crossing the Mississippi River into Iowa around 9:00 P.M. Kansas City and Topeka come and go during the night, and by the time you wake up the next morning, you'll be just about in Dodge City. Boot Hill is a bit up the way from the old brick station.

The country will stay fairly flat for a short while, but by midmorning the *Chief* has crossed into Colorado and is climbing up toward Raton Pass and the New Mexico border. You've been following the original route of the Santa Fe Trail for quite a while by now, and off and on the trail is still plainly visible from the right side of the train. Once through the pass, the third stop is Lamy, New Mexico, which is the station serving Santa Fe. Santa Fe is a very old town and much worth visiting for a few days. This was the final destination on the old Santa Fe Trail, but the *Chief* still has almost a thousand miles to go.

Next comes Albuquerque. The train stops for almost a half hour here for servicing and window-washing, so you'll have time to get off and look at some of the jewelry being sold, mostly silver and turquoise, on the platform. During most of the year, someone from the New Mexico Historical Society boards the train here and provides commentary over the lounge-car P.A. system about the history and geology of the area all the way to Gallup. (Other volunteers do the same thing on the eastbound train.) The *Chief* gets to Flagstaff around 10:15 P.M., and if you're making a side trip to the Grand Canyon, this is where you'll leave the train. Otherwise, you'll probably sleep through all of Arizona, waking up in time for your arrival into Los Angeles.

It's close to a toss-up, but I think the westbound trip is a bit better, only because the eastbound train may run late. In that eventuality, passengers will miss some of those really beautiful mountains in Colorado because of darkness.

Empire Builder (7, 8)

Between:	Seattle or Portland and Chicago
Via:	Spokane, Glacier Park (MT), Fargo, Minneapolis–St. Paul, Milwaukee
Operates:	Daily
Distance:	Portland–Chicago, 2,261 miles; Seattle–Chicago, 2,209 miles
Duration:	Portland–Chicago, 45 hours; Seattle–Chicago, 45 1/4 hours
Equipment:	Superliner coaches, sleepers, dining car, lounge car

This is another of my favorite trains! I've taken the *Builder* in both directions, but I prefer the eastbound train because passengers can see more of both the Cascades in Washington and the Rockies in western Montana—especially if the westbound train should run late.

The run from Seattle to Spokane is very pretty—first north along the shores of Puget Sound to Everett, then east into the magnificent Cascade Mountains. In summer months it will still be light when you reach Wenatchee, justifiably called the Apple Capital of the World. Then you continue on through farm and ranch land toward Spokane. Sit on the left for this part of the trip. The Portland section heads north, crosses the Columbia River into Vancouver, Washington, then heads for Spokane, turning east and passing through the Columbia River Gorge (on the left) for more than fifty miles. These two sections meet in Spokane well after midnight, becoming one train for the rest of the trip to Chicago.

If you can, wake up early the next morning, because you'll be in Montana, skirting the southern edge of Glacier National Park. These are the Rockies now—less forested, but more rugged than the Cascades. About thirty minutes past the West Glacier stop is the little community of Essex. It's a flag stop, so chances are you'll just go right on by, but watch for the Isaak Walton Inn on the left side of the train. This little hotel sits smack on the Burlington Northern's busy main line and is a favorite train-watching spot for railfans. At least two or three of them will be out in front of the hotel taking your picture—guaranteed!—so get up close to the window and wave as you go by.

In the middle of the morning, you'll leave the Rockies and begin learning firsthand what the term "Big Sky Country" refers to. It will take all day to cross Montana, but don't let anyone tell you this is a boring ride. You cross a rolling terrain with vast fields of grain, grazing cattle, and later on oil wells. You'll stop at Cut Bank, just twenty-five miles below the Canadian border. Two stops later, you are at Havre. Get off the train and take a look at the magnificent steam locomotive on display at the station. You'll begin to see the Missouri River during the afternoon and will cross it several times.

The *Empire Builder* passes through North Dakota during the night, turning at Grand Forks and following the Red River south. Breakfast will be in Minnesota, perhaps somewhere between St. Cloud and Minneapolis–St. Paul. Just before lunch, the train will cross the Mississippi, quite wide here, and stop at La Crosse, Wisconsin. For the next few hours, you are in dairy country. Then comes Milwaukee and, just ninety minutes later, Chicago. What a ride!

Coast Starlight (11, 14)

Between:	Los Angeles and Seattle
Via:	Santa Barbara, San Jose, Oakland, Sacramento, Klamath Falls (OR), Eugene, Portland, Olympia
Operates:	Daily
Distance:	1,389 miles
Duration:	Los Angeles–Seattle, 34 1/2 hours; Seattle–Los Angeles, 35 1/4 hours
Equipment:	Superliner coaches, sleepers, dining car, lounge car, parlor car

You really get to see a bit of everything on this train, especially on the northbound run, which provides a bit more daylight for some of the scenic highlights. Heading north out of Los Angeles, most of the interesting scenery will be on the left, since the train runs along the shoreline part of the way. After the stop at Oxnard, you should be able to see the Channel Islands about twenty miles offshore—and the big platforms for the offshore oil wells, too.

In midafternoon, the *Starlight* stops at the old mission town of San Luis Obispo, then begins climbing up toward Cuesta Pass. If you've followed my suggestion and are sitting on the left, you'll see the entire train as it goes through two horseshoe curves, not to mention the California Men's Colony, a state penitentiary. The train is now entering the Salinas Valley, appropriately called the "Country's Salad

Bowl" and will be following the Salinas River, too. At the northern end of the valley you'll pass through Castroville. Take note if you like artichokes, because this is where most of them come from. By the time the sun goes down, you'll have a good idea how important agriculture is to California.

By the way, the *Coast Starlight* features a parlor car for use by passengers traveling in sleepers. You can wander in here, order a beverage, and chat with some of your fellow passengers whenever you like; about midafternoon, you'll be invited into the parlor car to sample some California wines and nibble from platters of fruit and cheese. Pretty nice!

If your destination is San Francisco, get off at Emeryville, one stop after Jack London Square in Oakland. Amtrak will have a bus waiting there to take you into the city that the late (and beloved) columnist Herb Caen called Baghdad-by-the-Bay.

If you're continuing north on the *Coast Starlight,* get to bed early tonight, because you'll want to be awake in time for a stunning view of Mount Shasta from the left side of the train soon after you leave Dunsmuir, California. In fact, this second day aboard is one wonderful panorama after another. Most of the truly spectacular views will be on the right side of the train today, after the train leaves Chemult, Oregon.

From Klamath Falls north is a big logging area, so you'll be traveling though forests of Douglas fir. After Chemult, the train climbs to the Cascade Summit, where you'll see Odell Lake below and Maiden Peak beyond. On a single track, the train runs along the western side of Willamette Pass and Salt Creek Canyon, giving you a constantly changing vista for many miles. Building this railroad was quite a project. You'll pass through twenty-two tunnels between here and Eugene. After a stop in Salem,

Oregon's capital, the train heads through the Willamette Valley toward Portland.

Hope for a clear day, because as you get closer to Portland, Mount Hood and Mount St. Helens will be on your right. You'll be able to tell which one is Mount St. Helens; the violent eruption in 1980 blew away a large part of the peak. It's quite obvious, even from this distance. Leaving Portland, the "City of Roses," the train crosses the Columbia River into the State of Washington and, a few minutes later, stops in Vancouver. Okay, everyone . . . back over to the left side of the train! From here on, you'll follow the Columbia River, then run along the edge of Puget Sound through Tacoma and right past the Kingdome into Seattle. Seattle is, as you will find, a wonderful city.

San Joaquins

Between:	Oakland and Bakersfield (CA)
Via:	Berkeley, Martinez, Stockton, Merced, Madera, Fresno
Operates:	Four times daily each way
Distance:	315 miles
Duration:	6¼ hours
Equipment:	Amfleet coaches, cafe car

Four *San Joaquins* run up and down through the middle of California in each direction seven days a week. Three of the four complete their runs during daylight hours, so viewing opportunities will be the same whichever way you travel. The trains stick pretty much to the huge San Joaquin Valley, with the Sierra Nevada off to the left on the southbound trip. Amtrak buses provide connections between Oakland and San Francisco and between Bakersfield and Los Angeles. To visit Yosemite National Park, you can connect with an Amtrak bus at the station in Merced.

San Diegans

Between:	Santa Barbara or Los Angeles and San Diego
Via:	Fullerton, Anaheim, San Clemente, Del Mar
Operates:	Several times daily
Distance:	Santa Barbara–San Diego, 232 miles;
	Los Angeles–San Diego, 129 miles
Duration:	Santa Barbara–San Diego, $5^3/_4$ hours;
	Los Angeles–San Diego, 3 hours
Equipment:	Amfleet coaches, cafe car

The *San Diegans* run right along the coast for most of the way between Los Angeles and San Diego, and on most days you'll see lots of swimmers and surfers. You can pick from among several trains that run during daylight hours to enjoy the great scenery in either direction. Just try to get a seat on the right side of the train if you're heading southbound, because that's where the ocean will be. There are also some offshore oil platforms visible several miles off the coast.

This train is a "push-pull" operation—that is, if the locomotive pulls the train from L.A. to San Diego, it will push it from San Diego back to L.A. This eliminates the need to turn the entire train around in San Diego. The engineer simply moves from the locomotive cab to a little compartment at the end of what had been the last car. From there he operates the locomotive with a duplicate set of controls during the return trip. It can be a bit startling to see one of these trains go whizzing "backwards" through a grade crossing at seventy or so miles per hour, but it's really a more efficient operation. The engineers are not overly fond of this configuration, feeling (quite correctly, I think) that they are much more vulnerable in the event of a grade-crossing collision while operating from the auxiliary cab. With this concern in mind, Amtrak has recently begun using converted locomotives at the opposite end of some of these trains.

They're really just "shells" with space to carry baggage where the diesel motors used to be, but they do afford the crews some additional safety.

Transcontinental Train

Sunset Limited (1, 2)

Between:	Orlando (FL) and Los Angeles
Via:	Jacksonville, Tallahassee, Pensacola, Mobile, New Orleans, Houston, San Antonio, El Paso, Tucson
Operates:	From Orlando: Tuesday, Thursday, Saturday; from Los Angeles: Sunday, Tuesday, Friday
Distance:	2,765 miles
Duration:	Eastbound, 73$^1/_2$ hours; westbound, 74$^1/_4$ hours
Equipment:	Superliner coaches, sleepers, dining car, lounge car

The *Sunset Limited* was a very ambitious undertaking for Amtrak. It is, in fact, the first true transcontinental train in the nation's history, because other cross-country trips always required either the passenger or the railcar to change trains somewhere along the way. It's hard to say whether the eastbound or the westbound train offers the most or the best scenery, since you'll miss some nice areas in either direction. On balance, I think you'll get to see a bit more on Train 1, the westbound *Sunset,* although the best solution to that dilemma would be a round-trip.

Depending on the time of year, your first onboard sunset will occur about the time you depart from Orlando. At first, the train travels north to Jacksonville, then swings west and heads across the state's panhandle through the night.

Mobile, Alabama, arrives about the time you're heading for breakfast in the dining car (ask for grits with your eggs and bacon), and you can see Mobile Bay on the left. This is a gracious city and worth taking some time to explore. Angling a bit more to the south, the *Sunset* will nip across that little "tab" at the bottom of Mississippi, stopping at Pascagoula (bird-watching area to the left after leaving), Biloxi (shrimp boats), and Gulfport (big seaport). Last stop in Mississippi is Bay St. Louis, an art colony and very large recreation area. About a half hour after leaving Bay St. Louis and before the New Orleans skyline comes up on the left, you'll pass through Honey Island Swamp. Yes, there are indeed alligators in there, and you'll probably see them sunning themselves if the sun's out.

The *Sunset* has quite a long stop scheduled in New Orleans in both directions, and if its arrival is close to on time, you'll be able to leave the train and spend some time walking around the French Quarter, perhaps even taking time for lunch (eastbound) or dinner (westbound) in one of the many great restaurants this town has to offer.

Continuing the westbound journey and just after leaving New Orleans, you'll pass the Superdome (on the right), then cross the Mississippi River on the Huey Long Bridge. This bridge is four and a half miles long, some 200 feet high, and must be seen to be believed! The eastbound *Sunset* crosses after dark, which is one more reason I recommend taking the westbound train. For the next several hours you'll be traveling through bayou country. Since the ground is pretty soggy through much of this wetland, most of the tracks were built on pilings. As a matter of fact, you'll notice that the cemeteries all through here are above ground because the water table is so high. Sunset number two happens an hour or so before you cross into Texas.

Houston comes and goes around midnight, and just before dawn there's an hour-long stop in San Antonio, where the restoration of its wonderful old station is just about completed. The Rio Grande is to the left and, on the opposite bank, Mexico. You'll see Laughlin Air Force Base on the left side of the train just before arriving in

Del Rio, Texas, and about forty-five minutes after leaving that city, you'll cross the Pecos River on a very high bridge—320 feet down to the river. This is pretty dry country, and lots of cacti and mesquite can be seen now. About twenty minutes farther on, the *Sunset* rolls through the town of Langtry, once the home of the legendary Roy Bean. He wasn't really a judge but nevertheless proclaimed himself the "only law west of the Pecos" and dispensed his own unique version of justice here for a number of years. Somewhere along the way, ol' Roy became infatuated with Lily Langtry, a famous British actress, and named the town for her—a dubious honor at best.

The *Sunset* heads a bit more to the north now, climbing into the Del Norte Mountains. Just after a stop in Alpine, Texas, you'll cross Paisano Pass, over 5,000 feet in elevation and the highest point of the entire trip. It'll be late afternoon when you reach El Paso, located on the Rio Grande and surrounded by the Franklin Mountains. The railroad station here dates back to 1904 and has been handsomely restored. You'll cross the Rio Grande and into New Mexico just a few minutes after leaving El Paso. It's here that the *Sunset* passes literally within a few feet of the Mexican border, which is marked by a white post just to the left of the train. All those orchards you've been seeing are pecan trees.

You cross the Continental Divide shortly after leaving Deming, New Mexico, and reach the Arizona border an hour later. Mining is big in these parts—gold and silver and copper. Your third sunset on board comes as Amtrak's Train 1 heads for Tucson, where you can catch an Amtrak bus for Phoenix.

During the night, the *Sunset* crosses the Arizona–California border; if it's running close to on time, you'll arrive in the early morning into Los Angeles. Three sunsets, three time zones, and nearly three thousand miles. Quite a journey!

VIA Rail—Canada

VIA Rail's heaviest traffic occurs in the busy 725-mile central corridor between Windsor (just across the Detroit River from Detroit) and Quebec City. VIA trains run at speeds up to 100 miles per hour on much of this track. LRC equipment is used on these routes, and both standard and VIA1 class service is available on all trains. For these corridor trains, I've provided a listing of major routes and travel times to help in planning an itinerary. For specific train numbers, along with departure and arrival times, refer to a VIA timetable, access the web page at *http://www.viarail.ca,* or telephone VIA at 800-561-3949.

Trains Between	Distance	Duration
Montreal and Quebec	169 miles	2 1/2 hours
Montreal and Ottawa	116 miles	2 hours
Montreal and Toronto	335 miles	4–4 1/2 hours
Ottawa and Toronto	277 miles	4 hours
Toronto and Windsor	223 miles	4 hours

Eastern Trains

Ocean (14, 15)

Between:	Montreal and Halifax
Via:	Lévis, Mont-Joli, Matapédia, Moncton
Operates:	Daily, except Tuesday
Distance:	840 miles
Duration:	18 hours
Equipment:	Coaches, dome/cafe/lounge car, sleepers, dining car, observation car

The *Ocean* leaves Montreal in the early evening, immediately crosses the St. Lawrence, and then swings due east along the river's southern banks. The St. Lawrence is really a major waterway. It will be on the left side of the train for nearly eight hours; by the time the train turns south at Mont-Joli, the river is nearly thirty miles wide. During summer months, whales are often seen in the river, although because of the train's schedule it will be dark through most of this area.

About the time you wake up, you'll be crossing into the Province of New Brunswick. After making a stop at Campbellton, the train runs south along the coastline with the Gulf of St. Lawrence off to the left. The famous Bay of Fundy is much farther south, but this entire region is known for its extraordinary tides, which rise and fall as much as fifty feet twice a day. At Bathurst, the *Ocean* turns inland, passing through forests and farming country. After leaving Newcastle, the train crosses the upper part of Miramichi Bay, a mecca for fisherman looking for Atlantic salmon, then continues south across country to Moncton and into the Province of Nova Scotia. The *Ocean*'s final destination, the city of Halifax, was the jumping-off point for many convoys heading across the North Atlantic for England and Russia during World War II, and it's still a busy seaport. If you're into seafood, you've come to the right area! Like the *Canadian,* this train features VIA's refurbished stainless-steel cars. What a treat.

Chaleur (16, 17)

Between:	Montreal and Gaspé
Via:	Lévis, Mont-Joli, Matapédia, Carleton
Operates:	From Montreal: Sunday, Wednesday, Friday; from Gaspé: Monday, Thursday, Saturday
Distance:	654 miles
Duration:	16 hours
Equipment:	Coaches, sleeping cars, dining car

The *Ocean* and the *Chaleur* are really two trains in one between Montreal and Matapédia, where the coaches and sleepers that form the *Chaleur*'s consist get their own locomotive and head down along the southern shore of the Gaspé Peninsula. That big body of water you'll see off to the right when you wake up will be Chaleur Bay (*chaleur* is French for "warm"; personally, I'll take their word for it). By the time you get to Chandler, Chaleur Bay has become the Gulf of St. Lawrence. This area is heavily forested, with many lakes and rivers, and it is a very popular area for hiking, camping, hunting, and fishing. The *Chaleur* reaches the centuries-old town of Gaspé itself just in time for lunch—seafood, of course! There are several wilderness parks in the immediate area, and many tours are available. This is a great place to hole up and write a novel. On the return trip, the *Chaleur* meets the *Ocean* in Matapédia and it again becomes one train from there back to Montreal.

Polar Bear Express (423, 624)

Between:	Cochrane and Moosonee
Via:	Fraserdale, Coral, Moose River
Operates:	Daily (except Friday), third week of June to first week of September
Distance:	186 miles
Duration:	4¹/₂ hours
Equipment:	Coaches, dining car, snack/lounge car

This train is operated by the Ontario Northland Railway, not by VIA Rail. It runs for only about ninety days during June, July, and August, but the experience is worth going out of your way . . . and you'll have to! First you'll travel to Cochrane from Toronto (also on an Ontario Northern train). The arrival time is about 10:00 P.M., so the connection with the *Polar Bear Express* will require an overnight stay. After departure the next morning, the train travels along the Arctic watershed, crossing both the Abitibi and Moose Rivers, and passing through a sparsely populated area of forests and lakes. You can spend about four hours in Moosonee, then make the return trip to Cochrane. Better yet, spend the night in Moosonee and take a bit of extra time to learn about the unique way of life there, pretty much isolated from the rest of the world. During the balance of the year, the Ontario Northern operates the *Little Bear* (Trains 421 and 622) between Cochrane and Moosonee. (By the way, despite its name—probably a creation of the railroad's marketing department—there are no polar bears to be seen in Moosonee. For that, you'll have to take VIA's train, the *Hudson Bay.*) The Ontario Northern offers a number of packaged tours built around the train ride up to Moosonee and back, and they're very much recommended. For details, call 800-268-9281.

Western Trains

Hudson Bay (692, 693)

Between:	Winnipeg and Churchill
Via:	Dauphin, The Pas, Wekusko, Wabowden, Thompson, Gilliam
Operates:	From Winnipeg: Sunday, Tuesday, Thursday; from Churchill: Tuesday, Thursday, Saturday
Distance:	1,055 miles
Duration:	33$^1/_2$ hours
Equipment:	Coaches, sleepers, dining car

Winnipeg, the *Hudson Bay*'s southern terminus, has a population of some 600,000 people and is one of Canada's major cities. Churchill is at the far end of the train's route and is at the opposite end of the urban spectrum as well. It's a community of 1,200 souls located on the shores of Hudson Bay and just 600 or so air miles below the Arctic Circle. Between Winnipeg and Churchill, the train passes from prairie into dense forests and finally onto the tundra before reaching Hudson Bay itself. Along the way, it makes twenty-six scheduled stops, although the timetable lists another fifty-five "flag stops," where the train will stop if someone wants to get on or off.

There usually aren't many passengers on the *Hudson Bay,* but every year in late September when polar bears appear in and around Churchill, the train runs full for four or five weeks. When the bay freezes over, the bears go out onto the ice floe in search of fish and seals. While they wait, however, the bears pretty much make themselves at home in Churchill and, in the process, trigger a mini-boom in tourism. Because it is the only practical way in or out of many very small communities in the northern part of Manitoba, VIA Rail is mandated by the Canadian government to operate this train, for which the rest of us should be grateful. This trip is an extraordinary experience.

Canadian (1, 2)

Between:	Toronto and Vancouver
Via:	Sudbury, Sioux Lookout, Winnipeg, Saskatoon, Edmonton, Jasper
Operates:	From Toronto: Tuesday, Thursday, Saturday; from Vancouver: Monday, Thursday, Saturday
Distance:	2,776 miles
Duration:	70 hours
Equipment:	Coaches, dome/cafe/lounge cars, sleepers, dining car, observation car

This is VIA's premier train and deservedly so. In my opinion, the westbound trip is the one to take, because the scenery keeps getting more spectacular as you go. From the rich farmland around Toronto, the *Canadian* travels north before turning west to cross above Lake Superior through a wilderness of lakes, each surrounded by birch and pine forests. Then you go across the vast plains—cattle and wheat country—and into the Canadian Rockies to Jasper before reaching Vancouver and the Pacific. During my memorable trip on VIA's Number 1, passengers competed to see how many different species of wildlife could be spotted from the train. The final tally included geese, loons, osprey and eagles, deer, moose, wild sheep and goats, and a bear or two. (One traveler claimed to have seen a yeti, although that was after several hours in the lounge car.)

It's an absolutely sensational trip, which is really enhanced by the quality of the train itself. The stainless-steel coaches and sleepers have been completely refurbished, and the dome cars—there are three on each train—are the best possible way to enjoy the scenic beauty. During the very busy times of year, meaning roughly May through September, this train runs quite full and, as a result, the dining car is reserved for the use of sleeping-car passengers only. Meals for coach passengers are served in one of the two glass-domed Skyline lounge cars that are part of the consist. During other times of the year, there is no food service in the lounge cars, and all passengers are served in the dining car.

Skeena (5, 6)

Between:	Jasper and Prince Rupert
Via:	Prince George
Operates:	From Jasper: Wednesday, Friday, Sunday; from Prince Rupert: Tuesday, Friday, Sunday
Distance:	721 miles
Duration:	$20^1/_2$ hours
Equipment:	Coaches, dome/cafe/lounge cars

I have the feeling I've overused the word "spectacular" in describing some of these train rides, but the word certainly applies to the area surrounding Jasper. You can get to Jasper on VIA's Train Number 1, the *Canadian,* and it's well worth stopping here for a few days before catching the *Skeena.* There is no longer a sleeping car on this train, which now makes an overnight stop in Prince George, B.C. That adds one night in a hotel to the experience, but there's a very big upside: Except during the winter months, the *Skeena* now operates almost entirely during the daytime hours.

From Jasper, the *Skeena's* route takes it northwest through the Rockies crossing into British Columbia and through the Bulkley Valley to meet the Skeena River, which it follows all the way to the Pacific Ocean. Its final destination, Prince Rupert, comes at the end of the second day. Fishing is the main industry here, and although the terrain is not as ruggedly mountainous as Jasper, it is truly beautiful country, well worth a few days for a visit. From here, I suggest taking the *Skeena* back to Prince George, then BC Railway through Kamloops to Vancouver.

Malahat (198, 199)

Between: Victoria and Courtenay
Operates: Daily
Distance: 140 miles
Duration: 4¹/₂ hours
Equipment: Self-propelled rail diesel cars

Vancouver Island is the largest island in the Pacific Ocean off the coast of North America, roughly 300 miles long, and this train is an excellent way to see a good part of it. In fact, very few train rides pack as much fabulous scenery into such a short period of time as this one does. From the town of Victoria, the *Malahat* passes through some heavily forested areas before beginning to climb up toward Malahat Pass. The train will be crossing some deep gorges, and a VIA Rail booklet suggests that anyone who gets a bit queasy from heights might prefer sitting on the left side of the train (they aren't kidding, folks!).

After descending from the pass, the train goes by a number of lakes followed by some very picturesque farming country. You cross a number of rivers for the next several miles. If you like to fish, just get off anywhere along here. Whatever spot you pick will be the right one. About halfway through the trip, the train will cross the Nanaimo River. There's another bridge, higher and off to the west, and it's a favorite spot for those who hook themselves to a big rubber band and jump off. If a bungee-jumper happens to be poised on the railing as you go by, the *Malahat* will stop on the bridge to give everyone aboard a ringside seat.

From many spots along here you can look east off to the right and see Washington State across the Strait of Georgia and to the left the mountain range running down the center of the island. Fishing has always been important to the local people and, for that matter, to the wildlife, too. Keep your eyes peeled for bald eagles in this area, by the way. The last stop is Courtenay, a town of 10,000 and a jump-off point for hikers and skiers.

If you want to, on most days you can leave Victoria fairly early in the morning, spend a half hour walking around the town of Courtenay, then catch a return train that will get you back before 8:00 P.M. The most recent schedule has a noon departure for the Sunday train, which doesn't return to Victoria until close to 10:00 P.M. But do consider at least an overnight in Courtenay. You can savor the prospect of that return train ride over a nice dinner.

Mexico

As discussed in Chapter 14, there is really only one rail trip in Mexico that I feel comfortable recommending to anyone without hesitation at this time. The train listed following is operated by Ferrocarriles Nacionales de Mexico (Mexican National Railway), and it is a train that is available for use by the general public.

FNM operates a second daily train in each direction (the locals call it *El Pollero,* "the Chicken Train"). It's a good deal more colorful, and there's no serious reason to avoid it. However, it's much slower, leaving later in the morning and making quite a few more stops. As a result, much of the really spectacular scenery will occur after dark.

In addition, two private trains operate along this same route. The *Sierra Madre Express* operates between Nogales (about an hour's drive south of Tucson) and Creel. The *South Orient Express* operates between Chihuahua and Los Mochis, although the company offers other, more extended itineraries. There are significant differences among these three options involving itineraries, equipment, and cost—refer to Chapter 14 for those details. Just be aware that the really spectacular parts of the route will be the same whichever choice you make.

El Nuevo (73, 74)

Between: Chihuahua and Los Mochis
Via: Creel, Divisadero
Operates: Daily
Distance: 400 miles
Duration: 14 hours
Equipment: Coaches; in-seat food service

At 7:00 every morning, a first-class train, *El Nuevo,* leaves from each end of the line to begin a 400-mile, four-teen-hour journey over what must be one of the most amazing rail lines in the world. After departing from Chi-huahua, *El Nuevo* heads south and west and begins its long, gradual climb into the Sierras. This is farm country, with broad fertile valleys, apple orchards, and grazing cattle. There is a good-size and quite prosperous Mennonite community here, centered in the town of Cuauhtemoc, which comes about two hours after the train's departure from Chihuahua. Mennonite cheeses are justly famous and popular throughout Mexico.

The train keeps climbing after Chihuahua, and the terrain becomes more rugged, with orchards giving way to pine forests. About 12:30, the train reaches the logging town of Creel, at an elevation of more than 7,500 feet. The Tarahu-mara people, some 60,000 of them, are scattered throughout these mountains and canyons, many living pretty much the same lifestyle as their pre-Spanish ancestors. The town centers around two churches in the main square, a bank, a few restaurants, a small museum, and a lumber mill.

Soon after it's departure from Creel, the train passes through a horseshoe curve and starts up a steep grade. You can see it best from the left side of the train. In fact, unlike their American or Canadian counterparts, the Mexican train crews leave the top half of the double doors in the vestibules open throughout the trip. This makes for absolutely great viewing and is the place to be for taking pictures during the trip. But a serious warning: Be very careful about leaning out! Much of the train's route is through wooded areas, and tree branches frequently come very close to the railcars—occasionally they actually brush the cars as they pass.

You first see the canyons at Divisadero, a little town about an hour and a half from Creel. The train station is within 100 yards of a lookout from which there is a stunning view into not one but three interlocking canyons. I recommend staying overnight here—the view must be seen at several different times of day.

From Divisadero west you really begin to appreciate the incredible engineering that went into the construction of this part of the rail line. There are some thirty-five bridges and trestles; the one crossing the Rio Fuerte is 1,637 feet long, and another one, over the Rio Chinipas, is 1,000 feet long and 335 feet high. Then there are the tunnels—eighty-eight of them altogether. One is 3,074 feet long and, while passing through it, the train makes a full 180-degree turn and descends several hundred feet—inside the mountain!

Finally descending from the mountainous area, the terrain flattens out, and soon the train stops at Sufragio, the station serving El Fuerte. From there, it's another twenty-five miles to Los Mochis.

It's certainly possible to make this trip in one fourteen-hour day, but the country is so incredible, I really recommend taking the time to stop overnight along the way. It will be a lot cheaper if you travel on the FNM first-class train, but there is so much that is different and truly unique about this trip that it cries out for a more leisurely approach, and either the *Sierra Madre Express* or the *South Orient Express* will offer that. Whatever your choice, do it! If this isn't the most spectacular train ride in the world, it surely must be one of the top five.

CHAPTER 16

Is There a Train in Our Future?

Most Americans are surprised to learn that people in other parts of the world are riding trains in comfort and safety at speeds approaching 200 miles per hour. What's really amazing is that it's all being done with traditional technology: electric locomotives taking power from an overhead wire to pull cars with steel wheels along steel rails. That's the way railroads have been running their fastest trains for fifty years, and although exotic new technology is well on the way, that's probably how they'll be doing it for a while to come yet. It's equally amazing to many that so far the United States is not part of this train renaissance. After all, the U.S. has been a leader in the transportation field for 200 years, dating back to John Fitch's steamboat and including the Wright brothers, Henry Ford, Neil Armstrong, and a thousand others in between.

Is Everyone Else Wrong?

The fact is that every other industrialized country in the world has seen the advantages of a rail passenger system that moves people rapidly and efficiently. Most countries have already built such systems and are now busy expanding and updating them. The rest are planning and building high-speed rail lines as fast as they can.

Japan began its famous "bullet train" service in 1964. The first trains ran at 125 miles per hour along a 320-mile route between Tokyo and Osaka. That original system has since been expanded to more than 1,300 miles and carries 400,000 passengers every day at speeds up to 170 mph. The on-time performance of the Japanese trains is extraordinary, to say the least. In his definitive book, *Supertrains,* Joe Vranitch notes that in 1989 the Japanese compiled figures for all trains that had reported late arrivals. The average was twenty-eight *seconds.*

In France, the famous TGV (*train à grande vitesse*—literally "high-speed train") now routinely operates at speeds up to 186 mph with trains running as close as ten minutes apart during the busiest times. (In a 1990 test run, a TGV set a new record by attaining a speed of 325 mph, and plans are now under way to introduce a new generation of TGVs that will operate at 225 mph.) A ride on the TGV is quite remarkable—it is smooth, quiet, and without any real sensation of traveling at such speed. On-time performance is 98 percent. Neither the French nor the Japanese system has ever experienced a serious accident.

High-speed trains are also running in Germany, Great Britain, Spain, Austria, Sweden, and Denmark, among other countries, all at speeds of 140 mph and up. New high-speed rail lines are being planned in Portugal, Russia, Turkey, Greece, Taiwan, Australia—almost everywhere except here.

Have you ever made that grueling four-hour drive across the desert from Los Angeles to Las Vegas? A train like the TGV could get you there in two hours. It's an idea that makes sense and has been discussed. There's been talk about high-speed trains for other areas, too: in the Northwest, connecting Portland, Tacoma, Seattle, and Vancouver; back east, linking Philadelphia with Harrisburg and Pittsburgh; in Florida, taking people from either Tampa or Miami to Disney World in Orlando; and in Canada, along the corridor from Windsor through Ottawa and Montreal to Quebec. Several other areas are also being considered.

The trouble is, until there is real commitment from Washington, D.C., for the U.S. rail system or from the Canadian government for its rail system, no significant progress will be made. It will certainly not happen in the United States as long as influential voices in Congress still seem willing to let Amtrak wither and die. It's a position that's hard to understand, given the obvious success high-speed trains have had in these other countries. Under similar circumstances within his own field, I've often heard a shrewd and successful banker friend of mine ask, "What do they all know that I don't know?" It's a sensible and obvious question. Why aren't we asking that question regarding high-speed rail?

Do We Really Need High-Speed Trains?

Let's start with what would seem to be two safe assumptions. First, our population will continue to increase. Second, all those people will want the same kind of mobility we enjoy now. If those assumptions prove to be true (and they will, of course), it will invariably mean more cars on more highways. It will also mean more airplanes flying around, but in the same amount of sky. In other words, we will have more congestion, more pollution, and more safety concerns.

What if we didn't commit those megabillions to support and expand our auto/plane transportation habit? What if, as a nation, we threw our resources into building a nationwide passenger rail system instead, with high-speed trains operating in and around fifteen or twenty of the major urban areas? The answer is, people would travel just as efficiently, just as fast, and in greater safety. Furthermore, we could stop and probably reverse the degradation of our environment caused by our out-of-balance addiction to the automobile and the airplane. The catch is, it can only be done if people can be convinced that the high-speed train is indeed a reasonable transportation alternative.

Trains Are As Fast As Planes

Well, all right, a train certainly won't get you from New York to California as fast as a passenger jet, but it quite possibly will be comparable for a trip under 300 miles. That's a two-hour run for a high-speed train, and from city center to city center it will give the commercial jet a run for its money.

It's hardly state of the art, but consider Amtrak's Metroliner service between New York City and Washington, D.C. Even today, those trains will take you from Washington's Union Station (just a few hundred yards from the Capitol) to midtown Manhattan in just a tad under three hours. Try doing that by air! You'll be hard-pressed to make it any quicker (taxi from the Capitol to the airport; wait to check in, board, take off; another very long cab ride into Manhattan). No wonder almost half of the people traveling between New York and Washington are now doing so, relaxed and in comfort, on the train. Running over the same tracks, a European-style, high-speed train could cut the time between those cities by another twenty to forty minutes.

It could, and will: Amtrak has been evaluating high-speed trainsets from Denmark, Sweden, and Germany. A preferred design will be selected, and the first truly high-speed trains are expected to go into service sometime in 1999. Furthermore, Amtrak is electrifying the final portion of the Northeast Corridor between New Haven, Connecticut, and Boston, and it is also spending a good deal of money to straighten out many of the curves along that section. The eventual result will be faster running times all the way from Boston to Washington, D.C.

The fact is, when we fly, 300 to 400 miles is the distance most of us travel most often. That's certainly the case at Chicago's O'Hare Airport, the busiest in the nation, where over 40 percent of the arriving flights are from destinations 300 miles away or less. (O'Hare is typical, not unique: The number is almost the same for Los Angeles International, and it is over 50 percent at San Francisco International and New York's Kennedy Airport.) Proponents of high-speed rail have long argued that trains could carry people between Chicago and other nearby cities in the Midwest—Milwaukee, St. Louis, Indianapolis, Ft. Wayne, Toledo, Detroit, Cincinnati, and a host of smaller towns— faster, cheaper, and safer than planes. They're already doing it in Europe, after all. Alas, because of crowded skies around Chicago from air traffic at O'Hare and Midway airports, and because of pressure to provide even more flights, a third major airport south of the city is being pushed by some political leaders. The cost would be staggering—billions of dollars, thousands of acres of land, displacement of homes and businesses, not to mention the impact on the environment.

High-Speed Rail Is Cheaper to Build

Yes, it is! Depending on the terrain, it costs anywhere from $50 million to $200 million per mile to build a typical interstate highway. New modern airports are currently costing $2 billion to $5 billion each, and depending on which expert you talk to, this country supposedly "needs" from ten to twenty new ones. You and I will be paying for those airports, of course, either with our tax dollars or in the form of higher airfares, which the airlines must charge to cover the increased landing fees they'll be forced to pay. The cost for building a high-speed rail system? Again, depending on the terrain, it will cost about $30 million per mile—and that includes the trains themselves. Even exotic new maglev (magnetic levitation) systems are cheaper to build than highways or airports.

Trains Are Better for the Environment

This one is a slam dunk for rail. New highways and airports gobble up thousands of acres of land (land that never again generates property taxes for the local governments, by the way). Particulate pollution from automobiles and jet planes fills the air in most of our major cities, where it's measured and actually calculated by the ton. In his foreword to *Supertrains,* author Tom Clancy offers an extreme but illustrative example. He points out that "the Concorde . . . weighs 400,000 pounds when it takes off from the United States and 200,000 when it lands in England, having left 100 tons of fuel in its supersonic wake." Then there's the problem of noise pollution.

Electrically powered high-speed trains, on the other hand, have no exhaust and therefore emit no pollution. The amount of land used by two parallel tracks is obviously a great deal less than would be required for an interstate highway—in fact, in many instances, the rail line would be built along the existing highway's right-of-way. As far as noise is concerned, a high-speed train is roughly as loud as a stream of traffic, the difference being that noise from the automobiles is virtually continuous, while the train passes quickly once every twenty to thirty minutes.

Trains Are More Energy-Efficient

This is another easy one. Calculated on a per-passenger-mile basis, a high-speed train uses less than two-thirds the energy consumed by an automobile and only about one-fifth as much as a jet plane. We can really begin to see the potential benefits by comparing energy consumption in the U.S. with areas in Europe where high-speed rail is a viable alternative to the private automobile. On a per capita basis, Americans use almost 450 gallons of gasoline a year, while residents of a typical European city use just over 100 gallons.

Trains Are Safer, Too

Most of us are painfully aware of the carnage that occurs year after year on our highways—roughly 40,000 are killed and many times that number are injured. Statistically, planes are many times safer than automobiles, but there are serious concerns about our ability to maintain that high standard. The airlines of the world are now using about 12,000 planes to carry their passengers, but over the next ten years industry experts say about 7,000 new planes will be added to those fleets. The lion's share will be flying around in American skies. If there is legitimate concern about aviation safety now, how safe will we be with a 60 percent increase in the number of commercial aircraft? And if safety isn't a serious concern, why all the pressure for so many new multibillion-dollar airports?

So how safe are trains really? Well, if done right, a high-speed rail system is perfectly safe. Certainly in the case of the French and Japanese systems, we can take that statement literally—neither system has ever experienced a major accident. Here at home, it is true that Amtrak's safety record has been less than perfect, although I know of no serious accident involving a passenger train where responsibility has been laid at Amtrak's doorstep. In the worst incident, when some forty people were killed, a barge collided with a bridge in dense fog, knocking the tracks out of alignment just moments before the train started across. Over its twenty-six-year history, Amtrak has compiled an excellent safety record, and the fact remains that you're many times safer on a cross-country train ride than you are driving your own car to the local convenience store for a bottle of aspirin.

Ideally—and it's the way they do it in Japan and France—passenger trains should operate on their own exclusive rights-of-way. Except for most of the Northeast corridor, however, Amtrak is forced to share tracks with freight trains, meaning increased traffic operating at vastly different speeds. It's a safe arrangement, but one that often requires slower speeds or lengthy delays for Amtrak trains.

Small Towns Need Trains

Often overlooked in the plane-car-train argument are the thousands of communities all over the U.S. and Canada for which the train is the only public transportation link to the rest of the country. Canada's VIA Rail, for instance, runs a thrice-weekly train that passes through more than eighty tiny communities on its thousand-mile journey north from Winnipeg to Hudson Bay. Amtrak also serves countless little towns all over America that have no airports and are bypassed even by buses. Obviously, high-speed trains will never be a realistic option for most of these communities, but people in these small towns will be more than glad if they can simply keep their existing service—1950s technology and all.

Maglev Is Coming . . . Fast!

Just when we're beginning to grasp the idea of traveling up to 200 miles per hour on land, along comes yet another new transportation technology: magnetic levitation. Think it's some kind of exotic, pie-in-the-sky science fiction? Wrong! Maglev is already here, and it really works. As with so many great ideas, the basic concept is quite simple.

We've all held a magnet in each hand and, by turning them one way or another, felt them either attract or repel each other. In a nutshell, that's how maglev works. Large electrically powered magnets are built into both the train and the guideway; using the pushing and pulling forces, the train can be lifted free of its track and moved forward. As I said, this is not futuristic stuff. Maglev vehicles are currently being run on test tracks in several parts of the world, and one, in Japan, has reached a speed of 323 miles per hour. Engineers in Japan say that there is no reason why a speed of 600 miles an hour can't be achieved. (Perhaps passenger terror would be considered a valid reason. Clearly, there must come a point when, no matter how smooth the ride might be, extreme speeds at ground level become fearful for anyone without the psyche of a test pilot.)

Because the maglev train has literally no contact with the guideway, there is no friction and virtually no sound. Witnesses at a maglev test track in Germany reported being able to hear a pair of crows cawing nearby while the train was racing by.

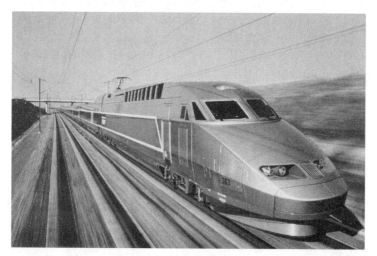

France's high-speed trains, the TGV, now routinely operate at speeds approaching 200 mph.

Although potentially able to travel much faster than today's bullet trains and France's TGV, a maglev system offers virtually the same benefits: It's energy-efficient, pollution-free, and quite safe. Furthermore, once all testing and certification have been completed and maglev trains can be ordered up "off the shelf," best estimates now say that the cost of building a maglev system will be about the same as for high-speed rail. Even if you have just a casual interest in this futuristic stuff, stay tuned—you ain't seen nothin' yet!

First, Some Little Steps

Maglev is all well and good, but the more immediate problem is to keep our conventional rail system up and running until a few more people in power see the light. To that end, Amtrak has some modest plans for the near future, which could mean some significant improvement in rail service for at least a few parts of the country. The short-term goal is to find a way to increase the average speed of its trains along some of the busier eastern routes. Too many curves along some stretches of track are now preventing trains from going faster; where the track is straighter, the existing equipment is already operating at top speed.

Within the past few years, Amtrak has tested two European trains for possible use in this country. First was the Swedish X-2000, which features computer-controlled cars that tilt as the train rounds curves, helping to neutralize the effects of centrifugal force on passengers and allowing the train to travel at higher average speeds. Soon after the X-2000, Amtrak tested a German ICE (Intercity Express), which is now operating at speeds up to 186 miles per hour on some of the new rail lines in that country. Amtrak put both the Swedish and the German trains into service on regular runs in several areas. The results, including reactions from passengers, have been analyzed and will be used to prepare specifications for high-speed equipment to be built specifically for Amtrak's needs. The problem, as always, will be money.

What About the S-Word?

That's S for subsidy, which is still considered a dirty word by many. Strangely, there are those who see nothing wrong with heavy government support of municipal bus systems but are opposed to any subsidy where Amtrak is concerned. Yet in one way or another government subsidizes every form of public transportation. There are no exceptions. Government builds highways for cars and buses; government builds airports for planes; government even builds bike paths and sidewalks.

But wait, you say, government doesn't subsidize American or Delta or United Airlines, so why should the taxpayers assist Amtrak? Ah, but government *does* subsidize the airlines. There are lots of examples, but the most obvious is our nationwide air traffic control system, which is run by the FAA, an agency of the federal government. Amtrak and all the other private railroads have traffic control systems, too, but they pay all the costs themselves. Cities and states float bonds to build and expand airports (Honolulu International Airport has been under construction to one degree or another without interruption since the early 1960s). Remember, too, that you and I pay a special tax on every airline ticket we buy. That money goes into a separate trust fund and is spent to advance the aviation industry.

Not one rail system in the world, which is intended for the use of the general public, is not subsidized by government. So why do some politicians continue to insist that Amtrak should be able to provide a nationwide rail transportation system without assistance from the government? The answer is ignorance, misinformation, and lack of vision, because it's so clear to many of us that for some very important reasons—environmental, economic, and social—rail should be the one means of transportation government encourages, not discourages.

Amtrak Is (Probably) Going to Make It

There are those in this country—people who know a great deal about trains and the transportation industry—who are worried about the future of rail travel in North America. And well they should be. After all, for twelve years it was a stated goal of the Reagan and Bush administrations to do away with any subsidy for Amtrak, and there are plenty of anti-rail people left in Congress at a time when budget cutting is on everyone's mind. Still, in spite of it all, there is some cause for hope if not optimism.

First and foremost, I suppose, given even passable equipment and service, Americans have made it abundantly clear that they like trains. Long-distance trains in particular run full much of the year, particularly in the sleeping cars. During the summer months, even Amtrak critics agree that the company could double the number of trains and still fill them up.

Second, in spite of tremendous handicaps, Amtrak is getting its act together little by little. In fact, Amtrak can actually lay claim to being the most cost-efficient national rail system in the world by at least one very important yardstick: The company's revenue now covers a full 80 percent of its operating costs. No other public rail system anywhere can come close to that. By comparison, VIA Rail Canada recovers about 60 percent of its operating costs from revenues.

Make no mistake, however: Amtrak will always need support from federal and state governments. Indeed, eleven states already subsidize certain Amtrak trains operating within their borders because they recognize that those trains are providing essential transportation links for their citizens.

What Amtrak really needs—in fact, all Amtrak has ever needed—is a stable source of adequate funding. The key words are *stable* and *adequate*. How can Amtrak be expected to plan for the orderly replacement of worn-out equipment, for example, if it has no idea from one year to the next how much support it will be getting from the federal government?

With stable and adequate funding, however, Amtrak could do what it wants to do: buy new equipment, reduce mechanical breakdowns, provide more trains on its popular routes, run them at more convenient times, improve on-time performance, and (this is my own personal addition to the list) wash every window on every train every day.

What You Can Do

There is a lot every one of us can do to preserve a national rail passenger system in both the U.S. and Canada, and none of it is very difficult.

Write letters   In the U.S., we all get to vote for (or against) one member of Congress, two U.S. senators, and the president. Letters from constituents are effective. Nothing will have more impact. Keep each letter short and to the point. Tell them you think the United States should have a decent passenger rail system and that you favor consistent adequate support for Amtrak by the federal government. North of our border, elements in the Canadian government have also been chipping away at VIA Rail. Here again, letters from constituents directed at elected representatives are the single most effective means of affecting any government policy.

Join the club   There are many nonprofit groups around the country that actively promote rail transportation at the state and local levels. I include a list of these groups in Appendix E. The organization focusing on Congress and the current administration in Washington, D.C., is the National Association of Railroad Passengers, more commonly referred to as NARP. If you're interested in supporting Amtrak and advancing the cause of high-speed rail, I encourage you to join. For more information, call 202-408-8362. Annual dues are $24 and half that for those under twenty-one or over sixty-five years of age. Mail your check to National Association of Railroad Passengers, 900 Second Street, NE, Washington, D.C. 20002.

Take a train ride!   Amtrak needs the money. For that matter, VIA Rail does, too. Besides, now that you've read this book, you'll certainly know how to get the most possible enjoyment from the trip.

Okay, then . . . *All Aboard!*

A Few Suggested Itineraries

ere are some examples of long-distance train trips that will provide plenty of great scenery plus an opportunity for some sightseeing along the way. You won't need many suggestions from me before you begin plotting your own adventures. It will help if you refer to the Amtrak and VIA Rail system maps on pages xvi–xvii and 215. You can begin these trips from any of the principal cities included in the itinerary. For instance, in the Big City Tour, you can start your trip from New York or Boston just as easily as you can from Chicago.

For more detailed information about specific trains mentioned here, refer to Chapter 15, "Now, Where Would You Like to Go?" A number of these itineraries have been specifically suggested because they include only three stopovers and therefore qualify for an Amtrak Explore America fare. Don't worry too much about meeting the three-stop criteria, however. A knowledgeable travel agent can often figure out ways to minimize any extra charge. In fact, I'll show you one of the best ways in a couple of the itineraries following.

Finally, you should also get a hold of the latest edition of Amtrak's Travel Planner, which includes a good variety of preplanned rail tours. You can obtain a free copy by calling Amtrak's Great American Vacations at 800-321-8684.

Big City Tour

CHICAGO–WASHINGTON, D.C.–
NEW YORK CITY–BOSTON–CHICAGO

Take the *Capitol Limited* from Chicago to Washington, because the very pretty stretch east from Pittsburgh will all be during daylight hours and you'll have a convenient, early afternoon arrival in Washington. Plan to spend at least several days in Washington, then head up to New York City. Take a Metroliner so you can experience a 125-mile-per-hour train ride. New York is worth several days, too: museums, Broadway shows, great restaurants. Train 172, the *Mayflower,* is a good choice when you go up to Boston. It's more scenic, as it runs along the Connecticut shoreline and has a nice midafternoon arrival. Italian food in the North End, the Red Sox at Fenway Park, and colonial history all over town—Boston has got it all! From here, take the *Lake Shore Limited* across New York State, along three of the Great Lakes, and back into Chicago.

This trip stays entirely within the eastern zone and includes three stopovers, thus qualifying for the lowest fare.

Glaciers to Glitz

SAN FRANCISCO–SEATTLE–GLACIER PARK–
CHICAGO–TRUCKEE–SAN FRANCISCO

If you want variety, this itinerary certainly has it. First, hop the northbound *Coast Starlight* for one of the more scenic rides in the Amtrak system, through the Cascade Mountains on up to Seattle. From there, board the *Empire Builder;* after more of the Cascades, get off at either Essex or Glacier Park in Montana while you're still in the

Rockies. Catch the same train a few days later, whenever you're ready, and head east to Chicago. See the sights in the Windy City, then head west on the *California Zephyr* through the Rockies and across the desert to Truckee, a wonderful little town in the Sierra Nevadas. After a day or so, catch the *Zephyr* once again and continue over Donner Pass and into San Francisco. (Actually, you'll get off in Emeryville, near Oakland, and an Amtrak bus will take you into San Francisco.)

Sharp eyes will note that this itinerary includes four stops (Seattle, Glacier Park, Chicago, and Truckee), which is not permitted on an Explore America fare. The solution is to use that special fare from San Francisco as far as Truckee, which includes most of the itinerary. Then buy a coach seat on a regular fare for the relatively short daytime ride from Truckee to San Francisco. That's one of the tricks of the trade a smart travel agent can help you with.

Oh, Canada!

CHICAGO–TORONTO–VANCOUVER–
SEATTLE–SAN FRANCISCO–CHICAGO

Let's plug VIA Rail into this itinerary, specifically that famous ride across the Canadian Rockies. From Chicago, take the *International* through Battle Creek (home of the cornflake) to Toronto. Try the glass elevator to the top of the CN tower, or see a baseball game at Sky Dome. Then settle into those great sleeping-car accommodations on the *Canadian* for the 3,000-mile trip across Canada to Vancouver. From there you take Amtrak's *Mount Baker International* back across the U.S. border to Seattle, where you can spend a few days before catching the *Coast Starlight* down through the Cascade Mountains to San Francisco. Then catch the *California Zephyr* back through our own Rockies and across the Corn Belt to Chicago.

The Santa Fe Trail

CHICAGO–DODGE CITY–SANTA FE–
GRAND CANYON–LOS ANGELES–CHICAGO

Here's one trip that takes advantage of the special air/rail fares Amtrak has worked out with United Airlines. It also involves just one train, the *Southwest Chief,* but what a trip it is. You leave Chicago in the late afternoon, crossing the Mississippi just after dark. If you are a western history buff, you'll enjoy spending a day in Dodge City and visiting Boot Hill. Then move on to Santa Fe, where you'll be dazzled by the silver jewelry made by Native American craftspeople. Two or three days here is a must. Get back on the *Chief,* this time getting off at Flagstaff, Arizona. The Grand Canyon is just eighty miles away, and an Amtrak bus will take you there the next morning. (Do they think of everything, or what!) It will be bedtime when you reboard the train a day or so later, so get a good night's sleep and be ready for an early morning arrival in Los Angeles. Take your time seeing the sights in L.A., then fly straight back to Chicago—it's all part of your air/rail fare. If you live on the West Coast, you can take this same trip in reverse order. The one thing you can't do, of course, is begin this itinerary somewhere in the middle.

The Grand Tour

NEW YORK CITY–WASHINGTON, D.C.–ORLANDO (DISNEY
WORLD)–NEW ORLEANS–LOS ANGELES–SAN FRANCISCO–
SEATTLE–CHICAGO–BOSTON–NEW YORK CITY

With this trip, you can say you traveled around the country and mean it literally. From New York, take the *Silver Meteor* south along the Atlantic coast to Washington and then on to Disney World in Orlando. Then hop the *Silver Star* for a short ride up to Jacksonville and a connection with the *Sunset Limited,* which will take you along the Gulf of Mexico, across the mighty Mississippi at New Orleans, and within a few feet of the Mexican border near El Paso. In Los Angeles, connect with the *Coast Starlight* and travel north with the Pacific Ocean in plain sight off to your left. From Seattle, head east across Big Sky Country on the *Empire Builder,* which comes within twenty-five miles of Canada. From Chicago, you'll run along the shores of three of the Great Lakes on the *Lake Shore Limited,* and from Boston you will end up back at Long Island Sound on the *Yankee Clipper.* When you stop and think about it, that's really quite remarkable, especially when you consider the variety of people and cultures and activities you'll encounter in all those cities along the way.

Semi-Grand Tour

SEATTLE–CHICAGO–NEW ORLEANS–
LOS ANGELES–SAN FRANCISCO–SEATTLE

For this abbreviated version of our round-the-country trip, we just lop off the eastern part of the country. We start in Seattle, heading east on the *Empire Builder* to Chicago. There, we take the *City of New Orleans* due south to that very same city. After at least several days of good food and great music, you take the *Sunset Limited* to Los Angeles, connecting with the *Coast Starlight* for the run up the California coast to San Francisco, then on up through Oregon and back to Seattle.

Fall Colors I

PHILADELPHIA–PITTSBURGH–CHICAGO–
WASHINGTON, D.C.–PHILADELPHIA

If you can time things so you hit the peak of the fall colors, this will be a sensational trip. Take the *Pennsylvanian* from Philadelphia to Pittsburgh, because the entire ride is done during daylight hours. Stay over for a day or so if you wish, or have a nice dinner while waiting for the *Capitol Limited,* which comes through later in the evening en route to

Chicago. From there, take the *Cardinal* back to Washington, D.C. It's a glorious trip any time of the year, but it's really something special in the fall. After a few days in Washington, zip back to Philadelphia on a Metroliner.

Fall Colors II

NEW YORK CITY–SARATOGA SPRINGS–
TICONDEROGA–MONTREAL–NEW YORK CITY
You can wait until the foliage is at its peak, then take this trip on a weekend with just a shoulder bag. Take the *Adirondack* north out of New York City up the Hudson River to Albany, then cross into Canada. Spend the night in Montreal—there's an excellent hotel that's actually part of the station complex (see Appendix B). Take the same train back to New York the next day.

Take this same train during the summertime if you have a week or ten days, and it becomes quite a different trip. First stop is Saratoga Springs, which is quite the spot during racing season. Next, soak up some history in the museum at Fort Ticonderoga, and spend a day or two in the Lake George area. Lake Placid is just a few miles away, too. Then meet up with the *Adirondack* again and head up to Montreal. While there, if you're interested in historical sites, visit Quebec City. It's less than three hours away by VIA Rail's Train 24, the *Chaudière*. This eighteenth-century city will keep you fascinated for at least two or three days. Then it's back to Montreal, to catch the *Adirondack* home to New York.

Southern Comfort

WASHINGTON, D.C.–ATLANTA–NEW ORLEANS–
MOBILE–JACKSONVILLE–CHARLESTON–WASHINGTON, D.C.
You start this tour of our southern states aboard the *Crescent,* which leaves Washington, D.C., at dinner time and reaches Atlanta just after breakfast. Stop for a visit

here if you wish, or stay aboard all the way to New Orleans. When you're finally ready to leave (it could be several days), catch the eastbound *Sunset Limited*. You can either get off in Mobile (they say the Deep South is actually north of this city!) or stay aboard across the Florida panhandle to Jacksonville. As long as you're here, you really should take an extra day for a visit to St. Augustine, just thirty miles to the south. Back in Jacksonville, you catch the *Silver Meteor* north for Charleston, South Carolina, then board the *Silver Palm* a day or so later for the ride back to Washington. You travel through all that beautiful Carolina and Virginia countryside during daylight hours, arriving in time for dinner.

Travel with a Reason

Somehow, train trips seem to be more successful if a specific purpose is woven into them. Think about putting together a rail itinerary based on a special interest or hobby: the Old West, the Civil War, major league baseball, rail museums, prospective colleges for your sixteen-year-old son or daughter, visits to old friends, and so on and so forth. As you can see, the opportunities and possibilities are almost endless. Take your time. The only thing more fun than the planning is the doing.

Good Places to Stay

Elsewhere in this book I've warned against trying to make close connections when changing trains on long-distance train trips. For many different reasons, trains can be late—sometimes very late—and missed connections are often the unpleasant result. If that happens, at the very least you will be inconvenienced and your carefully planned train excursion will be badly disrupted. It's just much safer to break up your trip with an overnight stay.

You can choose to stop and spend a few nights anywhere along the way during a rail journey, but the cities included here are the most common connecting points in rail itineraries. A look at the system maps for Amtrak and VIA Rail will show you at a glance how the routes intersect.

All of the hotels mentioned are close to the railroad station, and while only a few are what I would call "ritzy," you will find them all to be clean, well-appointed, and quite satisfactory. Some even offer rather special experiences, which have been so noted. Please bear in mind that the principal criteria here is convenience to the railroad station. To me, that's of primary importance if you're overnighting in a city—perhaps arriving in the afternoon on one train and leaving the next morning on another. If you're going to be in one of these cities for several days, however, proximity to the station could be of less importance than being more centrally located.

I have provided only a general indication as to what you might expect to pay at any of these hotels. For one thing, rates can change dramatically, depending on the day of the week or the season. Furthermore, it's all relative, anyway. A room rate of $100 might be expensive in one city and very moderate in another. As a general rule, though, you can expect to pay somewhere between $75 and $150 per night at most of these hotels. Some of them will be more, however.

Chicago, Illinois

THE MIDLAND HOTEL
172 West Adams (at LaSalle)
Chicago, IL 60603
312-332-1200

If you're traveling by rail from almost anywhere in the east to almost anywhere in the west, you'll probably have to change trains in Chicago, which explains why more rail connections occur here than at any other point in the Amtrak system. Consider that a real plus, because Chicago itself is all the reason you need for breaking your trip for a day or so. Union Station, which has recently undergone extensive renovation, is smack downtown on Canal Street, literally in the shadow of the Sears Tower. Also nearby on the shore of Lake Michigan is an outstanding aquarium, not to mention a galaxy of shops and stores and museums. Then, of course, there are the Cubs, the White Sox, the Bulls, the Bears, and the Blackhawks!

The Midland Hotel is closest to Union Station, and happily, it's a delightful hotel: reasonable rates, not too big, and recently redone in original art deco, which seems to fit well with the Golden Age of train travel. The staff is genuinely friendly, from the hotel's telephone operator to the general manager. Guests get a complimentary full breakfast buffet (including made-to-order omelets) and a free drink during the afternoon cocktail hour. The hotel's other restaurant, called The Exchange, is really outstanding. It's a bit of a walk to the station, but the hotel will take you there free in its own English taxi, as long as you give them some advance notice.

Chihuahua City, Mexico

HOTEL SICOMORO
411 Boulevard Ortiz Mena
Chihuahua, Chih. C. P. 31230
Telephone: (14) 13-54-45; 800-448-6970 (in the U.S.)

Chihuahua City is the eastern jump-off point for the rail trip through the Copper Canyon, and you'll almost certainly want to spend at least one night here before embarking on that trip. The Hotel Sicomoro is not within walking distance from the railroad station, but never mind—the taxi ride will take less than ten minutes and will cost less than U.S. $2. The rooms in this low-rise hotel are not deluxe, but they are quite comfortable and comparable to most medium-priced U.S. hotel chains. If you're not conversant in Spanish, don't worry about it. The hotel staff is genuinely friendly, and whether at the front desk or in the restaurant, most everyone speaks enough English that you'll have no problem communicating. There is a nice pool, which you'll appreciate, because Chihuahua can get very hot! There is also quite a good restaurant. The hotel bar features live entertainment almost every night.

Creel, Mexico

THE LODGE AT CREEL
61 Lopez Mateos
Creel, Chih. C. P. 33200
Telephone: (14) 56-00-71

As noted in Chapter 14, Creel is a logging town, and quite appropriately, this little hotel is comprised of a number of log structures scattered around a rather dusty parking area. But don't let the initial impression discourage you. First of all, the people who greet you are fluent in English and extremely cordial. The main building is a combination reception/dining area with a very comfortable if rustic feel to it. The individual units are spacious, quite comfortable, and even include television sets with CNN available. The town's water supply is questionable, but the hotel—part of the Best Western chain—supplies bottles of purified water in every room. You can get breakfast in the hotel, but for other meals they will direct you across the street to El Caballo, which I was told—and do not doubt—is the best restaurant in this little town. They serve excellent food at very reasonable prices.

Denver, Colorado

THE OXFORD HOTEL
1600 17th Street
Denver, CO 80202
800-228-5838

One of Amtrak's biggest and most popular trains, the *California Zephyr,* passes through Denver. A lot of people elect to get off here and continue their journey after a few days of touring in and around the Mile High City.

The Oxford Hotel is, in my humble opinion, worth an overnight stay in Denver. Located literally a few hundred yards from the main entrance to Denver's Union Station, it's undeniably the city's oldest hotel, first opening in 1891. If it's possible for a small hotel to be grand at the same time, this one is. The owners spent a great deal of money restoring the Oxford in the 1980s, and the result is a wonderful, tasteful elegance. For example, sherry is served to hotel guests every afternoon at 4:00 in the lobby. No two rooms are alike, each being decorated individually, and many come with very nice antique furniture. Oh, yes, there are real down pillows on the beds—always the mark of a hotel that goes a step or two beyond the cosmetic. The rates are reasonable, too.

Divisadero, Mexico

HOTEL DIVISADERO BARRANCAS

This hotel is located within 100 yards of the railroad station, and is literally within inches of the canyon's rim—I'm not exaggerating! You can step out of your room, take three paces to a railing, and gaze out on a view that includes not one but three interlocking canyons. Look down—almost straight down—and you'll see buzzards circling lazily a thousand feet or more below. The main dining area features two huge picture windows with sofas and chairs arranged around them. No wonder: Guests sit there for hours, just absorbing the view as the shadows change on the canyon walls. The rooms are comfortable, but there are individual peculiarities in many of them. For example, I'm an even six feet tall but had to duck when walking through the doorway into the bathroom to avoid whacking my head (I became aware of that the hard way!). You eat all your meals at the hotel, unless you buy some of the tasty snacks served up by vendors who appear magically whenever a train arrives. There is no television here, although the hotel does have a separate lounge with a VCR. And forget about the telephone! The only communication is by radio, and it's sometimes a hassle getting through. In an emergency, contact the hotel's sales office in Chihuahua: (14) 16-51-36 or (14) 10-33-30.

Essex, Montana

ISAAK WALTON INN
Essex, MT 59936
406-888-5700

Okay, so this isn't one of the great railroad centers of our country, but Essex is a kind of mecca for rail enthusiasts, because it's located right on the Burlington Northern's main line and a lot of rail traffic, including Amtrak's *Empire*

Builder, goes through here all day long. By the way, Essex is located on the southern edge of Glacier National Park, which means it's smack in the middle of some truly glorious country.

The Isaak Walton Inn is perfectly situated just a 100 yards or so from the tracks; railfans/guests hang out at the hotel watching, waving, and clicking away with their cameras as the trains rumble by. The hotel staff gives new meaning to the word "friendly," the rooms are rather plain but spotless, and the price is right. Several "deluxe" units have been created from old cabooses. Clearly, this hotel isn't for everyone, but I do think most folks who spend a day or so here will agree that it was worth doing.

Los Angeles, California

THE NEW OTANI HOTEL & GARDEN
120 South Los Angeles Street
Los Angeles, CA 90012
800-421-8795

Three of Amtrak's long-distance trains originate in Los Angeles: the *Southwest Chief* to Chicago, the *Coast Starlight* to Seattle, and the transcontinental *Sunset Limited* to Sanford, Florida. In addition, the *San Diegan*s depart several times daily on their three-hour trip to the south. All of this rail activity means you may well have need to spend a night or two here between trains. Of course Los Angeles is so sprawled out, it makes even more sense to pick a nice hotel as near as possible to Los Angeles Union Passenger Terminal as your headquarters. (By the way, while you're there, take a few minutes to enjoy a look around this great old station.)

The New Otani is just 4¹/₂ blocks away and is a doable walk from the station, unless you're weighed down with baggage. I recommend taking a taxi from the station to the New Otani late at night, even though it's a fascinating part of town. The hotel is in an area known as Little Tokyo, but quite close by is Oliveira Street, well known for food booths and shops selling clothing, food, jewelry, and many other items mostly with a Latin American flavor. The hotel itself features well-appointed rooms, excellent restaurants, and a lovely Japanese garden.

Los Mochis, Mexico

HOTEL SANTA ANITA
Leyva and Hidalgo
Los Mochis, Sinaloa
800-896-8196

The railroad station serving Los Mochis is not located near the center of town, and it's probably a fifteen- to twenty-minute ride to the Hotel Santa Anita. Taxis are very inexpensive, and (at least on the night I arrived) the hotel had a free shuttle bus waiting for passengers staying there. The hotel itself is a high-rise building, and the rooms are quite nice, including television offering both English and Spanish language channels. Also, as I had come to expect, the staff was helpful, genuinely friendly, and conversant in English.

Montreal, Quebec

THE QUEEN ELIZABETH
900 René Levesque Boulevard
Montreal, Quebec H3B 4A5 Canada
514-861-3511

This is a wonderful city in which to find yourself between trains. Many Americans are surprised to discover that it is very much a French city. In fact, Montreal is the second largest French-speaking city in the world (yes, Paris is number one). Coming into Canada by train from the U.S., you'll either end up here or in Toronto. Whether your rail itinerary has you going from here to Toronto and points west or east to New Brunswick and Nova Scotia, you'll probably want to lay over here.

The Hotel Queen Elizabeth is actually part of the huge Montreal railroad station complex, and you can literally walk from your hotel room to your train or the local subway without going out of doors (for four or five months a year, that's a distinct advantage!). In fact, the hotel sits right above an eighteen-mile network of underground promenades, with a large variety of shops and restaurants. The hotel is well furnished, offers two excellent restaurants, and has every amenity you would expect from a top-quality hotel. Royalty from many countries have stopped here—including Queen Elizabeth II. The hotel has quite a spread of rates, so you can opt for the very plush if you wish. Rates for the rest of us begin at about U.S. $100.

New Orleans, Louisiana

MAISON DUPUY
1001 Rue Toulouse
New Orleans, LA 70112
800-535-9177

I include New Orleans on this list of cities, because this is where you will get off the *Sunset Limited* coming from Los Angeles and other cities in the Southwest before connecting with the *City of New Orleans* (for Chicago and other cities along the Mississippi) or with the *Crescent* (for Atlanta, Washington, D.C., Philadelphia, and New York City). I trust it's not necessary to talk about why you should consider a stopover here.

The Maison Dupuy (pronounced doo-PWEE), which is located in the French Quarter, has almost 200 rooms. The atmosphere, however, is very much that of a small, intimate hotel. It has just undergone a complete renovation, with a lovely courtyard that's an ideal spot to sit and relax with a cool drink on a steamy afternoon. There's no need to leave the hotel in search of a great meal, either; its restaurant,

Dominique's, is absolutely outstanding, even in a city noted for exceptional cuisine. Maison Dupuy will be a bit pricey for some, but there really isn't another hotel that I would recommend within walking distance of the Amtrak station. This hotel is just a bit over a mile from the station (a quick taxi ride), and it's a charming place for an overnight stay in what is certainly one of America's more charming cities.

New York, New York

HOTEL PENNSYLVANIA
401 Seventh Avenue
New York, NY 10001
212-736-5000

Lots of rail connections are made here, too, since New York is the terminus for trains originating in several cities, including Boston, Montreal, Toronto, Chicago, New Orleans, and Miami. For years, trains from the north and west arrived in New York at Grand Central Terminal, while Florida trains and those from other southern cities ended up at Pennsylvania Station. More often than not, passengers making connections in New York City had to deal with a crosstown cab ride as they transferred bag and baggage from one station to the other. No more. After a bypass was completed in 1994, all of Amtrak's long-distance trains now use Penn Station. It's certainly more convenient, but a magnificent era ended when Grand Central was relegated to serving only northbound commuters, and veteran rail travelers still suffer real pangs at that thought.

The Hotel Pennsylvania is probably the best choice for rail travelers coming to New York City, especially if you'll be continuing on to another destination the following day. It's neither new (it was built in 1919) nor swank (although a $20 million renovation is under way), but the rates are reasonable and it does have a wonderful kind of brassy ambiance that's somehow just right. The hotel is also directly across the street from Penn Station, and if like me you put a high value on convenience, this is where you should land for a night or two in New York City. At the hotel, you will find two restaurants (one is an Irish pub), and a number of other restaurants are nearby. The hotel is a stone's throw to the new Madison Square Garden, home of the Rangers and the Knicks, and not much farther to the Broadway theaters. Fans of the big bands from the 1940s and 1950s will find it easy to remember the hotel's phone number: *PEnnsylvania 6-5000!*

Oakland, California

WATERFRONT PLAZA HOTEL
10 Washington Street
Oakland, CA 94607
800-729-3638

The old Oakland station was damaged beyond repair by an earthquake several years ago and it may have been a blessing in disguise. It was located in a not-so-nice neighborhood with no decent nearby hotels. That's all changed now. The Amtrak station for Oakland is now smack in the middle of Jack London Square, a shopping/dining/entertainment complex . . . and quite a good place to be if, for example, you're overnighting in Oakland to make a connection from the *Coast Starlight* to the *California Zephyr.*

The Waterfront Plaza is an integral part of Jack London Square, meaning you're within walking distance of some forty-five shops and twenty restaurants. It's located right on San Francisco Bay and just two blocks from the railroad station. This is not a large hotel and, although there are 144 rooms, it has the feel of a much smaller place. The rooms themselves are very nice and some have balconies overlooking the bay. And fireplaces! The hotel's restaurant is quite good and room service is offered. If you'll be there long enough for a trip into San Francisco, there are numerous public transportation alternatives, including a ferry which departs almost literally from the hotel's doorstep.

Portland, Oregon

THE BENSON HOTEL
309 SW Broadway
Portland, OR 97205
503-228-2000

This is another of America's very nice cities and a good place for a stopover—perhaps you will be connecting from the *Coast Starlight* to the *Empire Builder*. The Benson Hotel is about ten blocks from the Amtrak station, so you'll probably want to take a taxi if you're toting any more than a shoulder bag (as in Seattle, taxis are very inexpensive, and city buses in the downtown area are free).

The hotel was built by Simon Benson, one of the area's great lumber barons. When it opened in 1912, the Benson was the tallest building in the city, as well as the first to boast electric lights and elevators. There was a major renovation just a few years ago, which did a wonderful job of restoring the hotel's original luster. There are two very good restaurants in the hotel, particularly the London Grille. Best of all, the rates are affordable, which makes it the obvious choice for an overnight stay if you're making rail connections in Portland.

Seattle, Washington

INN AT VIRGINIA MASON
1006 Spring Street
Seattle, WA 98104
800-283-6453

Seattle is a wonderful place to layover between trains for a few days. For example, you could come up from Southern

California on the *Coast Starlight* and, after spending a few days here, head east on the *Empire Builder*. In any event, there's a lot to see and do in a fairly compact area. It's easy to be a tourist in Seattle, too, because cab rides are very inexpensive and buses operating in the downtown area are free.

The Inn at Virginia Mason isn't within walking distance from Seattle's railroad station, but it is quite close—not more than a five-minute cab ride. I found it quite by accident several years ago, and I wouldn't stay anywhere else in Seattle. Everything is very tastefully done in a style that's a bit 1920s. The rooms are comfortable, spacious, and reasonably priced. There's a very nice restaurant—it's small, but the food is well prepared and presented. If you want glitz and glamour, you should probably stay someplace else, but something about this little hotel makes you feel at home right away.

Toronto, Ontario

THE ROYAL YORK HOTEL
100 Front Street West
Toronto, Ontario M5J 1E3 Canada
416-368-2155

This is Canada's second largest city and, we're told, the most ethnically diverse city in North America. This is where you can board VIA Rail's premiere train, the *Canadian,* for one of the world's great train rides—through the wilderness and across the western mountains en route to Vancouver on the Pacific Coast. What could be more fitting than to spend a night or two in a wonderful hotel before embarking on a wonderful ride on a wonderful train?

The Royal York Hotel is one of several magnificent hotels built by the Canadian Pacific Railroad along its route across that country. The hotel is very dignified, very elegant, and—yes, I'm afraid so—pricey. It is, however, an experience worth having at least once. The Royal York is located smack across the street from Toronto's cathedral-like train station. In fact, when you check out of the hotel, the bellhops will place your luggage on a brass cart and roll it right across the street for you, setting your bags down where you check in for your train.

Washington, D.C.

PHOENIX PARK HOTEL
520 N. Capitol Street, NW
Washington, D.C. 20001
202-638-6900

If you travel by train, chances are you'll pass through Washington sooner or later. It's the logical place to make connections when you're traveling between the Midwest and the South or from New Orleans to any-where in the northeast. For goodness sake, take advantage of that! This city is worth a visit of at least several days. The renovation and restoration of Union Station was completed several years ago, and it is once again a magnificent edifice. In its own right it has become a gathering place for Washingtonians working on the Hill—and justly so. There are numerous shops and several excellent restaurants. From the station, you can also walk to the Capitol and the buildings that house the Congressional and Senate offices. Before you leave home, contact the office of your congressperson or senator. One of his or her staff people will be glad to take you on a tour of the Capitol and can also arrange for visits to the White House, FBI headquarters, and other interesting places. Then there's the Smithsonian Institution, which alone is worth several days of your time.

The Phoenix Park Hotel is almost literally a stone's throw from Union Station, and it will without question be your most convenient choice if you're just going to be in Washington overnight between trains. The owners of the hotel are Irish, and that's the theme throughout, including live Irish music every night in the Dubliner restaurant. The building itself has undergone a renovation, and all the rooms have been redecorated very attractively. However, I'm afraid its convenient location is really the only reason I mention it here. Some of the rooms are very small with rates that are high even by Washington's inflated standards. On a recent visit there, my wife and I were put in a room so tiny it was able to accommodate just one standard-size double bed. And there was no window! Unfortunately, the hotel was full that night and no other rooms were available. The next morning, I was told that renovations had not been completed on that particular room and that eventually a window would be added . . . either that, said the desk clerk matter-of-factly, or they would convert the room into a closet! (That certainly would be my recommendation.) Those circumstances notwithstanding, I was charged the full, regular rate of $165. My best advice, therefore, is to consider this hotel if you're arriving late in the day and departing early the next morning; even then, ask to see the room before settling in. Otherwise, shop around for another place to lay your head.

Excursion Trains and Railroad Museums

In preparing this list of scenic train rides throughout North America, every effort was made to be complete and accurate. Nevertheless, it should be used as a guide only, since fares, schedules, and other details of an individual railway's operations can and do change frequently. All of these excursion trains have up-to-date printed material available at no cost, so call or write for current information before making plans for a visit. It should also be noted that this is not a complete list. A number of companies were contacted and asked for information, and they either did not respond or did not do so in time to meet my publication deadline. A more detailed list of excursion trains and rail museums may be found in the *Steam Passenger Service Directory,* which can be ordered through local bookstores or by writing to Great Eastern Publishing, P.O. Box 246, Richmond, Vermont 05477 (or call them at 802-434-2351).

United States

Alaska

ALASKA RAILROAD
P.O. Box 107500
Anchorage, AK 99510
907-265-2494

The Alaska Railroad provides both scheduled passenger and freight service. Since other railroads offer either one service or the other but not both, that makes Alaska Railroad the only full-service railroad in North America. The railroad is also unique because it's a private corporation owned by the state of Alaska. The company operates from the deep-water port of Seward through Anchorage to just beyond Fairbanks, a distance of some 500 miles.

The railroad offers more than a dozen one- and two-day rail/tour packages, which originate in one of those three cities and include a choice of hotel accommodations where appropriate. The departure days and times of these rail tours are so varied, the only practical way to get valid, up-to-date information is to call and ask for one of its comprehensive brochures. In addition to offering tours for visitors to this spectacular state, the trains of Alaska Railroad also provide transportation links for local residents. Equipment is modern and includes coaches, observation dome cars, and dining cars.

Operates:	All year; daily from mid-May to mid-September; winter hours and operations vary, so call for details
Features:	Tour guides travel aboard many trains
Reservations:	800-544-0552

WHITE PASS & YUKON RAILROAD
P.O. Box 435
Skagway, AK 99840
907-983-2217

The train runs from Skagway at sea level to 2,865-foot White Pass summit and beyond to Lake Bennet, a total distance of forty-one miles. Considered an engineering marvel, the route features spectacular mountain scenery, crossing several impressive trestles. At Fraser (mile twenty-eight), the train connects with a bus for White Horse, another eighty-three miles inland.

Operates: Mid-May through mid-September
Features: Gift shop at depot
Reservations: From the U.S.: 800-343-7373; from north-west Canada: 800-478-7373

Arizona

GRAND CANYON RAILWAY
518 E. Bill Williams Avenue
Williams, AZ 86046
602-635-4000

Steam locomotives pull fully restored 1920-vintage passenger cars. This trip begins at the Fray Marcos Hotel & Depot in Williams, Arizona, and terminates at the Grand Canyon Log Depot. Both buildings are on the National Register of Historic Places. The route covers sixty-four miles of high desert plateau country, beginning in the tall ponderosa pine forest around Williams at an elevation of 6,700 feet. From there, the train descends 1,500 feet to the desert grassland area of Willaha, then climbs a 3 percent grade into the forests of Coconino Canyon, finally reaching the 6,800-foot level and its destination at the South Rim of the Grand Canyon.

Operates:	Daily, mid-March through the end of the year; call for schedule at other times of the year.
Features:	Gift shop, railroad museum, breakfast cafe, Wild West entertainment, strolling musicians
Reservations:	800-843-8724

California

CALIFORNIA STATE RAILROAD MUSEUM
111 I Street
Sacramento, CA 95814
916-445-7387; 916-552-5252, ext. 7245 (recorded information)

This is one of the really outstanding railroad museums in the country (probably the world!) and is definitely worth a special trip. It's run by the State of California's Department of Parks and Recreation and hosts more than 600,000 visitors a year. There are twenty-one locomotives and railcars on display, each of which has been meticulously and lovingly restored. In addition, there are numerous displays and exhibits that will keep everyone in the family fascinated for the better part of a day.

Operates:	Museum and library, year-round; steam train rides, April through September
Reservations:	Not required

CALIFORNIA WESTERN RAILROAD
P.O. Box 907
Fort Bragg, CA 95437
707-964-6372

More commonly known as the Skunk Train, steam or diesel locomotives haul passengers from Fort Bragg on the California coast some forty miles inland to Willits. Trains may be boarded at either terminus. The route passes through two deep mountain tunnels, follows the Noya

River, and crosses some thirty bridges and trestles as
it climbs up through the giant redwood forests. Trains
feature coaches and an open observation car. Most trips
during winter months are made in restored sixty-five-
passenger motorcars from the 1920s and 1930s.

Operates: Year-round
Reservations: 707-964-6371

NAPA VALLEY WINE TRAIN
1275 McKinstry Street
Napa, CA 94559
707-253-2111

Passengers enjoy a nonstop gourmet dining experience
aboard lavishly restored 1915 Pullman dining and
lounge cars while following a three-hour, thirty-six-
mile route through the heart of the picturesque Napa
Valley. There is a variety of charges for both the train
ride and the meals, so call for specifics and a schedule
of departures.

Operates: Daily, year-round
Features: Wine shop, art gallery, and boutique
                 at Napa Station
Reservations: 800-522-4142

PORTOLA RAILROAD MUSEUM
P.O. Box 608
Portola, CA 96122
916-832-4131

Visitors to the museum may ride in a diesel-powered
caboose train on a one-mile loop track around the
facility. Museum includes twenty-five locomotives
and more than fifty railcars. With prior arrangement and
at additional fee, visitors can "rent" and operate diesel
locomotives under instruction from a qualified engineer.

Operates: Museum open daily year-round; train rides,
                 Memorial Day to mid-September
Features: Gift shop, snack bar, artifact displays
Reservations: Not required

ROARING CAMP & BIG TREES NARROW GAUGE RAILROAD
P.O. Box G-1
Felton, CA 95018
408-335-4400

Several different steam locomotives haul trains through a
giant redwood forest, past a logging town dating back to
the 1880s, to the top of Bear Mountain. The ride, which
takes about an hour and a quarter, includes the steepest
narrow-gauge railroad grade in North America and some
of the tightest turns.

Operates: Daily except Christmas; may vary January
                 through March
Features: 1880s general store, chuck wagon barbecue,
                 country music; other special activities
                 scheduled periodically
Reservations: 408-335-4484

SANTA CRUZ, BIG TREES & PACIFIC RAILWAY
P.O. Box G-1
Felton, CA 95018
408-335-4400

These trains operate during the summer months, carrying
passengers along the San Lorenzo River between the redwood forest near Felton, California (Roaring Camp) and
Santa Cruz on the coastline. Trains depart from both
Roaring Camp and Santa Cruz several times a day. It's a
one-hour trip each way, and passengers may ride in
coaches or on open flatcars. Railroad also hauls freight
along the same route.

Operates: Mid-May through late November, plus
                 special excursions
Reservations: 408-335-4484

SIERRA RAILWAY COMPANY
(Railtown 1897 State Historic Park)
P.O. Box 1250
Jamestown, CA 95327
209-984-3953

Several steam locomotives haul the "Mother Lode Cannonball" on a twelve-mile ride through the heart of California's Gold Rush country. The company also offers two extended rides: the *Twilight Limited,* with snacks and drinks aboard and a western BBQ upon return; and the *Wine & Cheese Zephyr,* serving a variety of cheeses with selected California wines during the trip.

Operates: Saturday and Sunday only, March through
                 November
Features: Roundhouse, repair and maintenance shop
                 complex, turntable
Reservations: 209-984-3953

WESTERN RAILWAY MUSEUM
560 Railroad Avenue
Hercules, CA 94547
707-374-2978

Rides are confined to antique electric railway cars, but a variety of elegant Pullman cars are on display, along with steam and diesel locomotives.

Operates: Saturday and Sunday, year-round; Wednesday
                 through Sunday during summer months
Features: Carbarns, volunteer guides, bookstore,
                 picnic areas
Reservations: Not required

YOSEMITE MOUNTAIN SUGAR PINE RAILROAD
56001 Highway 41
Fish Camp, CA 93623
209-683-7273

From 1899 to 1931, the Madera Sugar Pine Lumber Company used wood-burning Shay locomotives to haul logs to the sawmill at Sugar Pine. The line has been restored and runs through the scenic Sierra Nevadas at 5,000-feet elevation, winds down a 4 percent grade into Lewis Creek Canyon, and passes through several horseshoe curves—about a forty-five-minute ride altogether. Restored locomotives haul passengers in both open and covered cars; Jenny railcars (self-propelled, trolley-like cars) are used on most weekdays. From June through early October, the railroad operates an evening excursion called the Moonlight Special, which includes a barbecue dinner and music.

Operates:	Jenny railcars: daily, March through October; steam train: daily from mid-May through September, weekends only in October
Features:	Museum, bookstore, gift shop
Reservations:	209-683-7273 (required for Moonlight Special only)

Colorado

CUMBRES & TOLTEC SCENIC RAILROAD
P.O. Box 668
Antonito, CO 81120
719-376-5483

See a description of this railroad in the New Mexico section.

DURANGO & SILVERTON NARROW GAUGE RAILROAD
479 Main Avenue
Durango, CO 81301
303-259-3372

This coal-fired, steam-powered narrow-gauge railroad has been in continuous operation since 1881. The spectacular forty-five-mile route between Durango and Silverton crosses valleys surrounded by red rock cliffs, climbs along mountain ridges with rushing Animas River 400 feet below, and offers vistas of the million-plus-acre San Juan National Forest. The one-way trip takes about three and a half hours; the round-trip is nine hours from start to finish and includes a two-hour layover in Silverton. Overnight layovers may be arranged. An additional train makes one round-trip each day between Durango and Cascade Canyon at special times during the year.

Operates: Mid-April through October, Thanksgiving Day through January 1
Features: Yard tours (additional fee), gift shop, concession car on train
Reservations: 303-247-2733 (four to six weeks in advance)

GEORGETOWN LOOP RAILROAD
P.O. Box 217
Georgetown, CO 80444
303-670-1686

Powered by a steam locomotive, the train runs between the towns of Georgetown and Silver Plume, both rich in mining and railroad history. Route passes through spectacular scenery of pines, aspens, and mountain vistas, including a crossing of the Devil's Gate High Bridge. The ride lasts about one hour and fifteen minutes.

Operates: June 1 through September 30 (dates vary slightly, year to year)
Features: Gift shop, restaurant at Old Georgetown station; optional silver mine tour
Reservations: 303-670-1686

LEADVILLE, COLORADO & SOUTHERN RAILROAD
P.O. Box 916
Leadville, CO 80461
719-486-3936

The train leaves from the Leadville depot and travels through Colorado's high country, following the headwaters of the Arkansas River to a spectacular view of the Fremont Pass and on to a view of Mount Elbert, the highest peak in Colorado. The round-trip lasts about two and a half hours.

Operates: Memorial Day weekend through the first weekend in October
Features: Historic depot, museum/gift shop, concessions
Reservations: 719-486-3936

MANITOU & PIKE'S PEAK RAILWAY
Box 351
Manitou Springs, CO 80829
719-685-1045

This is the world's highest cog railway, operating for more than 100 years from Manitou Springs to the 14,110-foot summit of Pike's Peak. Cars depart every eighty minutes starting at 8:00 A.M. over a route that follows a rushing stream through steep canyons, finally emerging onto Alpine vistas above the timberline. The total number of daily trips varies according to the time of year.

Operates: Daily from the last week of April through the end of October
Features: Gift shop and restaurant at summit
Reservations: 719-685-5401 (advance reservations strongly advised)

Connecticut

THE VALLEY RAILROAD COMPANY
Railroad Avenue
P.O. Box 452
Essex, CT 06426
203-767-0103

Steam and diesel locomotives haul passengers through the Connecticut River Valley in old-fashioned comfort, including a vintage parlor car. At Deep River, passengers can opt to extend their trip by transferring to a river cruise on a multidecked riverboat. The train ride lasts an hour; the train and boat together lasts two and a half hours.

Operates:	Daily, mid-June through Labor Day; call for specifics for other times during the year
Features:	Gift shop, working rail yard, exhibits; snacks available in parlor car en route
Reservations:	203-767-0103

Delaware

QUEEN ANNE'S RAILROAD
730 King's Highway
Lewes, DE 19958
302-644-1720

This company operates an excursion train and the Royal Zephyr Dinner Train through the southern Delaware countryside over what used to be Pennsylvania Railroad track. The excursion trains use open-air heavyweight coaches; the dinner train treats passengers to former New Haven Railroad coaches, which have been completely refurbished. Both diesel and steam locomotives are used.

Operates:	Mid-May through October (days and times vary considerably, so call for details)
Reservations:	302-644-1720

Hawaii

LAHAINA, KAANAPALI & PACIFIC RAILROAD
P.O. Box 816
Lahaina, Maui, HI 96767
808-661-0089

This steam-powered train carries passengers between the old whaling town of Lahaina and the resort area of Kaanapali on the island of Maui. The six-mile trip takes about a half hour in each direction and passes through sugar plantations, with the ocean on one side and the mountains of west Maui on the other.

Operates: Daily, except Thanksgiving and Christmas
Features: Singing conductor, narration, sightseeing packages
Reservations: 808-667-6851

Illinois

ILLINOIS RAILWAY MUSEUM
Union, IL 60180
815-923-4000

Visitors can see a variety of rail equipment, including steam and diesel locomotives, electric streetcars, and "L" trains. Other historic railway equipment is on display, from vintage passenger coaches to modern streamliners. Train rides take about forty-five minutes, and there are brief trolley car rides available, too.

Operates: Daily from Memorial Day to Labor Day; call for details for other times during the year
Features: Bookstore, museum shop, refreshments
Reservations: Not required

MONTICELLO RAILWAY MUSEUM
P.O. Box 401
Monticello, IL 61856-0401
217-762-9011

This attraction features not only a rail museum and a rail yard but a fifty-minute train ride that includes wooded areas and farmland. Passengers may board or layover at either the Illinois Central Depot (museum site) or at the Wabash Depot in Monticello, which was built in 1899. Visitors may walk through the display cars at the museum and are permitted to walk through the Camp Creek Yard, where there are numerous pieces of equipment.

Operates: Weekends and some holidays from the first
               weekend in May through October
Features: Gift shop in the Illinois Central Depot,
               light snacks
Reservations: Not required

Iowa

BOONE & SCENIC VALLEY RAILROAD
Box 603
Boone, IA 50036
515-432-4249

A twelve-mile, ninety-minute ride through the Des Moines River valley, crossing two bridges (one is 156 feet high). Railroad features diesel and steam locomotives (the latter operates weekends and holidays only).

Operates: Memorial Day weekend through
               the end of October
Features: Museum (free), gift shop, snack bar
Reservations: 800-626-0319

Kentucky

BLUEGRASS SCENIC RAILROAD & MUSEUM
P.O. Box 27
Versailles, KY 40383
606-873-2476

The five-and-a-half-mile route runs between Versailles and the Kentucky River, passing through horse, cattle, and tobacco farms and over three wooden trestles. Passengers may detrain at the Kentucky River, where there is an overlook that includes the Wild Turkey Distillery, the Kentucky River Valley, and Young's High Bridge, a railroad bridge built in 1889 by the Louisville Southern Railroad. This is a ninety-minute trip, start to finish.

Operates: Saturday and Sunday, May through
                  October; Christmas trains in December
Features: Museum, gift shop
Reservations: 800-755-2476

MY OLD KENTUCKY DINNER TRAIN
P.O. Box 279
Bardstown, KY 40004
502-348-7699

The train follows a thirty-five-mile route through very scenic countryside, including Bernheim Forest, a private 13,000-acre reserve, crosses an old all-timber trestle, and passes the historic Jim Beam Distillery. The trip takes about two hours.

Operates: Daily except Monday, April through December
Features: Gift shop in depot
Reservations: 502-348-7300

Maryland

WESTERN MARYLAND SCENIC RAILROAD
13 Canal Street
Cumberland, MD 21502
800-872-4650

The excursion trains are pulled by a 1916 Baldwin steam locomotive or a diesel-electric from the 1960s. From

Cumberland, the train heads into the Allegheny Mountains for the thirty-two-mile trip to Frostburg, passing through a horseshoe curve and 900-foot-long tunnel en route. Of course, the countryside is quite lovely, especially in the fall.

Operates:	May through December
Features:	Former Coca-Cola Corporation lounge car
Reservations:	800-872-4650

Massachusetts

CAPE COD SCENIC RAILROAD
252 Main Street
Hyannis, MA 02601
508-771-3788

The two-hour scenic ride begins and ends in Hyannis, with stops at the historic village of Sandwich and at the Cape Cod Canal. Diesel-electric locomotives haul passengers in classic coaches. Route takes the train through historic Cape Cod villages, past cranberry bogs, the Great Salt Marsh, and along Cape Cod Bay. A narrative is also provided. This railroad also operates a very nice dinner train—a three-hour trip—for which a coat and tie are required (this is Hyannis, after all!).

Operates:	Both trains run daily (except Monday), from mid-June through mid-September; call for specifics for other times during the year
Reservations:	508-771-3788

Michigan

ADRIAN & BLISSFIELD RAIL ROAD COMPANY
P.O. Box 95
Blissfield, MI 49228
517-486-5979

From Blissfield, excursion trains travel over track of the Erie & Kalamazoo Railroad, which first began operations in 1836. Passing through rich farmland of southeastern Michigan, the train finally stops at Lenawee Junction, once a major rail stop, before returning to Blissfield. The company also operates a fine-dining dinner train, a murder mystery train, a ghost train, and snow trains.

Operates: Schedule varies considerably during the
                 year, so call for details
Reservations: 517-486-5979

COOPERSVILLE & MARNE RAILWAY
P.O. Box 55
Coopersville, MI 49404
616-949-4778

This scenic thirteen-mile ride is along one of Michigan's oldest rail corridors in the middle of west Michigan, a premier tourist destination. The route crosses two bridges, passes through farmland and wooded areas, then follows Interstate 96 for several miles. Several special trains are run at special times during the year, including a murder mystery dinner train.

Operates: Saturday during July, August, and September;
                 Saturday and Sunday in October and December
Features: Gift shop
Reservations: 616-949-4778

KALAMAZOO, LAKE SHORE & CHICAGO RAILWAY
P.O. Box 178
Paw Paw, MI 49079
616-382-4244

The train takes passengers on a half-hour, thirteen-mile round-trip through Michigan's wine country, passing through woods, wetlands, vineyards, and along the shore of Lake Cora. There's an optional stopover at Bonamego Tree Farm, where you can picnic or hike until a later train comes along. Between Thanksgiving and Christmas, Santa Trains provide a chance to cut your own Christmas tree.

Operates: Saturday and Sunday during May, June, and September; daily (except Monday) in July and August; daily in October
Features: Sandwiches and drinks available on the train
Reservations: 616-382-4244

MICHIGAN STAR CLIPPER
COE RAIL SCENIC TRAIN
840 N. Pontiac Trail
Walled Lake, MI 48390
810-960-9440

This company has two very distinct operations: A three-hour scenic ride passes through some commercial sites but features residential and wooded areas, plus wetlands, a bird sanctuary, lakes, and ponds. Equipment includes restored 1917 coaches from the Erie Lakawanna Railroad. The dinner train is made up of Pennsylvania Keystone cars, with two dining cars separated by a kitchen car. The food is rated four-star and is served by folks decked out in formal attire. Male passengers are requested to wear coats and ties; ladies should dress comparably. Jeans or shorts are not acceptable. This is a special experience—the way it used to be in the golden age of fine rail dining and travel.

Operates:	Scenic train: April through October; dinner train: year-round
Features:	Scenic train available for special charters, field trips, fall color tours; dinner train features murder mystery, musical review, and illusionist (call for details and schedule)
Reservations:	810-960-9440

Nebraska

FREMONT & ELKHORN VALLEY RAILROAD
1835 N. Somers
Fremont, NE 68025
402-727-0615

This train is run by a local chapter of the National Railway Historical Society and operates fifteen miles of former Chicago & Northwestern track passing through the Platte and Elkhorn Valleys to Hooper, Nebraska. At one time, this track extended through Wyoming and into the Black Hills, prompting people to call it the Cowboy Line. Passengers ride in either former Chicago & Northwestern heavyweight coaches or in an air-conditioned streamlined coach once owned by the Milwaukee Road.

Operates:	April through December
Features:	Museum, souvenir shop
Reservations:	800-942-7245

Nevada

VIRGINIA & TRUCKEE RAILROAD COMPANY
P.O. Box 467
Virginia City, NV 89440
702-847-0380

The train is hauled by a steam locomotive and follows the original right-of-way past some of the most famous

Comstock gold and silver mines. Passengers may ride in either open cars or an enclosed caboose. The round-trip takes thirty-five minutes, but you may get off at the mid-point, if you wish.

Operates: June through September
Features: Gift shop
Reservations: 702-847-0380

New Hampshire

CONWAY SCENIC RAILROAD
P.O. Box 1947
North Conway, NH 03860
603-356-5251

An eleven-mile route goes through Mount Washington Valley, with passengers able to choose enclosed coaches, open-air cars, or luxury seating in a restored 1898 Pullman parlor-observation car. Both diesel and steam-powered trains are available for the one-hour trip.

Operates: Early April through late December
Features: Dining-car seating available; working rail-road yard with turntable; museum, gift shop, model railroad
Reservations: 603-356-5251 (for dining-car reservations, ask for extension 19)

HOBO RAILROAD
P.O. Box 9
Lincoln, NH 03251
603-745-2135

Passengers travel in former New York Central coaches along the Pemigewassat River and through very scenic country-side in the White Mountains. A variety of wildlife is usually seen, and the fifteen-mile trip is especially worthwhile during the fall color season. Depending on which trip is selected, optional lunch or dinner is served. The 7:00 P.M. train features a five-course fine-dining service in the Cafe Lafayette, a New York Central dining car originally built in 1924 and now completely restored. A number of special trains are also operated.

Operates: Mid-March through December
Features: Hobo picnic lunch offered on most trains
Reservations: 603-745-2135 or 603-745-3500

WINNIPESAUKEE SCENIC RAILROAD
P.O. Box 9
Lincoln, NH 03251
603-745-2135

This train runs for one- and two-hour trips over former Boston & Maine track between the towns of Meredith and Lakeport and along the shore of Lake Winnipesaukee, the largest lake in the state. The scenery is delightful year-round and is spectacular during the fall, when a three-hour excursion is offered. A dining car is available as an option for passengers during summer months.

Operates: Daily, from July 1 through Labor Day; the schedule in May and June and from Labor Day to the end of October is irregular, so call for details
Reservations: 603-745-2135 or 603-279-5253

New Jersey

MYSTERY EXPRESS
c/o Murder To Go, Inc.
92 Ridgedale Avenue
Florham Park, NJ 07932

Guests board the Mystery Express for drinks and appetizers, dinner, dessert, and coffee. During the three- to four-hour trip, as passengers relax and dine in restored vintage railroad cars, one or more "murders" occur. The plot thickens, then unfolds, and—just before the train reaches its destination—is solved.

Operates: Usually on Saturday in the spring and summer
Reservations: 201-301-0562

New Mexico

CUMBRES & TOLTEC SCENIC RAILROAD
P.O. Box 789
Chama, NM 87520
719-376-5483 or 719-376-5493

Narrow-gauge trains, each hauled by steam locomotives, depart daily from both ends of this 64-mile route and meet halfway at Osier, Colorado. You can board at Chama, New Mexico, 110 miles north of Santa Fe on US 84, or at Antonito, Colorado, which is 28 miles south of Alamosa on US 285. You also have the option of returning to your point of origin or changing trains and continuing on to the opposite terminus with return provided by van. Depending on your choice of itineraries, the trip will take six to eight hours. This railroad is one of the spectacular examples of mountain railroading in North America and is highly recommended.

Operates: Memorial Day weekend through mid-October
Features: Restaurant and gift shop at Osier; snack car on both trains
Reservations: 505-756-2151

New York

NEW YORK & LAKE ERIE RAILROAD
P.O. Box 309
Gowanda, NY 14070
716-532-5716

From the Gowanda station, the train travels up a steep grade and through Old Stone Tunnel, which has been in use on the rail line since the 1860s. Continuing on historic Erie Railroad track through scenic rural countryside, the train passes through the towns of Dayton and Markhams Corners. The train stops at the South Dayton station before beginning its return trip. In all, the trip lasts about two and a half hours. The railroad also operates the Blue Diamond Dinner Train and a Murder Mystery Dinner Train, both of which extend their runs beyond South Dayton to Cherry Creek.

Operates: Memorial Day weekend through the last
weekend in October
Reservations: 716-532-5716

North Carolina

NORTH CAROLINA TRANSPORTATION MUSEUM
P.O. Box 165
Spencer, NC 28159
704-636-2889

Steam and diesel locomotives pull trains on a tour around this large complex, the Historic Spencer Shops, once Southern Railway's largest steam locomotive servicing facility. Included are a large roundhouse with turntable and other accessory facilities—all operated under the jurisdiction of the state of North Carolina.

Operates: Daily (closed Monday, from November 1 to
March 31)
Features: Museum includes many examples of other
transportation modes
Reservations: 704-636-2889 (call in advance due to the
irregular schedule for the train rides)

Pennsylvania

BELLEFONTE HISTORICAL RAILROAD
Train Station
Bellafonte, PA 16823
814-355-0311

The railroad operates scheduled excursions and charters over more than sixty miles of track in Centre, Clinton, and Blair counties. Equipment used is self-propelled rail diesel cars. Scenic attractions include Bald Eagle Valley, Nittany Mountain, Sayers Dam, and Big Spring in Bellafonte. This route (the round-trip takes about an hour and a half) is really exceptional during the fall with its colorful foliage. Wildlife is also abundant in the area.

Operates: Saturday and Sunday, from Memorial Day
                 through Labor Day
Features: Dinner trains and a Santa Claus Express
                 operate periodically
Reservations: 814-355-0311

GETTYSBURG RAILROAD
106 N. Washington Street
Gettysburg, PA 17325
717-334-6932

Passengers ride in enclosed coaches pulled by a Baldwin steam locomotive. A sixteen-mile ride goes through the first-day battlefield in Gettysburg and then on to Biglerville, Pennsylvania. A fifty-mile Fall Foliage trip goes through Adams and Cumberland counties to Mount Holly Springs, passing through wooded areas, mountains, and orchards. Special theme trains are operated during the year and include dinner trips, a Christmas train, and, as would be expected, several different rides with Civil War themes.

Operates: April through October, with several special
                 trips in December

Features: Gift shop and snack bar
Reservations: 717-334-6932 (especially recommended for
              Mount Holly Springs trip)

MIDDLETOWN & HUMMELSTOWN RAILROAD
136 Brown Street
Middletown, PA 17057
717-944-4435

Passengers ride in vintage Pullman coaches during an
eleven-mile trip through wooded areas along the Swatara
Creek. During the northbound portion of the trip, a narra-
tor gives a brief history of the railroad and the Union Canal,
pointing out historic landmarks, including the remains of a
canal lock, century-old lime kilns, an operating stone quarry,
and Horse Thief Cave. On the return trip, there's a wonderful view of the Swatara Creek Valley as the train crosses
a thirty-five-foot-high bridge. Passengers may leave the
train to tour Indian Echo Caverns. Coaches are pulled by
either diesel-electric or steam locomotives. The railroad also
operates a dinner train.

Operates: Saturday and Sunday, in May, June,
              September, and October; Tuesday, Thursday,
              Saturday, and Sunday, in July and August
Features: Gift shop on train, collection of streetcars
              and other rolling stock on premises
Reservations: 717-944-4435

STEAMTOWN NATIONAL HISTORIC SITE
150 S. Washington Avenue
Scranton, PA 18503
888-693-9391

Steamtown is operated by the National Park Service, and
the facility here is well worth a special trip. The focus is the
Golden Age of Train Travel, from the mid-1800s to about
1950. In addition to the visitor center, there's a working

roundhouse and turntable, a museum, and a fascinating shop where vintage rail equipment is restored. Special trains, pulled by steam engines, operate between here and Moscow, Pennsylvania, about twenty-five miles away.

Operates: Year-round (call for information about train rides)
Reservations: Not required for admittance to grounds

Utah

GOLDEN SPIKE NATIONAL HISTORIC SITE
P.O. Box 897
Brigham City, UT 84302
801-471-2209

This site commemorates the linking of the two rail lines that completed the transcontinental railroad in the United States. No train rides are offered, but I included this listing because of the great historical significance of the site. The magnificent replica locomotives are very much worth seeing.

Operates: Visitor center open year-round; locomotives operate from about May 1 until the end of September
Reservations: Not required

Washington

LAKE WHATCOM RAILWAY
P.O. Box 91
Acme, WA 98220
360-595-2218

Passengers ride in several restored and refurbished passenger cars (dating back to a period between 1910 and 1926) that were originally part of the Northern Pacific's rolling stock. The steam locomotive is typical of those that operated in the area during the first several decades of this century. After leaving Wickersham, the train heads into a tunnel, passes alongside Mirror Lake, then goes through a forest.

Operates: Tuesday and Saturday, from mid-June
                through August, plus some holidays
Features: Gift shop, coffee shop on train, handcar
                rides in summer
Reservations: 360-595-2218

West Virginia

CASS SCENIC RAILROAD
Box 107
Cass, WV 24927
304-456-4300

This is an old logging railroad—or, more precisely, it's what's left of a much larger logging operation from the early 1900s. Passengers ride on original flatcars that have been refurbished and converted into coaches. The train passes through some very pretty wooded countryside, but the vintage Shay steam locomotives are what railfans come to see. These engines were originally designed to haul very heavy loads up steep grades and around tight curves, and this ride certainly gives them a chance to show what they can do. The route includes switchbacks and an almost unbelievable 11 percent grade, meaning an increase in altitude of 11 feet for every 100 feet of track. Putting that into perspective, the steepest grade on any main-line track in the country is 4.7 percent. The train stops at Whittaker Station, then continues to Bald Knob, a lookout over 4,800 feet above sea level.

Operates: End of May through October
Features: Country store, museum, theater, overnight
                accommodations
Reservations: 304-456-4300 or 800-225-5982

Wisconsin

NICOLET SCENIC RAIL
P.O. Box 310
Laona, WI 54541
715-674-6309

This train operates through the Nicolet National Forest, which lies south of the Michigan border and includes much of six Wisconsin counties. The regular twenty-mile excursion passes through lovely countryside and stops for passengers to detrain in Wabeno. The fifty-four-mile ride to Tipler runs during the height of the fall foliage and stops in Long Lake. As would be expected, it's a spectacular trip. Railcars are from the post–World War II "streamliner" era and include lounge and dining cars.

Operates: To Wabeno: from mid-June through August; to Tipler: from mid-September through the first week of October
Features: Buy lunch in the dining car or bring your own food aboard
Reservations: 800-752-1465

Canada

Alberta

HERITAGE PARK HISTORICAL VILLAGE
1900 Heritage Drive, S.W.
Calgary, Alberta T2V 2X3
403-259-1900

A great many restored buildings and numerous exhibits combine to re-create a typical settlement in western Canada from around the turn of the century. Many of the exhibits are railroad-oriented, including a number of restored railcars of historical significance. Both streetcar and train rides are offered, the latter in coaches pulled by one of several steam locomotives.

Operates:	Daily, from late-May through early September; Saturday, Sunday, and holidays until about the middle of October
Reservations:	Not required

FORT EDMONTON PARK
P.O. Box 2359
Edmonton, Alberta T5J 2R7
403-496-8787

More than sixty-five authentically re-created buildings depict life in Edmonton from the time of the fur trade in the mid-1800s through the 1920s. Staff people in period costumes help to provide a very realistic atmosphere. Train rides are offered, with passengers riding in three coaches pulled by a restored Baldwin steam locomotive built in 1919.

Operates:	Daily, from late May until Labor Day; Sunday, through September
Reservations:	Not required

British Columbia

BC RAIL, LTD.
P.O. Box 8770
Vancouver, British Columbia V6B 4X6
604-631-3500

This is a six-hour, eighty-mile trip from Vancouver to Squamish, passing along the shores of Howe Sound and through spectacular mountains. The trip includes a two-hour layover in Squamish, which provides time for sight-seeing and shopping. The consist includes a truly splendid steam locomotive, a maroon and black Royal Hudson built in 1940, along with coaches and two club cars.

Operates: Sunday, Monday, Wednesday, and holidays, from June 1 through mid-September
Reservations: 604-631-3500 (make them well in advance by phone)

ROCKY MOUNTAINEER
340 Brooksbank Avenue, #104
North Vancouver, British Columbia V7J 2C1
800-665-7245

These trains operate in either direction between Vancouver and Banff, Jasper, or Calgary. The Canadian Rockies provide some of the most magnificent scenery in all of North America, and wildlife sightings are numerous. The company offers a wide variety of tour packages from two to fourteen days. They can originate from several points, and all include at least some transportation in very comfortable coaches of the Rocky Mountaineer. The rail portions of the tours are all in daylight, and the packages include overnight stays in hotels, plus continental breakfasts and lunches on board. Schedule and prices vary considerably, so please call for an information packet.

Operates: Roughly from mid-May until early October
Reservations: 800-665-7245

Manitoba

PRAIRIE DOG CENTRAL
Vintage Locomotive Society
P.O. Box 33021
Winnipeg, Manitoba R3G 0W4
204-832-5259

Several interesting steam locomotives are on display here. One, built in the 1880s and operated by the Canadian

Pacific until 1918, pulls passengers in restored wooden cars on a two-hour, thirty-six-mile round-trip to the town of Grosse Isle.

Operates: June through September
Reservations: Not required

Ontario

SOUTH SIMCOE RAILWAY
P.O. Box 186
Tottenham, Ontario L0G 1W0
905-936-5815

This excursion train operates on an eight-mile circuit and features a wonderful steam locomotive built for the Canadian Pacific Railroad in the 1880s. It pulls passenger cars originally built in the 1920s, most of which have recently been restored. Other locomotives and a variety of rolling stock are also on display.

Operates: Sunday (and sometimes Monday and Tuesday), from late May to early October
Features: Railfan Day in early July, plus other special events
Reservations: Not required

Land Cruises

AMERICAN ORIENT EXPRESS
UW Travels
1415 N.E. 45th Street
Seattle, WA 98105
206-543-0540

This is a relatively new idea: the traditional concept of an ocean cruise applied to rail travel. The pioneer in this area is the now-famous *Simplon Orient Express,* which has been running a luxury train throughout Europe for some time.

This luxury excursion train is now operated by a Seattle-based company, which acquired a consist of magnificently refurbished classic railcars. The *American Orient Express* offers a number of different itineraries over the course of a year, ranging from a four-day trip between Los Angeles and Santa Fe, New Mexico, to nine-day transcontinental excursions, crossing Canada between Montreal and Vancouver or coast-to-coast in the U.S. from Los Angeles to Washington, D.C. Other excursions cover the Rocky Mountains, the Pacific Northwest, Glacier National Park, and the Grand Tetons.

The onboard dining is gourmet all the way, and the accommodations evoke all of the best from the *belle époque* of train travel. Each itinerary is selected for the scenery and is enhanced by leisurely stops at various locations along the way for sightseeing excursions. In addition, guest lecturers are usually brought along to provide real authoritative commentary. Passengers sleep on the train—sometimes in transit, sometimes not—and the package also includes hotel accommodations, plus all meals, sightseeing tours, lectures—pretty much everything but personal expenses. Make no mistake: This is a deluxe experience, with a price tag to match. However, if you can afford it (and even if you can't), any one of these trips will be an unforgettable experience!

Operates: Periodically; call for dates and itineraries
Reservations: 800-289-2586

APPENDIX D

Golden Spike Travel Agents

As noted in Chapter 4 on planning your rail trip, I've found that most travel agents are really not familiar with the intricacies of booking a long-distance train trip—especially if you're traveling in sleeping-car accommodations. If your hometown travel agent flunked the simple one-question test suggested in Chapter 4, you might wish to contact one of the following rail travel specialists. Each has a toll-free number for just that purpose.

Stan Barriger
Ascutney Travel
44 Pleasant Street
Claremont, NH 03743
800-872-4674

Ted or Sylvia Blishak
Accent on Travel
112 N. Fifth Street
Klamath Falls, OR 97601
800-347-0645

CARL FOWLER
Rail Travel Center
9 Congress Street
St. Albans, VT 05478
800-458-5394

GREG KUZMICK
Mon Valley Travel
100 Smithfield Street
Pittsburgh, PA 15222
800-245-1099

I'm sure there are other travel agencies around the country with toll-free numbers and people on their staff who specialize in booking rail travel. I will be more than glad to include them in future editions of this book, if they will simply contact me in care of the publisher.

I've also included here a list of travel agencies that have earned Amtrak's Golden Spike Award. These awards are given to travel agencies reaching a specific volume of sales in Amtrak tickets. That's still not an iron-clad guarantee that they know a lot about long-distance train travel, but it's a good way to start.

Don't worry if the travel agent you settle on isn't in your hometown. The entire transaction can be handled over the phone, and the agent will mail your tickets to you. So plan as much of the trip as you can yourself, then have the travel agent you select double-check your efforts and take care of the ticketing.

Arizona

PHOENIX:
American Express, 20022 N. 31st Avenue

Carlson Wagonlit Travel/G.E. Travel Center,
3200 N. Central Avenue

California

ALISO VIEJO:
XpoAmerica, 101 Columbia

COSTA MESA:
Auto Club of Southern California, 3333 Fairview Road

INGLEWOOD:
Your Man Tours, 8831 Aviation Boulevard

RIVERSIDE:
Let's Travel Tours, P.O. Box 2768

ROSEVILLE:
Roseville Travel, 201 Pacific Street

SAN FRANCISCO:
Grey Line, 350 8th Street

WALNUT CREEK:
Key Holidays, 1390 S. Main Street

Colorado

AURORA:
CUC Travel Services, 3033 S. Parker Road

DENVER:
RMA Travel & Tours, 1660 S. Albion

Rocky Mountain Motorist, 1400 E. Arkansas

Connecticut

HARTFORD:
American Express Travel, 450 Columbus Boulevard

Delaware

GREENVILLE:
Ambassador Travel, 3852 Kennett Pike

NEWARK:
AAA World Travel, 875 AAA Boulevard

Ambassador Travel, 109 Newark Shopping Center

American Express Travel, 500 Stanton Christiana Road

Travel One, 400 Christiana Drive

WILMINGTON:
Ambassador Travel, 3003 Concord Pike

American Express Travel Service, One Alico Plaza

Carlson Wagonlit Travel, 1800 Concord Pike

Delaware Travel Agency, 4001 Concord Pike

Holiday Travel Agency, 1100 N. Market Street

Professional Travel Planners, 302 W. 9th Street

Rosenbluth Travel Agency, Jefferson Plaza, Route 141 &
Henry Clay Road

District of Columbia

WASHINGTON:
AAA World Wide Travel Agency, 701 15th Street NW

ACT Travel, 1629 K Street NW

American Express Travel Service, 2201 C Street NW,
2001 M Street NW, 1150 Connecticut Avenue

Cal Simmons Travel, 1701 Pennsylvania Avenue NW

Carlson Wagonlit Travel, 3900 Wisconsin Avenue NW,
1661 K Street NW, Pentagon

Executive Travel Service, 1101 17th Street NW

The Lawyers Travel Service, 1615 L Street NW

McCabe Bremmer Travel, 1730 K Street NW

McGregor Travel, 1850 K Street NW

Metro Travel Service, 1200 18th Street NW

Omega World Travel, 600 E Street NW,
600 Maryland Avenue SW

Passport Executive Travel, 1025 Thomas Jefferson Street

Premier Travel Service, 1300 I Street NW

Sato Travel/U.S. Postal Service, 475 L'Enfant Plaza SW

Travel Department, 2100 M Street NW

Travel Horizons/Smithsonian Institution, Museum of
Natural History

Travelogue, 1201 New York Avenue NW

Travel On/GW Travel, 800 21st Street NW

Travel One, 1111 Constitution Avenue NW

Waters Travel Service, 888 17th Street NW

West End Travel, 11 Dupont Circle

Florida

BOYNTON BEACH:
Sand and C Travel, 9851 E. Military Trail

BRADENTON:
AAA Travel Agency, 6210 Manatee Avenue West

CLEARWATER:
AAA Travel Agency, 2170 Rainbow Drive

DELRAY BEACH:
AAA Travel Agency, 3075 S. Federal Highway

Kings Point Travel & Tours, 6626 W. Atlantic Avenue

Oriole Travel Station, 7431 W. Atlantic Avenue

FORT LAUDERDALE:
AAA Travel Agency, 4800 N. University Drive

Prestige Travel Agency, 7783 NW 44th Street

FORT MYERS:
AAA Travel Agency, 2516 Colonial Boulevard

HOLLYWOOD:
GAT Marketing & Travel, 3325 Hollywood Boulevard

JACKSONVILLE:
Bailey Tours, 3630 Rogero Road

Transcor Travel, 5230 Baymeadows Road

NAPLES:
AAA Travel Agency, 4910 Tamiami Trail

PALM BEACH GARDENS:
AAA Travel Agency, 9123 N. Military Trail

POMPANO BEACH:
AAA Travel Agency, 601 E. Atlantic Boulevard

PORT CHARLOTTE:
AAA Travel Agency, 21229-A Olean Boulevard

SARASOTA:
AAA Travel Agency, 3844 Bee Ridge Road

TAMPA:
Carlson Wagonlit Travel, 4511 N. Himes Avenue

VENICE:
AAA Travel Agency, 2100 S. Tamiami Trail

Georgia

NORCROSS:
Network Travel, 400 Pinnacle Way

Illinois

CHICAGO:
Vacation Village Travel, 1424 W. 95th Street

MACOMB:
Macomb Travel Center, 120 E. Calhoun Street

QUINCY:
Bergner's Travel Headquarters, Quincy Mall

SCHAUMBURG:
Signature Travel Services, 200 N. Martingale Road

Indiana

GOSHEN:
Menno Travel Service, 210 S. Main Street

Maryland

ANNAPOLIS:
Aladdin Travel Agency, 105 Forbes Street

American Express Travel Services, 67 Annapolis Mall

BALTIMORE:
Ramsay Scarlett Travel, 10 N. Calvert Street

Roland Park Travel, 600 Wyndhurst Avenue

Safe Harbors Business Travel, 25 South Street

Travel One/Alex. Brown, One South Street

T. Rowe Price Travel, 100 E. Pratt Street

World Travel Partners, 111 S. Calvert Street

BELTSVILLE:
Travel On Beltsville, 11750 Beltsville Drive

BETHESDA:
American Express Travel, 10400 Fernwood Drive

Cal Simmons Travel, 7700 Wisconsin Avenue

Ober United Travel Agency, 9000 Rockville Pike

Travel Coordinators, 7316 Wisconsin Avenue

CHEVY CHASE:
Ober United Travel Agency, 5420 Wisconsin Avenue

COCKEYSVILLE:
Roeder Travel, 9805 York Road

COLUMBIA:
Corporate Travel Concept, 9191 Red Branch Road

GAITHERSBURG:
AAA Travel Agency, 19200 Montgomery Village Avenue

HUNT VALLEY:
Travelogue, 11350 McCormick Road

Travel One, 225 International Circle

LINTHICUM:
American Express Travel Services, 1306 Concourse Drive

LUTHERVILLE:
AAA Maryland Travel Agency, 1306 Bellona Avenue

OWINGS MILLS:
American Express Travel, 10461 Mill Run Circle

Travel Destinations Management Group, 110 Painters Mill Road

Wright Travel, 11433 Cronridge Drive

POTOMAC:
The Travel Place, 11325 Seven Locks Road

WHEATON:
AAA World Wide Travel Agency, Wheaton Plaza

Massachusetts

CAMBRIDGE:
American Express Travel, 39 John F. Kennedy Street

Michigan

DETROIT:
KeyTours, P.O. Box 517

SOUTHFIELD:
Can-Am Travel, 3000 Town Center

Minnesota

MINNEAPOLIS:
Carlson Wagonlit Travel, 701 Lakeshore Parkway

OWATONNA:
Travel Headquarters, 143 W. Bridge Street

Missouri

FENTON:
Maritz Travel Company, 1385 N. Highway Drive

ST. LOUIS:
Maritz Travel, 1862 Lackland Hill Parkway

Montana

KALISPELL:
Flathead Travel Service, 500 S. Main Street

Nebraska

OMAHA:
American Express, 2840 S. 123rd Street

Nevada

CARSON CITY:
Frontier Travel, 1923 N. Carson Street

New Hampshire

CLAREMONT:
Ascutney Travel, 44 Pleasant Street

New Jersey

CAMDEN:
Rosenbluth Travel Agency, 1 Campbell Place

CHERRY HILL:
AAA International Travel Service, 201 Kings
Highway South

Rosenbluth Travel Agency, 57 Haddonfield Road

FLORHAM PARK:
New Jersey Auto Club, One Hanover Road

FORT MONMOUTH:
Carlson Wagonlit Travel, Riverside Route 1

FRANKLIN LAKES:
Becton Dickinson Travel, One Becton Drive

Stratton Travel, 795 Franklin Avenue

ISELIN:
Rosenbluth Travel Agency, Woodbridge Place

JERSEY CITY:
Astral Travel Service, 895 Bergen Avenue

LAWRENCEVILLE:
American Express Travel Services, 989 Lenox Drive

MONTVALE:
American Express KPMG Peat Marwick, 3 Chestnut Ridge Road

MOORESTOWN:
Barclay Travel Agency, 308 Harper Drive

Carlson Wagonlit Travel, 199 Borton Landing Road

Sato Travel, 199 Borton Landing Road

MOUNT LAUREL:
Travel One, 5000 Atrium Way

NEWARK:
American Express Travel, 745 Broad Street

NEW BRUNSWICK:
American Express Travel, Route 1 North Boulevard

NORTHFIELD:
AAA World Wide Travel, 901 Tilton Road

NUTLEY:
Travel Forum II, 54 Windsor Place

OCEAN:
AAA Travel Center, Ocean Plaza Shopping Center

PARSIPPANY:
American Express Travel, 2 Sylvan Way

PISCATAWAY:
American Express Travel, 220 Centennial Avenue

PRINCETON:
American Express Travel, 10 Nassau Street

Deluxe Travel, 219 Nassau Street

McGregor Travel, Route 206 Provinceline Road

ROSELAND:
American Express Travel, 1 ADP Boulevard

TOMS RIVER:
AAA Travel Agency, 864 Route 37 West

WAYNE:
AAA World Wide Travel, 418 Hamburg Turnpike

WEEHAWKEN:
American Express Travel, 1000 Harbor Boulevard

WILDWOOD CREST:
Festival Travel & Tours, 5501 New Jersey Avenue

New York

ALBANY:
Argus Travel, Stuyvesant Plaza

Fort Orange Travel, 90 State Street

Hudson Valley Auto Club, 618 Delaware Avenue

Travel Management Services, 23 Computer Drive East

BRONX:
Liberty Travel, 1385 Metropolitan Avenue

BROOKLYN:
Auto Club of New York, 1781 Flatbush Avenue

Calendar Travel Agency, 227 Utica Avenue

D L & W Travel, 530 Norstrand Avenue

Liberty Travel, 180 Montague Street

Me Again Travel, 66 Court Street

Odyssey Travel, 151 Seventh Avenue

BUFFALO:
AAA Western & Central NY, 100 International Drive

CATSKILL:
Empress Travel, 388 Main Street

CLIFTON PARK:
Carlson Wagonlit Travel, Clifton Country Mall

NFT Travel, 15 Park Avenue

CORNING:
American Express Travel Service, 23 W. Market Street

FAR ROCKAWAY:
Town & Country World Travel, 21-35 Mott Avenue

GARDEN CITY:
Automobile Club of New York, 229 Seventh Street,
1415 Kellum Place

JAMAICA:
Auto Club of New York, 186-06 Hillside Avenue

LATHAM:
CTN/Albany Travel Unlimited, 19 British American Boulevard

MANHATTAN:
American Express, 1585 Broadway, 380 Madison Avenue

American Express ETM, 200 Vesey Street

American Express Travel, 1120 6th Avenue,
130 Liberty Street, 1 New York Plaza

American Express Travel Services, 1251 6th Avenue,
37 Wall Street, 72 Wall Street, 7 World Trade Center,
2 Penn Plaza, 1 Chase Plaza, 388 Greenwich Street

Auto Club of New York, 1881 Broadway

BTI America's/Bear Stearns Travel, 245 Park Avenue

BTI America's Travel, 1140 6th Avenue,
342 Madison Avenue

Capital Cities/ABC Inc. Travel Dept., 77 W. 66th Street

Carlson Wagonlit, 363 6th Avenue, 225 Liberty Street

Continental-American Travel, 770 Lexington Avenue

Credit Suisse First Boston Travel Services, 11 Madison Avenue

Direct Travel, 1180 6th Avenue

DMS Travel, 317 Madison Avenue

Empire Blue Cross & Blue Shield/US Travel, 622 Third Avenue

Goldman, Sachs & Co., 85 Broad Street

Harlem Travel Bureau, 2002 5th Avenue

Humbert Travel Agency, 400 Madison Avenue

Japan Travel Bureau, 787 7th Avenue

Journeycorp Travel Management, 488 Madison Avenue

Kintetsu International Express, 1325 6th Avenue

The Lawyers Travel Service, 461 Park Avenue South

Liberty Travel, 2280 Broadway, 260 E. 72nd Street

Linden Travel Bureau, 41 E. 57th Street

Macey's East/Direct Travel, 151 W. 34th Street

Maritz Travel Company, 277 Park Avenue,
330 Madison Avenue, 399 Park Avenue

Maritz Travel Time Inc., Time-Life Building

MSW Columbia Travel Group, 630 5th Avenue

Park Avenue Travel Service, 60 E. 42nd Street

Pisa Brothers, Inc. Travel Bureau, 630 5th Avenue

Protravel International, 515 Madison Avenue

Stevens Travel Management, 432 Park Avenue South

Tzell Travel, 119 W. 40th Street

Valerie Wilson Travel, 475 Park Avenue South

VTS Travel Enterprises, 55 John Street

Zenith/McCord Travel, 16 E. 34th Street

SMITHTOWN:
Automobile Club of New York, 729 Smithtown By-Pass

North Dakota

LINTON:
Rosenbluth Travel, Highway 83 and 13E

WILLISTON:
Daryle's Travel, 407 Main Street

Ohio

SOLON:
CTN/Astro Travel Service, 6200 SOM Center Road

Oklahoma

NORMAN:
Travel Service, 2500 S. McGee

Oregon

KLAMATH FALLS:
Accent on Travel, 112 N. 5th Street

Pennsylvania

ALLENTOWN:
Lehigh Valley Motor Club, 1020 Hamilton Street

Rosenbluth Travel, One Windsor Plaza

ARDMORE:
Suburban Travel Agency, 41 Coulter Avenue

Travel One, 6 Greenfield Avenue

BENSALEM:
Omega World Travel, 450 Winks Lane

BLUE BELL:
Cherry Hill Travel Agency, 1425 Union Meeting Road

BRISTOL:
B&B Travel, 1159 Rodgers Road

BRYN MAWR:
Bryn Mawr Travel Agency, 933 Lancaster Avenue

Travel Answers (no address available)

COLLEGEVILLE:
American Express Travel, 500 Arcola Road

DOUGLASSVILLE:
World Travel, 1724 W. Schuylkill Road

HAVERFORD:
Keystone Travel Agency, 394 W. Lancaster Avenue

INTERCOURSE:
Rutt's Tours, 3564 Old Philadelphia Pike

JENKINTOWN:
Get A Way Travel, 111 Township Line Road

KING OF PRUSSIA:
American Express Travel Related Services, 200 N. Warner Street

MALVERN:
Cherry Hill Travel Agency, 51 Valley Stream Parkway

Rosenbluth International Travel, 200 Vanguard Drive

Travel One, 40 Great Valley Parkway

World Travel, 44 General Warren Boulevard

PHILADELPHIA:

AAA Mid-Atlantic Travel Agency, 2040 Market Street

American Express Travel Service, Two Penn Center Plaza, Center Square East, 1101 Market Street, 2000 Logan Square, 3000 Logan Square, 3451 Walnut

Carlson Wagonlit Travel, 217 South Street, 1601 Market Street, 22nd & Oregon Avenue, 30 S. 17th Street

Keystone Travel Agency, 6400 Bustleton Avenue

The Lawyers Travel Service, 1717 Arch Street

Manning Travel Agency, 1617 JFK Boulevard

McGettigans Corporate Planning Service, 100 Penn Square East

Monarch Travel Services, 2100 Walnut Street

Premier Travel Services, 217 S. 20th Street

Reliance Travel Services, 4 Penn Center

Rosenbluth Travel Agency, Two Liberty Place, One Franklin Plaza, 1500 Market Street, 2001 Market Street, 1515 Walnut Street, 2401 Walnut Street

Sampson Travel Agency, 10 Penn Center

Sato Travel/GSA, 841 Chestnut Street

Squires Travel Service, Two Logan Square, 1 Penn Center

Uniglobe/The Traveling Man, 1107 Walnut Street

United Nations Travel, 130 Chestnut Street

World Travel, 13th & Montgomery Avenue

PLAINS:
Kingdom Tours, 22 S. River Street

RADNOR:
American ExpressTravel, 100 Matsonford Road

Sampson Travel Agency, 100 Matsonford Road

RIDLEY PARK:
Mutual Travel/Boeing, Route 29 West

SAINT DAVIDS:
Carlson Wagonlit Travel, 555 E. Lancaster Road

VILLANOVA:
American Express Travel, Connelly Center

WEST CHESTER:
World Travel, 1365 Enterprise Drive

WEST POINT:
Rosenbluth International Travel, Sumney Town Pike

South Carolina

KINGSTREE:
Kingstree Travel Agency, 133-A E. Main Street

Texas

DALLAS:
World Travel Trade, 5420 LBJ Freeway

IRVING:
American Express, 31110 Skyway Circle South

Vermont

ST. ALBANS:
Rail City Travel, 2 Federal Street

Virginia

ALEXANDRIA:
Cal Simmons Travel, 111 Oronoco Street

ANNANDALE:
Metropolitan Travel Services, 4520 Old Columbia Pike

ARLINGTON:
Maritz Travel, 685 N. Glebe Road

FAIRFAX:
AAA Travel Agency, 12600 Fair Lakes Circle

FALLS CHURCH:
World Travel Partners, 3141 Fairview Park Drive

VIENNA:
AAA Travel Agency, 8300 Old Courthouse Road

Rosenbluth International Travel, 1604 Springhill Road

Washington

SEATTLE:
AAA Travel Agency, 330 6th Avenue, North

Mutual Travel, 1201 3rd Avenue

Wisconsin

EAU CLAIRE:
Holiday Travel, 2727 Henry Avenue

Pro-Rail Associations

The National Association of Railroad Passengers (NARP) is located in Washington and does battle on a daily basis with those who—because of political ideology, their own special interests, or just old-fashioned ignorance—would see our national rail passenger system go down the drain. Dues are $24 per year ($12 for those under twenty-one or over sixty-five years of age), and I would urge you to join. Every new member helps, and you will find the monthly newsletter informative. NARP's web page is located at *http://www.worldweb.net/~narp.*

NATIONAL ASSOCIATION OF RAILROAD PASSENGERS (NARP)
900 2nd Street, NE, #308
Washington, D.C. 20002
202-408-8362
e-mail: *narp@worldweb.net*

The common bond among the following organizations is that they have all been formed to support and promote rail transportation within their geographical areas. They would also welcome a few more dues-paying members.

ALABAMA ASSOCIATION OF RAILROAD PASSENGERS
325 Skyland Boulevard East
Tuscaloosa, AL 35405

ARIZONA RAIL PASSENGER ASSOCIATION
P.O. Box 7482
Phoenix, AZ 85011

ARKANSAS ASSOCIATION OF RAILROAD PASSENGERS
32 Fair Oaks
Conway, AR 72032

TRAIN RIDERS' ASSOCIATION OF CALIFORNIA
926 J Street, #612
Sacramento, CA 95814

(COLORADO)
COLORAIL
P.O. Box 480452
Denver, CO 80248

CONNECTICUT ASSOCIATION OF RAIL & BUS USERS
P.O. Box 891
Meriden, CT 06450

(DELAWARE)
DELMARVA RAIL PASSENGERS ASSOCIATION
P.O. Box 11102
Wilmington, DE 19850

FLORIDA COALITION OF RAIL PASSENGERS
1000 W. Horatio Avenue, #125
Tampa, FL 33606

GEORGIA ASSOCIATION OF RAILROAD PASSENGERS
P.O. Box 851
Decatur, GA 30031

ILLINOIS Association of Railroad Passengers
1609 E. Broadway
Monmouth, IL 61462

INDIANA Association of Railroad Passengers
5346 Chipwood Lane
Indianapolis, IN 46226

IOWA Association of Railroad Passengers
3349 Southgate Court, SW, #108
Cedar Rapids, IA 52404

(KANSAS)
MISSOURI-KANSAS Rail Passengers Coalition
P.O. Box 411192
Kansas City, MO 64141

LOUISIANA Association of Railroad Passengers
P.O. Box 30353
New Orleans, LA 70190

(MAINE)
TrainRiders/Northeast
P.O. Box 4869, Downtown Station
Portland, ME 04112

(MARYLAND)
Delmarva Rail Passengers Association
P.O. Box 11102
Wilmington, DE 19850

(MASSACHUSETTS)
TrainRiders/Northeast
P.O. Box 4869, Downtown Station
Portland, ME 04112

MICHIGAN Association of Railroad Passengers
P.O. Box 351
St. Clair Shores, MI 48080

MISSOURI-KANSAS Rail Passengers Coalition
P.O. Box 411192
Kansas City, MO 64141

ProRail NEBRASKA
3915 Apple Street
Lincoln, NE 68503

(NEW HAMPSHIRE)
TrainRiders/Northeast
P.O. Box 4869, Downtown Station
Portland, ME 04112

NEW JERSEY Association of Railroad Passengers
P.O. Box 5475
Somerset, NJ 08875

NEW MEXICO Association of Railroad Passengers
416 Columbia Drive, SE
Albuquerque, NM 87106

(NEW YORK)
Empire State Passengers Association
RD 4, Fish Road
Mexico, NY 13114

(NORTH CAROLINA)
Carolinas Association for Passenger Trains
6003 Teaneck Place
Charlotte, NC 28215

OHIO Association of Railroad Passengers
479 Humiston Drive
Bay Village, OH 44140

OKLAHOMA Passenger Rail Association
1120 S. 21st Street
Chickasha, OK 73018

OREGON Association of Railway Passengers
20585 SW Cheshire Court
Aloha, OR 97007

(PENNSYLVANIA)
Keystone Association of Railroad Passengers
P.O. Box 426
Harrisburg, PA 17108

(PHILADELPHIA AREA)
Delaware Valley Association of Railroad Passengers
P.O. Box 7505
Philadelphia, PA 19101

RHODE ISLAND Association of Railroad Passengers
P.O. Box 8645
Warwick, RI 02888

(SOUTH CAROLINA)
Carolinas Association for Passenger Trains
6003 Teaneck Place
Charlotte, NC 28215

TENNESSEE Association of Railroad Passengers
610 W. Due West Avenue, #421
Madison, TN 37115

VIRGINIA Association of Railway Patrons
P.O. Box 867
Richmond, VA 23207

WASHINGTON Association of Railroad Passengers
Security Bldg., Room 418
203 E. 4th Avenue
Olympia, WA 98501

(WEST VIRGINIA)
Retain the Train
P.O. Box 1162
Huntington, WV 25714

WISCONSIN Association of Railroad Passengers
Pleasant Valley
Stoddard, WI 54658

Railroad Terms and Slang

air brake   The standard braking system used on both passenger and freight cars. Compressed air is used to hold the brake shoe away from the cars' wheels. When air pressure is reduced, the brakes are applied. This concept has an important impact on safety because should anything go wrong with the system, the brakes are automatically applied. Every car on the train has its own brakes. The braking system for the entire train is controlled by the engineer in the locomotive. Often, when a train is backing into a station, the brakes are applied by the conductor, who operates a special valve in the vestibule of the last car (which, when backing, becomes the first car).

air signal   A separate air line runs the length of a passenger train, which, when activated by a valve at the end of each car, beeps in the locomotive cab. The conductor can use this means to signal the engineer—but seldom does, since normal communications are carried out by handheld radios.

alerter (also **deadman control**)   This device automatically applies the brakes and stops the train if the engineer should suddenly become incapacitated. If one of the train's controls (throttle, brake, whistle, and so forth) isn't touched during a specific period of time (usually twenty to thirty seconds), a horn will sound inside the locomotive cab. The engineer then has five seconds to respond before the brakes are automatically applied.

articulated car   Two railcars joined together to function as one unit, such as the articulated buffet cars operated by Amtrak on trains between New York and Florida. Passengers may move between the two cars without opening or closing doors, but the cars flex at the spot as the train rounds curves.

A-unit   There can be as many as four locomotives pulling a long freight train. This term refers to the first locomotive at the head of the train. Usually, it's the only one with an engineer. Also called the **lead unit.**

Automatic Train Stop System (also referred to as **ATS**)   If a train passes a signal calling for reduced speed without an electronic acknowledgment from the engineer, this system will stop the train automatically.

axle   The steel shaft on which the wheels of the railcar are mounted. Unlike most other wheeled vehicles, the wheels of a railcar are welded to the axle, which then revolves with the wheels. This is an extra safeguard to prevent the wheels from slipping off the rails, and it also transfers the weight of the car to the journal bearings.

axle generator   A small generator, run by the revolving axle, which provides electrical power for the specific car (lights or heat for a caboose, for example).

ballast   Coarse gravel or crushed rock used to form the roadbed on which tracks are laid.

blue flag   This signal (a flag is used during the day, a light after dark) displayed in front of and behind railcars means that people are working on or under that equipment.

bogie   The European term for a railcar's wheel assembly, which is called a **truck** on this side of the Atlantic.

boxcar   This is what most of us call a "freight car": a completely closed car with sliding access doors on each side, used for any kind of general cargo that can't be exposed to the weather.

brake (*see* **air brake**) There's also dynamic braking, which uses the locomotive's traction motors to produce electricity instead of consuming it. If the locomotive is a pure electric, this power is fed back into the system through the overhead wire; if it's a diesel-electric, it's blown out through vents in the top of the locomotive. Either way, the process slows the locomotive. Dynamic braking will only slow a train gradually and therefore is used in much the same way a driver downshifts a car to control the speed when heading down a hill.

cab A compartment in the locomotive where the crew sits and operates the train.

caboose A car at the end of freight trains for train crew members. Most of us think the caboose is where crew members can rest or sleep, but its primary function is as a rolling observation post from which the train can be observed and potential problems spotted—overheated journal bearings ("hot boxes"), for example. Regrettably, cabooses are gradually giving way to automatic detectors at trackside, which alert the crew to such problems.

cab ride What you and I would probably give a month's pay for!

cafe car This is sort of halfway between a dining car and a lounge car, with a small kitchen and seating area plus a lounge. Generally, cafe cars are used on small or short-haul trains.

catenary The overhead system of wires and supports from which electric engines draw the power to operate.

coach A railcar for carrying passengers. Normal configuration is rows of seats separated by a center aisle, with two seats on each side of the aisle.

coal car An open-topped hopper or gondola car used for carrying coal. Many of us incorrectly used this term for a **tender,** the car placed immediately behind a steam locomotive from which coal was shoveled into the firebox.

conductor   The onboard person ultimately responsible for the operation of the train and for the rest of the train crew.

consist (pronounced CON-sist)   The total number of cars, including the locomotive, making up the entire train.

container   The box-like "intermodal containers" that are filled with various commodities and then loaded on flatcars, swung aboard ships by cranes, or hauled to their destination by flatbed trucks.

continuous welded rail   These are rails that are welded together in long sections. For rail passengers, welded rails mean a smoother, quieter ride, although a few travelers still claim to prefer the clickety-clack of rails that are bolted together.

coupler   The device at each end of all railcars used to hook cars together. The standard coupler works automatically when cars are connected, but for safety reasons, the uncoupling process must be done manually. (Once the cars have been coupled together, a yard worker does have to connect cables and hoses for electrical power and brakes.)

crossbuck   The traditional signal at railroad grade crossings, with flashing red lights and the crossed signs forming a flattened X shape, usually saying "Railroad Crossing."

crossover   A track arrangement permitting a train to transfer from one track to another (usually parallel tracks).

cross tie   The wood or concrete structure to which the rails are fastened.

cupola (pronounced CUE-po-la)   The small observation dome on top of the caboose.

cut   The passageway cut through earth or rock through which the train passes. Also a **cut of cars,** referring to several railcars, coupled together, which are moved from one train to another as a unit.

derailment   When the wheels of a car or locomotive come off the rail. While derailments are usually accidental, they're sometimes deliberately caused for safety reasons. Watch for small signs in rail yards that say "DERAIL." They mark a special section of track that will derail (in other words, stop) an unattended car that may be rolling toward a main track where a collision could occur.

diaphragm   The ribbed fabric shield stretched between passenger cars, protecting you from the weather as you pass from one car to another.

diesel-electric locomotive   This is the most common kind of locomotive and the one which most of us mistakenly refer to simply as a "diesel" engine. There is indeed a diesel motor—and a very powerful one, too—but it doesn't actually move the train in the same way, for instance, that the diesel motor moves a bus. Instead, the diesel motor powers a generator, which in turn produces electricity, which powers the traction motors on each axle—and that's what moves the train.

dispatcher   The person who operates from a central location and is responsible for and directs the movements of all trains within a specific area.

dome   The round, raised opening on the top of a tanker car through which the car is filled. The dome also provides an area for the liquid in the tanker car to expand because of heat.

dome car   A passenger car with a glass-enclosed upper-level viewing area. None are left in the Amtrak system, but these cars are still found in VIA Rail consists and on several of the private excursion trains. A great place to ride!

driving wheel   Any of the locomotive's wheels that are turned by the engine to move the train.

electric locomotive   Any locomotive that is powered by electricity and that gets that electrical power directly from an outside source—that is, from an overhead wire (catenary) or from an electrified third rail.

engine   Although technically meaning the machinery that produces energy, in the context of this book the word "engine" is frequently used as a synonym for "locomotive."

engineer   This is the person who actually gets paid for sitting up there in the cab of that locomotive and driving it—something many of us are certain we'd do for free.

equipment   Engines and cars of all kinds. Anything that rolls along the tracks. Also referred to as **rolling stock.**

express train   A passenger train that operates with minimum delays, usually meaning it makes only a few stops on its route. An **express freight** operates in the same fashion, being routed from point A to point B as quickly as possible.

extra train   A train that does not appear on the published timetable. The airline equivalent is called an "extra section."

fireman   Except for special excursion trains powered by a restored steam locomotive, firemen are, alas, part of an earlier time. In the days of steam, the fireman was primarily responsible for keeping the firebox adequately fed with wood or coal. The second person in the locomotive cab is sometimes still referred to as the fireman, but on Amtrak trains that has given way to the more appropriate term, **assistant engineer.** The freight railroads are now using either that term or **coengineer.**

first class   In North America, this almost always means sleeping-car accommodations, although both Amtrak and VIA Rail in Canada offer forms of upgraded coach class that are sometimes referred to as first class.

flag stop   A station, usually but not always included in timetables, at which the train stops only in response to a signal.

flange   On the wheel of a railcar, this is the one-inch ridge on the inner rim of the wheel that keeps the train on the track.

flatcar   A railway freight car without tops or sides, used for hauling materials that may be exposed to the weather.

flat spot   As the term implies, a spot on a wheel that has been flattened, usually from the wheel sliding along the rail. If there's such a wheel on your car, you'll probably be able to hear and feel it. (That's one more reason to try securing space near the center of the car.) This is not just a matter of comfort, however. Freight cars with flat spots on their wheels cause more fuel to be used and, if left unattended for too long, can turn into safety problems. Once spotted, they're promptly taken out of service for repairs.

foamer   Railroad slang for a railfan; that is, someone so hooked on trains that he or she supposedly foams at the mouth when one appears. Not really derogatory, but not a compliment, either.

FRED   The automatic detector mounted on the rear of most trains to electronically alert train crews to any mechanical problems. It's an acronym for Flashing Rear End Device. They get the job done but have replaced the traditional cabooses on freight trains, which are sorely missed by most working railroad people. That helps explain why they generally translate the acronym as "F - - - - - - Rear End Device."

freight car   Any railway car used to transport almost anything: manufactured goods, fruits and vegetables, coal and other minerals, and so forth. The term does not apply to tanker cars.

frog   A special construction at the intersection of two tracks, permitting trains on one track to cross another track (as opposed to permitting a train to cross from one track to another). You can usually tell when you cross a frog from the clattering noise the wheels make.

fusee   These are basically the same type of flares that police use to warn cars to slow down for a highway accident.

They're used the same way by railroad people, dropped off the rear end of a slow-moving train to warn trains coming up from behind.

gandy dancer   Old-time railroad slang for anyone working on the tracks. The term comes from the brand name of the specialized track work tools made by the Gandy Manufacturing Company more than 100 years ago.

gauge (or **gage**)   In the railroad context, this refers to the distance between the rails, which throughout North America has been standardized at 4' 8$^{1}/_{2}$".

gondola car   A car with low sides and an open top for carrying just about anything that does not need protection from the weather.

grade   Refers to a change in elevation for a section of track. For example, a 2 percent grade means the track goes up (or down) a total of 2 feet over a distance of 100 feet.

grade crossing   A spot where a road crosses the train tracks at the same level (on the same grade).

green eye   Railroad slang for a clear signal, meaning the train may proceed at normal speed.

gross weight   The total allowed weight of a freight car and its contents. You'll see this with the appropriate numbers stenciled on the sides of most freight cars.

handcar   A small, four-wheeled vehicle, usually powered by a small gasoline engine, which carries workers and inspectors along the tracks.

head-end power   Electricity being provided to the entire train by a special generator located either in the engine or in an additional unit placed immediately behind the engine. Usually abbreviated HEP.

helper   Additional locomotives, usually unmanned and remote-controlled from the lead unit, which provide extra power to help the train over steep grades.

highball   A semi-slang term meaning a signal or a verbal instruction that authorizes the train to proceed at the maximum legal speed. The term originated from the old practice of hoisting a colored ball to the top of a signal pole to indicate a clear track ahead.

hopper car   These differ from gondola cars by having sloped sides and ends, permitting the contents to be dumped out through doors in the car's bottom. These cars carry bulk cargo, such as grain (in which case, they're covered) or coal (in which case, they're not covered).

hot box   A railroad term for an overheated journal bearing. If undetected for long, a hot box can mean serious problems—up to and including the failure of both the wheel and the axle.

hot box detector   These are the devices that have finally put the caboose out of business. They're sensitive to heat and are placed at various locations along the main tracks. Overheated bearings (hot boxes) are noted and the crew is notified, either by a recorded announcement or by an automatic signal.

hump yard   A railroad yard in which various cars are separated into different trains. A switch engine pushes freight cars, singly or in small "cuts," over a hump—literally a high spot in the yard. Once over the hump, the engine separates from the cars, allowing them to roll slowly by themselves, drawn by gravity, down the long, slight incline, being switched as they go, to join the proper train.

journal bearing   If there's a critical part common to all railcars, the journal bearing is it. There are two of these box-shaped bearings for each axle, and essentially they bear the weight of the car and help to distribute the weight of the car over the axle.

An overheated journal bearing is referred to as a **hot box** and, if unnoticed, can cause a serious breakdown.

lading   Another word for a freight car's load.

load limit   This is the maximum weight that a given car is permitted to carry. It's computed by subtracting the weight of the car, as it stands empty, from the maximum allowable gross weight. The load limit is stenciled on the side of every car.

locomotive   Frequently referred to as the "engine" by most of us, this is the self-propelled machine that hauls the train. If there is more than one locomotive in the consist, the first is called the A or the "lead" unit. Additional unmanned locomotives are referred to as B units.

main line   The tracks receiving regular, heavy use.

main track   The track on which scheduled trains are operated.

Metroliner   The electric-powered, high-speed trains operated by Amtrak in the Northeast corridor, between New York City and Washington, D.C.

milepost (also **mile marker**)   White posts with black numbers usually located at trackside that indicate the number of miles from that spot to or from a specific point. Sometimes these markers are signs fastened to metal posts by the track or attached to utility poles.

multiple unit   This term refers to two or more locomotives coupled together to increase hauling capability. Such locomotives are all radio-controlled from the lead unit.

narrow gauge (*see* **gauge**)   Any gauge that is less than the standard gauge of 4' 8$\frac{1}{2}$", although 36" is the most common. Narrow-gauge tracks are usually used in areas where the terrain requires the curves to be too sharp for the longer, standard-gauge railroad cars.

observation car   A passenger car specially designed to be the last car in a passenger train, featuring observation windows at the end of the car. These cars are usually fitted as lounge cars. VIA Rail Canada has several of these beauties and uses them on its long-distance trains. The *Sierra Madre Express,* an excursion train that travels the Copper Canyon route in Mexico, carries an observation car that actually has an open viewing area.

pantograph   This is the device that extends upward from the roof of an electric locomotive and presses against the overhead wire (catenary), collecting the electricity to power the locomotive.

parlor car   These were first-class coach cars, used for short-haul daytime travel, with large revolving seats and other features not available in ordinary coaches. There was an extra fare for the additional luxury, of course. Amtrak has added a parlor car to the *Coast Starlight*'s consist, in which those traveling in sleeping cars can relax, chat with fellow passengers, and enjoy snacks and beverages. Complimentary wine tastings are held in the *Starlight*'s parlor car as the train travels through the California wine country. What a nice touch!

piggyback cars   Railroad flatcars used for hauling semitruck trailers.

rail   Made of rolled steel, a rail is usually 39 feet long. The cross section of a rail can best be described as having an upside-down capital T shape. All rails look basically the same, but the larger and heavier rails are used where high-speed and/or heavy trains operate. Smaller, lighter-weight rails are used in rail yards where traffic is less frequent and slower.

rapid transit   Any high-speed rail system used for moving people in urban areas.

red eye   Railroad slang for a red (stop) signal.

refrigerator car (or **reefer** in railroad slang)   An insulated, closed car with cooling equipment designed to keep its contents at a specific temperature. Many of these cars are also equipped with heaters to keep fresh produce from freezing during extra-cold winter weather.

rerailer   A device used to guide a car's wheels back onto the track after a derailment.

right of way   The strip of land on which a railroad track is laid.

rim   The outer circumference of the wheel on a railroad car or locomotive; the part of the wheel that comes in contact with the rail.

rock and roll   Railroad slang for excessive side-to-side movement of rail cars; caused by poor track conditions.

sander   A device, operated from the locomotive cab, that applies sand to the tracks in front of the driving wheels to prevent them from slipping; used going up steep grades or if ice or snow has covered the tracks.

siding   A track located adjacent to the main track onto which one train is diverted to allow another to pass.

signal   A mechanical or electronic device that communicates instructions to the train crew relating to the train's speed, usually in connection with other rail traffic or track conditions.

slide fence   These wire fences are placed along the track in mountainous areas. If they're knocked down by a rock or snowslide, signals are automatically triggered to warn trains of possible obstructions on the tracks.

snow fence   You'll see a lot of these along the tracks in the open prairies of the west. They disrupt the wind patterns and, if placed properly, keep snow from drifting on the tracks.

spur   Unlike a siding, which is relatively short and is usually parallel to a main track, a spur can be of any length and runs off in another direction. Often, spurs are what freight trains use to provide service to towns or manufacturing businesses located in the vicinity.

standard gauge   The standard distance between the rails on track throughout North America: 4' 8^{1}/$_{2}$".

stock car   A car used for carrying livestock. Usually the same size and shape as a standard boxcar, but with slats on the sides for ventilation (which is needed!).

stopping distance   How far the train travels from the time brakes are applied until it comes to a stop. Examples: A 100-car freight train traveling at 30 mph could require over a mile to come to a stop; an Amtrak passenger train traveling at 80 mph has a stopping distance of about 4,000 feet.

Superliners   These are the bi-level cars used by Amtrak on its long-distance western routes and several eastern ones, too.

switch   A moving section of track, usually operated by remote control, which is used to transfer a train from one track to another.

switching locomotive (also called a **switcher**)   A locomotive used for moving individual cars or sections of a train from one track to another in a station or yard.

switchman   A railroad employee, also called a yard brakeman, whose primary job is assisting in the moving of railcars in a yard.

tank car   A railroad car used for transporting liquids.

terminal   More than just a station, this is by definition an important rail facility, where both passengers and freight are handled and where many other railroad activities are carried out.

third rail An additional rail, installed parallel to the regular track, through which electric power is supplied to the locomotive. The electricity is collected through a metal "shoe" that slides along the third rail.

throttle The knob or handle that is used to increase or decrease the amount of fuel (or electricity) going to the engine, with a corresponding effect on the train's speed.

tie More commonly called a cross tie, these are the wood or concrete pieces that are embedded in gravel and to which the rails are fastened.

timetable A published schedule detailing the movement of trains, both passenger and freight.

track The entire structure over which trains operate, including rails, cross ties, and the various fastenings that hold it all together.

traction motor Electricity, either taken from an overhead wire or generated by an onboard diesel motor, goes to the traction motors, which in turn power one set of the locomotive's wheels. There are several such motors in each locomotive.

traffic control system As with the airlines, this term refers to the system of signals, operated by railroad personnel, that controls the movements of trains.

train One or more locomotives pulling one or more cars.

trainman An onboard railroad employee who assists the conductor.

trainset A train that is not assembled and disassembled, but functions as a complete unit over a long period of time. Typically, a set number of cars with a locomotive at each end of the train (making it unnecessary to turn the entire train around at the end of its run).

trolley   The overhead wire that provides electric power for railroads or transit systems. (Generally, **trolley** is used when speaking of light-rail systems such as urban trolley cars, while the term **catenary** is used in connection with intercity trains.)

truck   This is the entire wheel assembly at each end of a railcar: wheels, axles, bearings, brakes, suspension, frame—the whole works.

trunk line   Much more than a spur line, this term refers to a rail line that can extend over many miles.

turntable   A kind of lazy Susan for trains, used to turn engines and cars around at rail terminals.

unit train   A train that carries only one commodity—coal, for instance—from point A to point B.

vestibule   The enclosed area at the end of each passenger car.

Viewliner   The newest generation of Amtrak sleeping cars now being used on many overnight trains in the east. Viewliners are easily spotted because of the second tier of windows designed to provide more light in the bedrooms and nighttime viewing for passengers in upper berths.

weigh bridge   The railroad equivalent of a weigh station along an interstate highway where officials check for overweight trucks.

welded rail   *See* **continuous welded rail.**

wheel base   The distance between the first and last axles on a railcar or locomotive.

wide gauge   Two meanings here: (1) a section of track that has spread wider than the standard 4' 8½", meaning there's potential for a derailment; (2) a term to describe tracks built to gauges wider than the North American standard, as in Russia.

work train   A train that doesn't generate revenue for the railroad; one that takes workers to a spot where track is being repaired, for example.

yard   A rail center where, within a specific area, train consists are made up, cars are moved about, and, in general, railroad activity is carried out.

yard engine   A locomotive that is assigned to a yard and functions only within the yard area. Almost always synonymous with **switching locomotive.**

yardmaster   The person in charge of all operations carried out within the yard. The nautical equivalent is the harbormaster.

yard speed   The speed that will allow the locomotive to stop within a distance equal to half the range of vision.

yellow eye   Railroad slang for a yellow (or caution) signal.

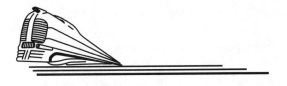

More Information About Trains and Train Travel

There are a lot of books, magazines, and videos about trains out there. The trouble is, most of them have a very narrow focus—which is great for the hard-core railfan but way beyond either the knowledge or the interest of ordinary folks who just like to ride trains and want to know a little more about them. With that in mind, here are some of the sources I discovered in compiling this book, which I think most of the rest of us will find interesting and enjoyable.

Books and Articles

Armstrong, John H. *The Railroad: What It Is, What It Does.* Simmons-Boardman Books, Inc., 1993.

Beebe, Lucius, and Charles Clegg. *The Trains We Rode.* Promontory Press, 1993.

Ditlefsen, Charles E. *Those Magnificent Trains.* Cedco Publishing Company, 1994.

Emeka, Marcus L. *Amtraking: A Guide to Enjoyable Train Travel.* Apollo Publishing Co., 1994.

Faith, Nicholas. *The World the Railways Made.* Carroll & Graff Publishers Inc., 1990.

Kisor, Henry. *Zephyr: Tracking a Dream Across America.* Times Books, 1994.

Maiken, Peter T. *Night Trains: The Pullman System in the Golden Years of American Rail Travel.* Lakme Press, 1989.

Porterfield, James D. *Dining by Rail.* St. Martin's Press, 1993.

Railroad Facts, 1996 Edition. Association of American Railroads, 1996.

Railway Age's Comprehensive Railroad Dictionary. Simmons-Boardman Books, Inc., 1992.

Reutter, Mark. "The Lost Promise of the American Railroad," *The Wilson Quarterly,* Winter 1994.

Train Journeys of the World. Barnes & Noble Books, 1993.

Vranich, Joseph. *Supertrains: Solutions to America's Transportation Gridlock.* St. Martin's Press, 1991.

Whistles Across the Land. Cedco Publishing Company, 1993.

Wilner, Frank N. *The Amtrak Story.* Simmons-Boardman Books, Inc., 1994.

Periodicals

A great deal of information on this whole subject may be obtained every month from several magazines. These are the most prominent publications, although all but *International Railway Traveler* are aimed at the hard-core railfan audience.

International Railway Traveler, P.O. Box 3747, San Diego, CA 92163

Railfan & Railroad, Carstens Publications, P.O. Box 700, Newton, NJ 07860

RailNews, Pentrex, Inc., 2652 E. Walnut, Pasadena, CA 91107

Trains, Kalmbach Publishing, P.O. Box 162, Waukesha, WI 53187

Videos

Literally hundreds of videos are now available on the subject of trains and railroads, although once again, most are not intended for someone who is simply interested in train travel. Nevertheless, I can suggest three sources for videos that have passenger train travel in their listings in addition to the narrow-focus material.

Green Frog Productions, 200 N. Cobb Parkway, Bldg. 100, Suite 138, Marietta, GA 30062

Pentrex, Inc., P.O. Box 94011, Pasadena, CA 91109

Revelation Audio-Visuals, 977 East Avenue, Tallmadge, OH 44278

Now here are some specific recommendations for videos dealing with trains and train travel, all of which are generally available from video catalogs.

America by Rail, CounterTop Video/James Entertainment

America's Scenic Rail Journeys, Acorn Media

The California Zephyr and *The Empire Builder,* Green Frog Productions

Great American Train Rides, Vols. I–IV, Pentrex

The Great Canadian Train Ride, International Travel Films

The Iron Road, Peace River Films

Last Train Across Canada, Cleo 24 Inc.

Locomotion: The Amazing World of Trains, A&E Home Video

Index